Job Search Letters

FOR

DUMMIES

A Wiley Brand

by Joyce Lain Kennedy

FOR

DUMMIES

A Wiley Brand

Job Search Letters For Dummies®

Published by: **John Wiley & Sons, Inc.,** 111 River Street, Hoboken, NJ 07030-5774, www.wiley.com

Copyright © 2013 by Joyce Lain Kennedy

Published simultaneously in Canada

For general information on our other products and services, please contact our Customer Care Department within the U.S. at 877-762-2974, outside the U.S. at 317-572-3993, or fax 317-572-4002. For technical support, please visit www.wiley.com/techsupport.

Wiley publishes in a variety of print and electronic formats and by print-on-demand. Some material included with standard print versions of this book may not be included in e-books or in print-on-demand. If this book refers to media such as a CD or DVD that is not included in the version you purchased, you may download this material at http://booksupport.wiley.com. For more information about Wiley products, visit www.wiley.com.

Library of Congress Control Number: 2013938102

ISBN 978-1-118-43641-7 (pbk); ISBN 978-1-118-43640-0 (ebk); ISBN 978-1-118-43642-4 (ebk); ISBN 978-1-118-43643-1 (ebk)

Manufactured in the United States of America

10 9 8 7 6 5 4 3 2 1

Contents at a Glance

Table of Contents

Introduction

R ight now, you hold in your hands a key to today's successful job search. *Hint:* Your challenge isn't like it was even five years ago.

Communications and technology are two gigantic change factors that are rapidly transforming both the materials and the methods of finding and nailing down a job. The two factors are connected.

Communications. Joining resumes as staples of employment tools, an explosion of job search messaging is emerging to benefit job seekers everywhere in any career field or industry.

For brevity, I use the term "job search letters" in this work to mean all messaging that promotes job finding and career health. I identify many *categories* of job search letters that you can write to get what you want. Key messaging *formats* include the following:

Letters	E-mails	Profiles
Memos	Text messages	Bios
Multimedia	Reports	Prezis
Video	Checklists	Mobile messages

Technology. An almost unimaginable amount of technological innovation is reshaping how messaging moves in the marketplace of jobs.
Most of it is digital, ranging from social media networking and public profile posting, to mobile job app responses and information intended to automatically match jobs and candidates.

 Despite mind-blowing change now and tomorrow, bear in mind that technology does not and cannot replace human interaction at every turn of the employment process. For that reason, a number of the sample job search letters in these pages are intended to be passed by hand, depending on the circumstances.

About This Book

This guide to modern job search communications wouldn't have been possible without the outstanding collaboration of 42 top-shelf professional career messaging writers who provided the message samples throughout its pages.

The professional writer's name is credited beneath each sample. Find the writer's contact information in the Directory of Job Letter Writers, which is printed in the appendix of this book.

Job Search Letters For Dummies replaces three editions of *Cover Letters For Dummies.*

Foolish Assumptions

I assume that you chose this book because your job search is on your mind, perhaps as a new graduate fresh from college with scant working experience, or as a career changer seeking to make a leap into a different field, or as a seasoned worker wondering how to get ready for the next future challenge.

More specifically, I'm also making these assumptions:

- ✔ You may feel as though good things never seem to happen in your job world. Have you considered the possibility that you don't market your abilities robustly enough in a tight economy?

  The arsenal of messaging samples in these pages offers new ideas about how to communicate your true worth.

- ✔ You're job hunting, but you've never written any kind of job search letter that landed you an interview. (Putting recruiters to sleep, are you?)

  Now you're ready to step up your game and learn from samples of how today's writing pros do it. You sense that this is the right guidebook to help you pick up the know-how to look job perfect to employers stuck in hiring paralysis.

- ✔ You're employed but concerned about or dissatisfied with your current work situation. You're looking for escape routes if push comes to shove — but you need the right message tools to look vibrant in modern times.

- ✔ You're ready to move up in rank and money, but all is quiet on the management front. You've heard a story about an audacious soul who won a nice promotion by writing a request justifying it, and of another individual who fired up her keyboard to ask for a pay bump, and the money flowed. You're ready to learn how to write letters like that.

Icons Used in This Book

For Dummies signature icons are the little round pictures you see in the margins of the book. I use them to call your attention to key bits of information. Here's a list of the icons you find in this book and what they mean.

This icon signals situations in which you may find trouble if you don't make a good decision.

Some points in these pages are so useful that I hope you'll keep them in mind as you read. I make a big deal out of these ideas with this icon.

This icon directs your full attention to compelling messages that make you stand out from the crowd.

Here I flag advice and information that can spark a difference in the outcome of your career message.

Beyond the Book

In addition to the goodies contained in this book, *Job Search Letters For Dummies* comes with some access-anywhere material on the web. Check out the free Cheat Sheet at `http://www.dummies.com/cheatsheet/jobsearchletters` for additional helpful letter-writing suggestions.

Where to Go from Here

If you're in a tight spot and don't have the time to start with Chapter 1 and read this book cover to cover, please allow me to make a few suggestions to get you off to a good launch.

When you need to dive into specific information, the Table of Contents is your guide to grab the immediate info you need. The Index is another place to cherry-pick the answers you want.

Additionally, here are several targeted call-outs:

- ✔ When you aren't up on the framework of mobile search and social media, read Chapters 2 and 8. I've tried not to go overboard on the techie talk, but offer only enough to get you onboard today's job search functions.

- ✔ When you've just spotted an advertised job opening you want, cut to the chase: Immediately read Chapter 4.

- ✔ When you need to make a move fairly quickly, but you have no advertised jobs you want to claim, head straight for Chapters 1, 2, 5, 6, and 8 through 12.

Your Treasure Hunt Begins

Within this guide's pages you'll find more than 40 valuable new types of documents to send your career soaring. Seek and find samples of these kinds of job search letters:

accomplishment statement, checklist comparison, resume addendum, specialty profile, first 90-day forecast, introduction letter, skills checklist, resume letter, job offer response, rejection follow-up, job return agreement, job ad reply, networking letter, prospecting letter, after-interview letter, social media message, mini-message text, branding statement, bio, bio flyer, professional profile, elevator speech, leadership initiatives summary, occupational highlights, cultural fit statement, industry experience statement, job training snapshot, project plan review, certifications list, performance snapshot, strengths summary, education achievements report, best work portfolio, sales skills index report, qualifications-job ad requirements display, reference list, reference compendium, recommendation letter, online work portfolio, prezi, and videoclip message.

Treasure hunts are great fun but this isn't a kid's game. A rewarding career is your grand prize in a changed job market where you need all the clues you can get.

Part I
New Tools for New Times

In this part . . .

Do you know what kind of power a well-crafted marketing message can bring to your search for a good job? Rather than allow a job search letter to merely introduce your resume, give it the wings to make your image soar! In this part, you find out how a job search letter can bring the right kind of attention your way.

Chapter 1 discusses all that job search letters can be and all that they can do for you. Chapter 2 leads you down the dynamic mobile path. Discover the new age of job search letters. Finally, Chapter 3 contains newcomers to the job search letter arena that not only give you extra help to get hired, but illustrates how a wise addition of collateral documents can add lift-off to your career future.

Chapter 1

Best Messages: Land Jobs and Leap Ahead

In This Chapter

▶ Saying hello to a bevy of winning messages in the New Digital Age

▶ Learning the ropes of writing great job search letters from top pro writers

▶ Guarding your new letters' good looks as they travel online to change your life

A new blast of recruiting technology is blowing the hinges off the way we once pursued a job search when we applied, got a call, went in for an interview, and either got hired or continued looking until we hit pay dirt.

Just as computers and the Internet forever changed the way job seekers *find* hiring companies, digital technology is forever changing the way job seekers *sell* hiring companies.

This book, aimed at virtually every job seeker, is rich with sample letters showing you how to sell companies on the benefits of hiring you. You'll find a wealth of letters to grow your know-how in Chapters 4 through 11.

There's more. After you're hired, you'll want to be rewarded for your valuable work with a boost in money and clout. That's why Chapter 13 contains more sample letters, to help you accomplish your career progression.

A Brief Kaleidoscope of Letter Types

More specifically, you may be amazed at the number of purposes you can accomplish with solid job search letters. The following thumbnail roster summarizes the kinds of career-growing letters that can speed you on your way and that you'll find in the chapters ahead:

✔ **Getting hired:** Job ad reply, online cover note, checklist match of qualifications with job requirements, accomplishments sheet, job fit statement, first 90 days work product goals projection, reference commentary, employee referral memo, contract and job-bidding application, prospecting letter, networking letter, after-interview letter, interview leave-behind supplement, and interest revival letter.

✔ **Getting modern:** Mobile text message, social media message, branding brief, bio, profile, online work portfolio, prezi, and video interview.

✔ **Getting ahead:** Internal requests for promotion, raise, company job vacancy, and lateral move within company.

Job search letters may be postal mailed, courier delivered, personally hand delivered, or, far more likely, moved by digital computer technology. Digital technology has become the leading method of delivering job search letters, as the following section observes.

Digital Is Destiny

Digital technology keeps churning out new ways for people to connect and communicate in the job market. Why isn't innovation slowing down or taking a breather?

Three words sum up the answer: *smarter, faster, cheaper.* That's essentially the motivation for recruiters (who pay the bills) and inventors (who sell to recruiters) to continue coming up with new technical twists in the job market.

What's more, digitally native generations represent a growing proportion of the working population. Young adults — who teethed on the Internet and texted most of their messages — represent an increasingly larger share of the labor market.

Among important contemporary categories of recruiting and job search technology are the following four headliners:

1. **Mobile.** The use of smartphones and tablets to job-hunt is spreading across the planet like wildfire, even among workers older than 30. Chapter 2 is devoted to the ins and outs of mobile job search.

2. **Social.** The explosion of social media means more information is available about candidates than ever before; it even elbows in on unfavorable data candidates prefer to keep out of public view. There are two sides to the social digital coin:

   Social discovery makes it easier for recruiters to find candidates for specific positions.

   • Social communication makes it easier for job seekers to find jobs and references in ways never before possible.

The growth in time spent on social media is largely tied to the skyrocketing spread of smartphones. Chapter 8 looks at letters for social media.

3. **Search automation.** Until two decades or so ago, job applications were filled with candidate-supplied, or *internal,* information and were kept in filing cabinets. Now they're kept on computers in applicant tracking systems (ATS). Hiring actions include *external* information gathered online in social searching.

   Contemporary ATS technologies automate a comprehensive review of candidates that includes both internal and external information by using computer formulas called algorithms.

4. **Predictive analytics.** In making hiring decisions, predictive analytics means sophisticated software used to predict a candidate's future performance. Statistics in candidate selection add to or complete with human judgment.

When a job change is on your agenda, it's essential to Google your name once a week to see what recruiters are spotting. This exercise means more than searching for embarrassing personal moments. It means updating your old profiles and revising any other data that can disqualify you for the type of job you're chasing.

Memorable Job Search Letters

The transforming power of digital technology encourages a strategy of writing your way forward with messages that ask for advice and information, help from professional contacts, assistance from a former business coworker, or consideration from a recruiter.

Digital technology makes it practical for you to take another bite of the apple in pitching a hiring manager after a turn-down, asking for a part-time gig, or helping in researching a potential job.

Your letters have to be worth reading, whether by a recruiter, a hiring manager, or an automated system. Three outstanding job letter examples follow.

Executive position letter

Very well-written job search letters are critical when you're chasing highly competitive employment positions, such as senior executive, scientist, technologist, upper-level government employee, college professor, attorney, or other upscale occupation.

The following sample letter by Debby Ellis, Phoenix Career Group in Houston, illustrates quality writing that's always appropriate for an executive position.

Gerald F. Fox _____ **Chief Operations Officer**

[Date]

Dennis Paige, Chief Executive Officer
XYZ Transportation
3100 Space Center Boulevard
Houston, TX 77059

Dear Mr. Paige,

America is innovating again. Just one important example is the successful landing of the Mars probe, *Curiosity*. But to be and stay competitive in today's global economy, *every* manufacturing enterprise is obliged to remain vigilant in their approach to operations … the challenge, always, is to outperform the competition. This is where I offer the most value.

XYZ Transportation offers everything the next stage in America's technology evolution requires, but it is my belief that to compete successfully and profitably deliver this business, you need an operations leader that can return your high-tech manufacturing to double-digit profitability. I know how it will work, because I've done it before. Specifically, I offer:

- Experience and success building and managing high-value manufacturing organizations.

- Expertise in leveraging lowest-cost supply chain processes to create competitive advantage, improve profits and enhance value.

- Mastery in the seamless setup and integration of globally centralized SAP platforms.

- Extensive experience, advanced degrees and current certifications in engineering, technology and program management.

To demonstrate my level of interest, I have developed a series of presentations outlining my ideas for: Implementing Engineering-Centric Manufacturing Methodologies; Reducing Supply Chain Cost While Maintaining Quality; and Leveraging Information To Improve Efficiency. I will deliver the work samples to your Executive Committee by courier over the next three business days.

If you are interested in discussing more details, I can be reached at 123-456-7890, or you can send me an email, jerry.fox@gmail.com, and I will respond quickly. I appreciate your time and consideration.

Sincerely,
Jerry Fox

POB 430, Houston TX 77030 ● (C) 123-456-7890 ● jerry.fox@gmail.com ● http://www.linkedin.com/in/jfox ●@jfoxcoo

Debbie Ellis, MRW, Phoenix Career Group — Houston, Texas

Alumni career fair letter

The main idea: When attending a college career fair, a simple tactic makes you stand out from the fair's endless flow of visitors: Leave your resume at each booth with a customized cover letter that features a facsimile of your college's logo.

Cast your eyes on the following sample letter from imaginative Atlanta-based resume writer Sharon M. Bowden.

Frank A. Strickland
Nashville, Tennessee 34968
(310) 555-1212• Email@email.com

Alumni Career Fair – Wednesday, April 18, 20xx

Thank you for participating in Vanderbilt's Alumni Career Fair. It is good to see [Company Name], such a well respected company, represented today. As a Class of 20xx graduate with a **Bachelor of Science in Accounting**, I have been working as a **CPA** for a small accounting firm for the last few years. While I enjoy my work, I have decided it is time to pursue additional challenges in the area of mergers and acquisitions, for which you are well known. Below are a few accomplishments:

➢ Provide comprehensive approach to tax planning for 16 companies with annual revenues that exceed $50 million

➢ Recognized in writing by clients for outstanding achievement in the areas of risk management, compliance and reporting

➢ Selected as a member of Vanderbilt's Distinguished Alumni Council

The odds are my financial acumen, discipline, and strong work ethic would be an asset to your organization. Additionally, I am interested in travel as I am fluent in English, French, and Spanish and lived abroad for a number of years. Again, thank you for your consideration, and I look forward to speaking with you in the near future.

Sincerely,

Frank A. Strickland

Attachment: Resume

Sharon M. Bowden, CPRW, CEIP — Atlanta, Ga.

Letter perfect design, now what?

Employers and various collectors of resumes, applications, and other job search letters use an applicant tracking system (ATS) to automatically read and process job communications and manage the hiring or storage process. All ATSs are not the same; they vary in their degree of sophistication.

You can send your resume letters by postal mail or by e-mail, but when your letter contains graphic design elements, postal mail is the safer choice. Here's why:

Sending design-dependent letters online may create "very ugly cover letters," Jim Lemke explains. Lemke, the technical reviewer for all of my *For Dummies* career books, reports that, while most applicant tracking systems retain the native format (MS Word, for example) for both resumes and cover letters, others do not.

"Cover letter formatting gets messed up in some systems because the system keeps only the resume in native format and converts cover letters to text," Lemke says.

"You can, of course, call the HR office at a target company where you plan to send a graphically enriched cover letter and just ask, 'Does your applicant tracking system retain cover letters in native format or convert them to text?'" Lemke notes, "and to double-check, ask the same question about resumes."

Renowned career coach Ralph Haas (careerdoctor.com) offers yet another reason for using postal mail: "After you have submitted your credentials through appropriate web-based channels, consider printing your resume and cover letter on high-quality white paper and sending it to an actual human being via snail mail. Your cover letter can refer to the fact that you have — as asked — submitted your resume via appropriate channels, but you hoped that this additional follow-up would underscore your interest in the position."

Career guru Susan Whitcomb (susanwhitcomb.com) advises, "Get your resume into a target company's database, have it hand-delivered by internal contacts in the target company to the hiring manager (not HR), and send it as a follow-up after meeting with networking contacts."

Networking letter

Countless surveys of job seekers rate networking as indispensable. Chapter 5 offers 15 excellent samples, and here's one more. The following sample, written by resume writer Joellyn Wittenstein Schwerdlin in Worcester, Mass., demonstrates vividly how effective messages can be constructed with brevity and clarity, as well as warmth.

From: Connie Anderson
To: Margaret White

Date: [Date]

Subject: Girl Scouts of White Plains, New York

Hi Margaret,

My name is Connie Anderson and I'm in a job search networking group facilitated by Jo Anne Schmidt.

When I mentioned my upcoming interview for the position of "Recruiter/Memberships" with the Girl Scouts of White Plains, Jo Anne thought you might be able to help me. She said you worked for this region for about two years as a business development consultant.

Of course, I buy Girl Scout cookies every year from neighbors and friends and am familiar with the Girl Scout mission. But I'd love to get an insider's perspective about the organization, to help me prepare for the interview.

Can we schedule a brief phone chat, to discuss further? I would really appreciate any insights you can offer me.

Thanks very much in advance. I look forward to hearing from you soon!

Sincerely,
Connie Anderson
c-anderson@anyisp.net
555-555-5555

Joellyn Wittenstein Schwerdlin, CCMC, JCTC — Worcester, Mass.

Should you use a template?

A cover letter makes your first impression on an employer. Show that your strengths fit the target job like green on grass. When you're tempted to scout the Web for one of those free cover letter templates for which the only heavy lifting required is filling in the blanks, remember the downside: You risk exchanging time saved for opportunity lost.

Why Job Letters Are the Future

The word is out about another technological gee-whiz product being tested as this book goes to press: *smartglasses.* Slipping a pair of smartglasses on your face can alert you to jobs in your area while you're moving about. Or as someone has observed, "Get ready for eyewear that brings computing to your corneas." (Personally, I'm holding out for dentistry that brings computing to your wisdom teeth.)

The serious job seeker can't brush off speed-racing of new digital technologies to automate hiring conclusions drawn from massive amounts of data. Just don't mistake the technological medium for the marketing message.

The message is how you communicate your value to employers who will pay you for it. The message is how you communicate your job fit to employers who insist on knowing it.

It's the message that's important, not the medium that delivers the message.

The strategy of using effective modern job search messages presents a golden opportunity to own the narrative of why you're a perfect choice for the job you seek. And after you write your way onto a payroll, keep writing your way forward with career-management messages. Please continue reading: You'll find 188 terrific samples to light your way.

Communications skills most people commonly use today for job finding and job growing aren't up-to-speed for the emerging world. If you're in the left-behind category, here's your chance to catch up and zoom into the future.

Technology meets autotranslation

How can you write your job search letters and resume in language A, your native tongue, but apply in language B for work in another country? The rise of new technology makes it happen.

Google Translate (translate.google.com) creates an automated translation of your written job search docs with a few clicks on a computer. Moreover, a host of jaw-dropping translation apps have descended on smartphones — you merely point your camera at a block of text and see it translated on your phone.

Chapter 2

Mobile Meets Job Search

· ·

In This Chapter

▶ Checking out job hunting in a smartphone world

▶ Discovering what mobile search offers you — or not

▶ Using today's job search apps to find work

▶ Welcoming mobile-enabled company career pages

▶ Creating great messages to use in mobile job search

· ·

*F*inding a job with a smartphone or tablet is no longer breaking news. Mobile job search is here right this very minute!

Even the formerly staid *New York Times* — nicknamed "The Old Gray Lady" — has adopted a mobile attitude. Joining countless numbers of today's media enterprises, the famous national newspaper has redesigned its popular online publication, *Today's Headlines*, to be more readable on the mobile digital devices you carry around with you.

Who else has mobile on the mind? Job seekers are racing to hunt for employment anytime, anywhere. A recent major breakthrough in recruiting technology made the mobile gold rush possible. Until that happened, candidates couldn't submit a complete job application on a mobile device.

Although substantial problems remain in mobile technology, job seekers can use it on any device that has Internet access. Typically, this means a smartphone or tablet, but it also means a laptop or desktop.

Companies that capitalize on mobile moves seem to knock on new digital doors every week. This chapter presents *job messaging* as currently shaped by the key basics of mobile development.

The FAQs of Mobile Job Search

What does *FAQs* mean? It's an acronym, abbreviation, or slang word that means "Frequently Asked Questions." Websites often post FAQs pages to share essential information about the site. Here's your chance to grab six fast answers to how to connect with a new job when you're on the move:

✔ **Which smartphones and tablets are most used in mobile search?**

Android (Google), iPhone (Apple), BlackBerry (RIM), and Windows (Microsoft) currently are the four leading smartphones and tablet computers job seekers use to search job boards, apply for jobs, obtain job interviews, video interview from their mobile device, and more.

✔ **Where can you find jobs via mobile devices?**

The three basic sources for mobile discovery of jobs are job boards, job search apps, and web-enabled company job pages.

✔ **Can I apply for all jobs from my mobile device?**

No. Chris Forman, online job search guru and CEO of Startwire.com, says some kinks remain to be worked out in mobile search:

"As of mid-2013, about one to two jobs in five were mobile enabled (optimized for a mobile experience, or offer a simple enough application process that they can be completed effectively on a small digital device)."

✔ **How easy is it to apply for a job and send your resume?**

Forman also cautions that ease of submission and resume access vary:

"A key benefit of mobile job search is the ability to submit your resume along with a job application. Check to see whether your smartphone's operating system allows you to save a resume on your phone. If so, is it easy to work with — or a pain to use?"

✔ **Can you send customized resumes and cover letters on a mobile device?**

Yes and no. If your device can handle resumes and cover letters, prepare in advance. Write and store a number of versions of key job search messages either in free job search apps (which I discuss later in this chapter) or in free file-sharing services, such as Dropbox (dropbox.com) and Google Drive (drive.google.com).

Matching your qualifications to a job ad's requirements is critical. When responding to a job ad, choose the version of your document that most closely meets the requirements of the specific job you seek, and then tailor it as much as possible. The key to being hired, whether or not there is an opening, is customizing your approach.

Don't expect to do serious, large-scale editing from your mobile device, especially one without a mouse-type pointer function. Editing is painstaking work and a tar pit for errors, especially when using miniature keyboards.

Career strategist and coach E. Chandlee Bryan suggests a speedy way to produce mobile messages: "Simply compose sentences or important phrases on a laptop or desktop — and cut and paste them into your smartphone or tablet."

✔ **Is there an advantage to being in the first wave of responders to a posted job opening?**

Mobile job search gives you the timing tools to jump out ahead of your competition. When you see a job that interests you, apply as soon as possible before the hiring authority is overwhelmed with a fire hose of responses, assumes it has plenty of qualified candidates to choose from, and shutters the search.

As job search app Proven.com CEO Pablo Fuentes says, "The early bird catches the work."

Fuentes explains that because the job seeker can respond on the fly to a new job posting within hours or the next day, the quick response time mobile technology facilitates can spell the difference between being hired or not.

Who Mobile Benefits Most

Mobile job search currently skews toward a younger crowd. Recognizing that dedicated mobile usage is correlated with age, many employers recruit via the mobile web for new college grads and other entry-level workers.

The mobile choice also is a natural for fields with well-defined requirements, such as health care, finance, and technology, and can include some professional jobs.

Mobile scouting continues to be a popular method of job finding in high-turnover industries, such as retail outlets, restaurants, theaters, hotels, and hair salons. Temporary and contract jobs are magnets for mobile.

But managerial and executive job seekers are more likely to gain interviews through traditional hands-on recruiting channels because the cost of a failed management hire can be disastrous to a company's profitability — and even to its survival.

What Mobile Offers Everyone

Mobile frees you to make updates and connections in real time. For example, suppose you just met someone at a party who works at a company you want to join. The minute you leave the party, you can find out if your new acquaintance has a professional profile on a social network and follow up the next day. (Jump to Chapters 8 and 20 for a discussion of social media in job search.)

Mobile search offers a number of positive factors. Among steps in the job search that you can achieve with mobile are the following:

- Search for jobs by location, company, and employment type
- Receive job alerts about openings you may want
- Apply for jobs
- Find friends in companies now hiring and request referrals
- Research companies and interviewers before an interview
- Research salaries
- Track the status of your application for each job you go after
- Calendar upcoming tasks, events, follow-ups, and interviews
- Keep track of accounts you create on company career pages and job boards when storing your resumes and cover letters
- Maintain notes from successful and unsuccessful interviews
- Pursue your job search during a commute or other down time so you're not missing opportunities

Say Hello to Job Search Apps

Apps are convenient programs that make your life easier when you're on the go. Apps turn your smartphone and tablet into little computers that you can hold in your hand. The word itself, *app*, is short for *application*, a software program used for a wide variety of purposes, including ones that make it super convenient to search for jobs wherever you are.

For more information about apps, hop on to the Department of Labor website OnGuardOnline.gov, and click on "Understanding Mobile Apps."

Want to use mobile apps on a laptop or desktop computer (not on a smartphone or tablet)? Make the technical switch on this website: BlueStacks.com.

Among the estimated hundreds of apps in modern job search, 15 of the best known or most advanced follow in alphabetical order. Find others by browsing for "mobile job apps:"

Career Builder	JobAware	Monster
Dice Job Search	Jobrio	Proven
GlassDoor	JobStreet	Simply Hired
Good Job	LinkedIn	StartWire
Indeed	LinkUp	TweetMyJobs

Greet Mobile Company Job Pages

Are mobile job apps here today but not tomorrow? Highly respected Internet pioneer Mark Mehler thinks so. Mehler, who's seen web technology bubbles come and go over the past two decades, co-owns the consulting firm CareerXRoads: The Staffing Strategy Connection. The firm regularly tracks recruiting trends within the largest American companies. A recent CareerXRoads study brings Mehler to the following perspective:

> *Apps to apply for a job are dead.*

As Mehler explains, "Major corporations now use new technologies so it is seamless to apply for a job using a mobile device. There is no reason to download an app. Our 2013 research with the Fortune 500 companies reveals that 85 corporations already have mobile-enabled career pages, and half of those allow job seekers to apply seamlessly."

Other experts in the job space are not convinced that apps will soon be road kill on the Information Highway. Here's the gist of an alternative outlook:

"Targeting a specific company and applying directly to its website job section is ideal. But the needs of a candidate who doesn't know which specific companies have open jobs to fill, and who would rather expand employment prospects by searching generally, make job apps a viable option."

Consider These Message Tips

Guidelines to writing for mobile devices differ from guidelines to writing for laptops or desktops. The main difference is one of size, like a modern one-room efficiency apartment compared to a traditional two-story house. Here are a few considerations to bear in mind:

- **Readability.** Because the screens of smartphones are about 3 to 5 inches, make sure you know how your resume and cover letter look on a small screen.

  Tablet screens can handle total resumes, but hold the size to one or two pages.

  A variety of digital devices can view resumes in PDF (portable document format).

  Keep resumes, cover letters, and other messages as short as you can while still delivering strong self-marketing communications. Send your resume and cover letter to yourself, and see if you can read it without injuring your eyesight.

✔ **Keywords.** Remember to include the same keywords as in any resume. Indeed.com analyzed millions of job postings and pulled out commonly requested professional attributes:

Leadership, interpersonal, problem solving, motivated, efficient, detail oriented, prioritize, teamwork, reliable, multitask, time management, passionate, listening, outgoing, and honesty.

Here's a super trick to quickly choose the most powerful keywords to include in your custom resume and/or its cover letter:

1) **Hop on a free *tag cloud generator* website, such as TagCrowd. com or ToCloud.com.**

    (A *tag* is a label; a *cloud* is a metaphor for the Internet; a *generator* is software.)

    Spend a few minutes observing how the tag cloud generator creates images from words.

2) **Choose a job ad that you like; copy and paste its job description into a tag cloud generator.**

3) **Note the keywords.** In mere seconds, the generator will respond with a visualization of the most powerful keywords for the job's must-have requirements. The visualization pictures the job description's major keywords in larger, bolder fonts than the keywords of lesser importance to the employer.

4) **Claim top keywords.** When you can claim 70 percent or more of the job description's heavy-hitter keywords, list them at the top of your resume in bullets, a spotlight that gives you a good shot at being contacted for an interview.

✔ **Overall quality.** Don't expect technological novelty to make up for an inferior message. Even when your resume arrives via mobile technology (which suggests that you're up-to-date in employment techniques), if it fails to address a job's requirements and lacks accomplishments that underscore your value, a mobile search doesn't do anything more for you than would a traditional online search.

✔ **Laptop or desktop backup.** Sometimes you come out ahead by doing parts of your job search on your desktop or laptop. No candidate is likely to build a powerful resume, cover letter, or job application on the phone with one finger poking around on a teeny-tiny keyboard. You'll know when e-mailing a job's link to yourself is a more practical move.

Check Out Sample Mobile Messages

While various formats work for constructing short messages for mobile job finding, here's one that I think works well for resume cover notes and more:

1. Subject of message

2. Space

3. Sender's name and contact information

4. Mobile cover note information

5. Closing and sender's name signature

The following three samples illustrate this format.

▮ ✔ Getting to know you

> Subject: Managerial CPA/credit, taxes, valuation/rock solid
>
> Herman B. Davis
> hbdavislowa@supermail.com
> 123-456-7890
> Des Moines, Ia.
>
> As a Certified Public Accountant with technology skills to match, I'm interested in moving into mobile marketing. For the past five years, I've worked in credit analysis, tax assessment reporting, and valuation analysis. During the last 12 months, I've been a manager of accounting professionals. My resume overviews how I can help.
>
> As a document is limited in the information it conveys, why don't we meet in person? If you need additional information before arranging an interview, please call me at 123-456-7890. Otherwise, I'll check back with you next week to confirm your interest.
>
> Yours truly, Herm Davis

▮ ✔ Showing you the money

> Subject: Fundraiser/Indeed.com, 9012-XX/Over-goal record
>
> Rita Nugent
> 090-777-8888
> rnuggest@comcast.com
> St. Louis, Mo. 55515
>
> As a highly motivated and energetic person ready to move up to the next level, I was thrilled to see your job post for a senior development specialist for Washington University. I am a seasoned foot soldier in the fundraising ranks; exceeded my goals by 12% and 29% in the last two annual campaigns.
>
> Please contact me by phone or by email. After looking me over, if you want to chat, let's do it!
>
> Sincerely yours, Rita Nugent

▌ ✔ **Scoring in the consulting business**

Subject: Strong HR candidatge/21 yrs./BS-HR Mgt.

Melanie Hill
melaniegill@earthlink.com
(400) 555-1111
Redondo Beach, CA 99999

Dear Shawn Miller:

After researching HR consulting firms in the LA area, I feel sure I have the experience (both client site and remote consulting) and education (bachelor's in HR management) to make a strong contribution to your organization. I'd like to work with you if you like the qualifications you see in my resume.

Sincerely, Melanie Hill

Leading with references

Year after year, annual surveys of big company hiring sources by CareerXRoads principles Mark Mehler and Gerry Crispin show that a candidate who's introduced with an employee referral is four to seven times more likely to be hired than a candidate who arrives unknown.

The referral magic also continues to boost your chances when you arrive with an introduction (an implied reference) from others the hiring boss knows.

The following mobile message opening samples mention a name or a connection that warms your welcome:

✔ Virginia Springer gave me your name today and recommended that I contact you ASAP. As a newly graduated dental hygienist, I am appreciative of being referred to a leading dentist for consideration as an addition to your staff. I am proficient in general prophylaxis, charting, patient education, ultrasonic scaling, and other modern dental office skills.

Can we explore an employment acquisition: me?

✔ Judge Edward Guevara of the 8th Circuit Court of Appeals, for whom I clerked, recommends me to you for inclusion in your law firm. Judge Marvin Helens of San Diego Superior Courts seconds that recommendation.

I'm enthusiastic about providing you with a close-up of my professional value. Until we meet, thank you for your consideration. My resume follows.

✔ Dr. Lee Payne, our mutual dentist, says you'll be happier spending time with me than with him. Aside from that lame joke, I do have demonstrated financial management skills you may be able to make good use of on a contract basis.

After running my own business for 25 years, I like the idea of working with younger people who could use someone with a broad range of financial and operations management experience to keep a small firm operating in the black. My resume follows.

✔ Jorge Luna Sandoval tells me you're in the market for a dependable, fully insured subcontractor who can do almost all types of construction to manage your tenant improvement projects. Yes, I can do it all: electrical, carpentry, painting, and all finishes. I know materials and costs. My references verify my on-time and on-budget results. Plus, my wife's job pays our health insurance. My resume follows. Can we schedule an interview?

✔ Yvonne Fischer certainly throws good parties, don't you think? I very much enjoyed talking with you at Yvonne's home and am responding to your kind invitation to send you my resume to be shown to your company's hiring managers. Yes, I'm definitely interested in upcoming openings at your office. Thanks very much. You already have my e-mail address, but my phone is 444-222-6666 — and I love its ring tone!

Replying to job posts

When you spot an advertised job on any recruiting platform (mobile, web, or print), consider responding with *a variation* on one of the following ten sample opening statements. Pair it with a strong closing statement (an assortment of closers appears later in this chapter), and you'll look like a candidate worthy of serious consideration:

✔ Checking Indeed.com paid off. Although I'm employed, I've been looking for the right opportunity to work for your company, and last night I found it! The requirements of your position #80440 for a regional distribution manager fit me exactly, from my B.A. in Economics to my fleet maintenance managerial experience.

✔ After spotting your need for a top-shelf multitasker and plate-spinner with a proven track record of project management, I have three words: Count me in. I can put a checkmark beside each requirement you list, as my resume confirms.

✔ Your posting on my job app to recruit a capable, self-motivated representative for customer service describes a position for which I am well credentialed. My record of increased and varied responsibilities in a pressure-cooker environment has prepared me for solving problems quickly and juggling multiple assignments with cost-saving success.

✔ When I saw your call for a mobile software engineer on Dice today, I thought someone had told you about my background and you were paging me: Excellent C/C++, 2+ years of software engineering experience from the mobile games industry, experience in Android, and much more. I hope that my resume will make your day, just as your posting made mine.

✔ RE: Executive Assistant, May 15 Craigslist Phoenix: My resume follows. I'm an experienced EA to senior management, offering strong digital skills, time management, organization, scheduling, prioritizing, and gate-keeping grace, as well as a reputation for loyalty and confidentiality.

✔ Please consider me for your advertised office administrator position (*Chicago Tribune,* June 7). As assistant office administrator, I have suc-cessfully introduced systems, processes, and techniques that boost productivity, save money, and promote satisfaction from support staff. Please find more information in my resume.

✔ Hello! Your recent posting for an entry-level accountant seems to be exactly the kind of position for which I have diligently prepared, and it appears to require the skills [identify a few skills] and experience I acquired in my previous internship assignments. My resume follows for your review.

✔ I am contacting you with enormous interest in your recent job post I found on the [name] app for [identify position]. My qualifications, as outlined in the following resume, appear to be a terrific match with the requirements listed for this position. I offer [identify several relevant skills] that should meet your challenging position with abilities to spare.

✔ [Name of] job app posted your attractive offer #120632, which is based in Portland. My wife and I are relocating to Portland because of her recent agreement to become the assistant administrator of St. Christopher's Hospital by September 1.

I relocate with an excellent reputation in the [identify industry] as a prod-uct manager who can deliver shareholder value and launch new products with flair. Some specific accomplishments are described in my resume.

✔ After reading your posting for an EXPRESS DELIVERY FACILITY OPERATIONS COORDINATOR, my qualifications should more than meet your requirements, as my resume confirms. I will leave the U.S. Marine Corps in two months. If you want to meet with me sooner, we could meet each other on Skype or video.

Mobile message closers

When you make closing statements in your mobile message, you have a choice in how assertive you want to be. Do you want to communicate with warmth and friendliness, such as "Hoping to hear from you soon about the job," or show confidence by closing with the type of statement sales teams and many experienced job seekers use? Maybe you'll aim for a closing state-ment somewhere in between.

Consider this assortment of closing statements to inspire you:

- ✔ My resume encapsulates my candidate package, but a personal meeting would better reveal my qualifications and fit for your company. Can we talk? Please call me at [smartphone number].

- ✔ If you like what you see on my resume, I'll be happy to hear from you on when we can meet and talk.

- ✔ I'd appreciate the opportunely to translate my past accomplishments into future benefits for your company. Please call me at [number] or e-mail me at [address].

- ✔ As you requested, here's my resume. I'll check back with you next week to flesh out any blank areas. Many thanks for your interest.

- ✔ My resume follows. I'll follow up by phone next week to answer any questions you may have.

- ✔ Thank you in advance for reviewing my resume. I enthusiastically look forward to discussing my qualifications in an interview. I'll e-mail you on Thursday to see when that might be possible.

- ✔ I hope to play an active role in the future prosperity of your organization. I'll contact you next week to talk about this job or related positions for which I have the qualifications to deliver A+ results.

- ✔ My school term will be over May 23 and I will be available to begin work the next day if you are considering adding me to your summer recreational staff. I appreciate your valuable time spent reading my resume. Many thanks.

- ✔ Analysis of your job ad suggests that I am well qualified to provide the education and teamwork fit that you specify. I look forward to hearing from you soon. My mobile phone number is [number]; my e-mail address is [address].

- ✔ My resume follows. Thanks for reading it and not letting it drop out of sight in an ATS. I can bring in revenue for your company. Please respond to me at [mobile phone number] or [e-mail address].

- ✔ I look forward to a discussion of why I'm the best candidate for this opportunity. My e-mail is [address]; my phone is [number].

- ✔ I hope to hear from you ASAP because I already have an attractive offer and need to reply, but your position sounds totally and incredibly perfect for my qualifications. My cell phone: [number].

- ✔ I very much enjoyed talking with you on video and look forward to meeting with you in person sooner rather than later. E-mail me at [e-mail address].

- ✔ Do you need more than my resume provides? Please call me at [number] at your earliest convenience. Thank you.

- ✔ I'm fired up about the employment opportunities within your organization and hope to explore contributions I can make. After checking out my resume, it would be great if you could e-mail me this week to let me know when your calendar is open. Looking forward to it.

✔ Your time is valuable, and I appreciate your consideration. That's why I'll call you next week to answer any questions you may have. Or if staffing this position is time sensitive, you can reach me at [number].

✔ I welcome a personal interview to discuss how my qualifications can augment your company's excellent reputation for marketing acumen. I'll e-mail you on Thursday to see if we can meet and when.

✔ My salary needs are in line with the [job title] description and what I bring in abilities and experience. I'll contact you this week to see when we can explore specifics. Or if you need to reach me sooner, my mobile number is [number].

✔ You're an ace for reading my resume. I ask to meet with you personally if you have an interest in my professional potential following my June graduation with a B.S.B.A. in Accounting. I will follow up with you next week to see if and when we can interview. Crossing my fingers.

✔ My internship experience and education [name of degree and major], coupled with my eagerness to learn and drive to achieve, make me a potential excellent hire decision for your company. Can we discuss available positions coming up after May?

Mobile Job Search in the Digital Age

Mobile offers an appealing fast tempo for people who don't want to waste a minute of their busy lives. Despite mobile technology's growing pains, the immediate reward for job seekers is their new ability to scout jobs whenever and wherever they have down time.

Studies of how recruiters and job searchers connect reveal the fluidity of the marketplace as mobile usage doubles from one year to the next. In fact, mobile job search figures are climbing as you read this.

Stretching tomorrow's digital screens

Question: How soon will a new generation of larger screen sizes on digital devices be available?

Answer: Within a decade, probably much sooner. At least two smartphone and tablet makers propose creating a larger viewable area by updating today's flat and rigid screens with displays that bend around the device's edges and eliminate physical buttons.

Why you care: The technology upgrade will provide more options in the size of your job search letters.

Chapter 3

Newcomer Letters that Persuade

In This Chapter

▶ Meeting new letters that market you now and later

▶ Appreciating how job letters give you career lift-off

▶ Nailing distinctive messages to remember and use

*F*ight for the job you want and the career security you need with *the persuasion of words*. Words, of course, are old friends, but they're showing up in new homes you want to know about. Persuasive words now fuel a wide variety of job letters that can help you.

The "persuasion of words" concept sits at the sweetest spot in the big tent of job search letters. The tent has room for letters and notes you can write to get a job, and for documents and memos that back up your claims. After you land a job, the tent has room for a similar array of letters you can draft to gain a promotion, a raise, extra leave time, or some other benefit.

Here's a preview of what the growing bevy of job search letters can do to bolster your job search and advance your career:

✔ Persuasive words are essential for letters you write to find a home in recruiters' candidate resource files.

✔ Persuasive words are required in personal statements you write to get into medical, business, or law school.

✔ Persuasive words are crucial in blogs you write to attest to your expertise in knowledge and skills that employers want.

✔ Persuasive words are rewarded in recommendations you write for yourself that others will be glad to sign.

✔ Persuasive words are vital in notes of appreciation you write to maintain solid relationships throughout your career, thanking people for professional favors.

13 Messages to Outrun Rivals

This chapter introduces a baker's dozen newcomer types of letters, notes, documents, and memos.

When a letter type is illustrated with a sample, I let you know by listing the last name, in all caps, of the particular sample that corresponds with the concept being discussed. You can find the samples at the end of the chapter.

Now it's newcomer letter time!

Accomplishment statements

The accomplishment statement of your winning moves commonly takes a full page. You can package it with a resume, hand it out at job fairs, or distribute it in networking activities. You can use it as a cheat sheet to prepare for interviews, share it with an interviewer to spark conversation, or leave it behind as a reminder of why you're the best candidate. (HOLDER)

See Chapter 10 for other kinds of leave-behind supplements.

Checklist comparisons

No document style more directly connects a job seeker's desirability for a position than a thorough point-to-point comparison of an employer's requirements with a candidate's qualifications.

Make your case by deconstructing a position statement, line by line. Then detail how you fill the bill, again going line by line. This chapter includes a sample two-page checklist in a straightforward two-column layout. (DUVALL)

Resume addendums

Career marketing letters have always been a balancing act. The busy reader wants information fast. The accomplished job seeker wants credit for all she's done. The resume addendum solves the dilemma.

The addendum zeros in on a facet of your background that may not stand out in a resume or may be buried in another type of job search letter. For example, an addendum may spotlight a competency or offer a convincing reason why an unconventional candidate should be considered.

This chapter includes two resume addendum samples.

Professional writer Don Orlando created the sample of a *leadership adden-dum* (for Carla L. Johnson). It provides compelling proof that you can solve your target company's problems. Orlando explains why it works:

> *In the resume, those proofs are concise. In the addendum, your skills can come alive in story form — specifically, a story about your value. Your description of the problem you solved, the actions you took, and the gain you achieved make the hiring authority think, "I need someone like that!"*

Professional writer Stephanie Clark created the sample of a *reading list adden-dum* (for Sonia Cher). It harmonizes with the alternative viewpoints of the holistic nutritionist and includes both colorful comments and a sprinkling of lowercase typefaces.

The focus of other kinds of resume addendums is limited only by your needs and creativity, such as a *technology summary, an industry-specific sales record, a professional credentials inventory, an office tools brief,* and *a computer skills overview.*

Two sample resume addendums are included in this chapter. (JOHNSON, CHER)

Specialty profiles

A specialty profile is a single-page document fastened to your resume that details a strength related to the position you seek. Examples of subject areas: paraprofessional healthcare specialties, training expertise, client sourcing, and project management.

Topics for special profiles sometimes overlap with topics in resume adden-dums; the distinction is in the eye of the beholder.

First 90-day forecasts

The purpose of preparing a document that projects early achievements is to show hiring decision makers that you truly understand the requirements of the position and the level of performance expected, and emphasizes that you will be immediately productive.

The forecast model of a job search letter is best suited for professional and managerial candidates who have the authority to make important policy decisions. These documents tend to run between 5 and 25 pages, headed by a 1-page executive summary. This chapter includes a sample executive summary for a 90-day forecast (HENDRIX).

Introduction letters

When you do a walking-around job hunt, consider using a portable job prospecting letter. Suggested by professional writer Judy Gillespie, the letter is packaged with a resume in a clear plastic folder.

The big idea is to canvas shopping, office, and industrial areas, and hand out your prospecting package to selected potential employers in their places of business. A Gillespie client relocating from out of state found a good position in a retail optical shop using this job letter technique illustrated by the sample letter. (LOWELL)

Professional education statements

As part of the competitive process of being admitted to a professional degree program, you'll likely have to submit a personal statement or application essay.

Even though you submit bricks of data, the admissions committees require statements and essays because their members want to see who you really are. Your formal but sterile application describes you only in terms of numbers and lists of accomplishments. In your statements, remember these tips:

✔ Show your motivations and why you're interested in the career field.

✔ Communicate your qualities, strengths, and accomplishments by illustration or story rather than factual statements.

✔ Include illustrations showing that you are responsible, energetic, and easy to get along with.

QR-coded letters

You've seen quick response codes (QR codes) virtually everywhere, from cereal boxes, to company websites, to store merchandise. They're the two-dimensional bar codes that can be scanned for data and decoded by a QR code reader on smartphones. The data includes words and numbers, or a hyperlink.

Consider four main benefits of using a QR code in job search activities:

✔ You have to be noticed to be hired. A quick response code helps you stand above the crowd of job candidates who've never heard of using them in job search letters.

✔ Ageism-bedeviled seniors can project an image of being technologically vital by incorporating a QR code in their search materials.

✔ Job seekers of any age can use QR codes to subtly say they're technically proficient, a trait especially desirable in marketing, technology, public relations, and social media.

✔ When attending a job fair or networking event where recruiters are working booths and collecting resumes, a QR code on your resume enables recruiters to scan more about you then and there.

The most common locations to embed QR codes appear to be cover letters, networking letters, prospecting letters, resumes, and business cards. You can make your own QR code for free. Search online for "QR code generators." Check out smartphone apps, searching for "QR code makers."

Job skills checklists

Skills are the coin of the realm when you're in the market for employment. A job skills checklist is a document you can use to customize resumes, prepare for job interviews, and perhaps use in an after-interview letter to remind the hiring authority of what you can contribute to the employer's game plan.

Some people prefer to build a master skills checklist that goes on and on; the master list isn't shared with employers, but is kept privately as a resource to draw upon when needed.

For instance, you can construct a checklist by career field, a checklist by industry, and a checklist for contract jobs, part-time jobs, and job-bidding website applications.

Find examples by searching online for "job skills checklists."

Resume letters

Resume letters are designed for targeted mail campaigns, online or postal, and are sent to people who can hire you. The sources of names for your list of recipients range from networking results to commercial mailing lists.

A first-rate resume letter addresses five classic concerns of a harried employer:

✔ I don't know who you are.

✔ I don't know your work and your reputation.

✔ I don't know what you have that I want.

✔ I don't know why I should read about you, wasting time I don't have.

✔ I don't know why I shouldn't trash your letter right now.

A resume letter works particularly well when a work history is riddled with hard-to-explain gaps and other problems. It attracts notice because it reads more like a story than a document.

This chapter includes a sample of a resume letter. (BAKER)

Job offer responses

What do you say when you receive a job offer? (Other than "Hallelujah!") No matter what your decision, remember to say that you much appreciate the offer. You have three basic options — "yes," "no," or "too late."

Offer acceptances

Thank the hiring manager for the job offer, mentioning the full job title, and formally accept it. Mention your understanding of the terms and conditions of employment: compensation, work hours, starting date, where you will report to work, and any special conditions, such as company-supplied uniforms, short-term or contract work, and required training. If the company's written offer covered all the important bases, you can cut it short like this:

> *I am happy to accept your offer as stated in your letter of [date]. The job offer letter contains the compensation we agreed to — [$ amount]. I'm very much looking forward to seeing you on my first day, which is [date] at [location].*

Offer declines

Politely and briefly decline the job offer, to maintain good relations with the employer and keep the door open for future offers. You never know what good fortune could develop if you handle a turndown with class. Mention that the decision was difficult to make and that you wish the employer all possible success. Your phrasing can be along these lines:

> *Thank you very much for your job offer of an engineering position in your R&D division. Unfortunately, I must decline your offer. After intense review, I just can't make the numbers come out right for me. Your job will not meet my financial needs, considering my student loans and living costs in San Francisco. I am sorry that I won't be working with the impressive people I've met at your excellent company. I appreciate the time and consideration*

you've given to me, and I sincerely hope we have the opportunity to meet in the future.

Name withdrawals

When you take another job before an offer comes through, write a short, respectful response telling the truth. Here's a sample note:

I was delighted to receive your interesting offer for [position title] at [organization]. Although I am impressed with both the position and your company, I've received another offer that I think more closely matches what I'm looking for. That's why, after giving it deep hours of thought, I must decline your fine job offer.

Thank you for your time and effort. I hold the best thoughts for you and your company's bright future.

Rejection follow-ups

When you don't get the job, send what some call the "suck it up and smile" letter as an investment in your reputation.

Graciously thank the hiring manager for the interview and consideration. Ask that you be kept in mind for future openings. Send a similar (but not duplicate) letter to the human resources representative or recruiter with the company. Personalize both letters by saying what impressed you about the company and the position.

Anything can happen. The new hire for the job you wanted may quickly and abruptly resign, and you'll get a call. The recipient of your letter may wish he could have hired both of you and recommend you to a colleague for another open position. Such occurrences are infrequent, but they do happen.

Job return agreements

You're surprised when a company that laid you off wants you back. You're wondering if a second act on the same stage is a productive move in your career. After investigation, you're willing to have a homecoming. Okay, but try to sweeten your deal by writing a job return agreement. Here's an example of asking for a pay raise and no waiting time for benefits:

I am looking for market rate compensation, considering that, since I left the company, I have gained several skills that will help me do my job even better (name the skills). Because I know the job and the company, I will be 100 percent productive as soon as I start. I ask that I resume all employee benefits immediately and that my seniority rights be restored as if there were no break in service.

Alexis Holder

Europe | alexis@newleaf.ca | Skype alexisHolder | +68 1604 2931
Available for Relocation – Canada, U.S., U.K.

Product Innovator |
International Partnership Builder |
Leader, Presenter, Writer, Communicator |

Me in a Nutshell |

Ideation* – I excel at seeing connections between things, people, ideas (in fact, I am fascinated by ideas and delight in innovating and creating, and need to keep myself mentally renewed).

Activator* – Not only is my mind a fertile ground of creative insights, I turn concepts into action, stir enthusiasm, champion projects, add momentum, take the lead, and affirm people's contributions.

Strategic* – Faced with multiple possibilities or challenged with an obstacle, I can conceive new ways, problem solve, identify opportunities, stimulate discussions, and make sense of it all for the best solution.

Input* – I crave more information, more involvement, can switch with ease from one topic to an unrelated issue, love to offer insight and perspective, and really relish a give and take brainstorming session.

Adaptability* – Inherently flexible, I am calm and this reassures others. I work best in a stochastic, unstructured environment where the need to respond well to constantly changing circumstances is a gift.

*My top strengths as discovered through Gallup Inc. StrengthsFinder

Achievements & Awards |

- Developed products as creative lead on the top-tier product in the TOYNAME® lineup: the award-winning TOYNAME® products.
- Nurtured long-term relationships with an extended list of multi-national partners that represent several industries, for example, (Names of Well-Known International Corporations).
- Presented to diverse audiences around the world – professional, purchasing public, academics, scientific – and frequently; and contributed to articles and books on creativity.
- Fluent in English and German; conversational levels of French, Swedish and Dutch.
- Recognized with **awards** for innovative product development.
  - ✓ (Name) Group Achievement Award, for contributing to annual student competition.
  - ✓ 200⁺ awards bestowed on TOYNAME® brand in which I participated in 10 product developments, and led an additional four product innovations.
  - ✓ Toy Industry Awards (TIA), 20xx, for TOYNAME® products in which I led the launch.

Additional Business Skills |

Project management	Strategic communications	MS Office Suite
Staff management	Public relations / Diplomacy	Final Cut Pro
Staff development	Cross-functional leadership	Mac & PC platforms
Prioritization	International partnerships	Adobe Creative Suite

Stephanie Clark, CRS, CIS — Nanaimo, B.C., Canada

Amanda Duvall

Page 1 of 2

You Require	Amanda Duvall Delivers
◆ Overall Administrative leadership, supervision, and control of large entity that provides variety of job training/employment services	✔ Am currently serving as Mayor of Crystal Valley, Texas, and Managing Director of StarPower Staffing Inc. Leadership, supervision and control of large departments that have provided information technology services to large companies. Included in this responsibility was the creation of individual training programs. Have led numerous seminars on job search for a number of public companies and for local trade associations.
◆ Budgets, fundraising, grant writing	✔ To finance the Local Train, made numerous trips to Washington to persuade staff of key members of congress and senate. Met with U.S. Transportation Secretary Robert Saxtra to secure federal dollars, as well as Crystal Valley congressional delegation (I meet with them yearly on transportation projects). As Workforce Partnership CEO and chief fundraiser, I will show you the money.
◆ Direct preparation, review, presentation, and control of annual operating, system and support and program policy budgets for the Policy Board	✔ Created budgets and completed detail reviews of budgets at StarPower Staffing Inc., Security Midwest, and City of Crystal Valley.
◆ Establish and maintain lines of communication with a wide range of community, contractor, and employer-based organizations	✔ As a government official and businessman, have worked with a wide range of the public. At StarPower Staffing Inc. and, earlier at Technology Finder, have worked with over 75 companies negotiating contracts with employers and providing over 500 contract employees.
◆ Effectively communicate orally and in writing	✔ Have created myriad of reports, statistical and analytical, throughout career; frequently speak and make presentations in boardrooms and auditoriums.
◆ Establish effective working relationship with management, employees, and the public representing the diverse cultures and backgrounds	✔ Public service, including being popularly elected three times as Mayor of Crystal Valley, speaks to my history of establishing effective working relationships with a wide range of people, from administrative assistants and letter carriers, to managers and high-ranking government officials. References will validate my unblemished track record in diversity hiring and respectful treatment of all.

Amanda Duvall, Cell (936) 555-0111

You Require	Amanda Duvall Delivers
◆ Prepare and give public presentations on Workforce Partnership initiatives	✔ Given well-received presentations for StarPower Staffing Inc., City of Crystal Valley and at many other organizations. Understand use of PowerPoint presentations and video technology.
◆ Treat employees, representatives of outside agencies and members of the public with courtesy and respect	✔ As references indicate, my interpersonal relationships are in good shape. Behavioral courtesy toward and respect for all is embedded in my personality and always has been.
◆ A graduate degree is desirable	✔ Hold master's degree in counseling with emphasis in organizational behavior and group dynamics. (University of Texas at Austin).
◆ Ten years of executive level experience working with senior level executives within government and private sector organizations as well as governing boards, councils and committees	✔ Over twenty years as an executive in seven organizations. Twelve years as an elected official.
◆ The individual appointed must have a reputation that reflects the highest public ethics, and personal integrity, as well as flexibility and creativity in meeting the needs of customers	✔ References document my reputation for the highest public ethics and personal integrity.
◆ Possess knowledge of current and future workforce needs	✔ First-hand experience "in the trenches" with a number of high tech, biotech and general business entities, determining staffing requirements. And am abreast of national and regional job trends and statistical sources of data.
◆ Possess knowledge of State and Federal employment and job training programs, contract administration, and grants management	✔ Created and negotiated three-blanket service contracts with the General Services Administration (GSA). Have passed a thorough audit of services provided to a federal agency. Have participated in federal training programs on GSA contracts. Have followed state and federal job training programs from the original CETA jobs program.
◆ Possess knowledge of public and private sector management practices and systems	✔ Maintain knowledge and awareness of managerial practices, systems and trends through reading of journals (such as *Business Week*, *Austin Business Journal*), reading of various books, attendance at seminars from Software Industry Council. Spot check website news and blogs as well.

Amanda Duvall, Cell (936) 555-0111

Carla L. Johnson 4140 Carter Lane Kansas City, MO 64101 ✉clj2006@knology.net ☎ 816.555.0111

To: Mr. John Markwell, CEO, BizJet

Leadership Addendum

> Please don't look for any generalized list of "qualifications" here. I thought you deserved to see documented proof of performance, aligned closely with the values I laid out in my letter to you. I hope these condensed examples encourage you to explore how I might serve BizJet.

Refocusing an established corporate culture by capitalizing on best technology and leadership practices:

The problem: I inherited a business that had slowly changed its self-image from "successful" to "comfortable." Our team thought we were in the business of just selling products and services. They saw each new sale as a discreet event, a number they hoped would grow. I just couldn't stand seeing our good people not getting satisfaction from what they did. No wonder we couldn't keep a stable sales staff. It bothered me that our customers often saw us as "order takers." In short, doing business at arms length was shortchanging everyone. I knew our team and our customers deserved a lot more.

The actions: First, I made sure every employee knew we sold *productivity*, not product. Then I reached out to our customers with the same message, but packaged in a way I knew would appeal to them: we wanted to be their success partners. Soon my staff was seeking out our customers to find *all* their wants and their needs. Our people became masters at what drove our customers' businesses.

We automated what we learned, instituted data mining, optimized inventory order points automatically—in short, I gave our people and our customers everything they needed to build mutual success.

The results: Soon our sales force's commissions were 300 percent greater than before. Market share doubled in just 18 months. Sales employee turnover dropped from 20 percent a year to less than 5 percent. Most of all, employees wanted to come to work, our competitor's top performers wanted to work for us, customers wanted to see our reps, and I couldn't wait to reward excellence all through our firm.

Getting ahead of customer perceptions to beat the competition:

The problem: We almost became the victim of our own success. We convinced our customers that we sold productivity they had to have. But when our products needed service, most customers accepted the established industry standard that dictated an eight-hour delay before they were up and running well again. That may have been the *industry* standard, but it sure wasn't mine.

*More indicators of return on investment **BizJet** can use...*

Carla L. Johnson

The actions: I had all the expertise right in house: our service engineers. I asked them how we could cut the eight-hour down time in half. It might have been the first time management recognized them for their expertise.

The results: Soon we were returning our customers to full operation in half the time. But by then, the relationship I built with our engineers, and they with our customers, had taken on a momentum all its own. Eventually, the time to return to service dropped from 8 hours to less than 90 minutes. We rarely lost a customer to service concerns from then on.

Motivating customers to help our cash flow:

The problem: Over time, we allowed our customers to take a casual view of our payment terms. We were telling people we wanted to be paid in 30 days, but we were accepting most payments 45 days or more after we delivered our products. That's why we could rarely forecast our cash flow well. That's why our ability to invest in growth was crippled.

The actions: I knew our administrative staff felt somewhat underappreciated. Could I transform collections—a job most people disliked—into a motivator for this group? I found the key in having them share in the rewards through a bonus system based on the amount they collected.

The results: Collection times soon fell to less than 30 days. I made sure everybody knew how our administrative staff had positioned us for better and faster growth.

Expanding into an unknown market to meet very aggressive growth targets:

The problem: The company that bought my firm demanded uncompromising growth: 25 percent a year! They asked me to help them expand into a new market, some 250 miles to the south, an area we knew very little about.

The actions: We soon identified two likely acquisition targets: one barely making a profit and another in the red. Of course, we went beyond the usual, rigorous due diligence to find what our new customers would want. We not only uncovered their wants, they helped us identify the local sales "stars." That's all we needed to apply the best practices we had learned on our home ground to our new market.

The results: We were up and running in just under 18 months. Revenue in this new growth market escalated from $1.8M to $6.0M in 9 years.

Don Orlando, CPRW, JCTC, CCM, CCMC, CJSS, MCD — Montgomery, Ala.

sonia cher

I live the holistic philosophy of mind-body-spirit connection

registered holistic nutritionist

I am a Registered Holistic Nutritionist with a profound knowledge of holistic nutrition and the holistic lifestyle - my recommendations are appropriate, comprehensive, and educational.

HolisticHealth Centers will benefit from my drive to serve and desire to inspire change.

my favorite reading list

✳ **Nourishing Traditions: The Cookbook that Challenges Politically Correct Nutrition and the Diet Dictocrats** - *by Sally Fallon with Mary G. Enig*
The author dispels the myths of the low-fat fad in this practical and entertaining book. It is the best cookbook I have found as it teaches how to cook from scratch in the most nourishing way possible, which goes along with my personal philosophy that short cuts don't lead to long term results. I endorse its focus on healing and nourishing foods as opposed to quick and easy meals.

✳ **When the Body Says No: The Cost of Hidden Stress** - *by Gabor Mate, M.D.*
Aptly described as a groundbreaking book, the author shows how emotion and psychological stress play a powerful role in the onset of chronic illness. His research substantiated my own innate belief that emotions play a huge role in physical health. This pivotal work has become a mainstay in both my personal and professional lives and I recommend it often.

✳ **Miracle of Water** - *by Masaru Emoto*
An intriguing book full of grippingly beautiful photography introduces and explains the concept of "resonance," or the transmission of life-force energy. This book introduced me to the impact thoughts have on the molecular structure of water. Given that we are 70% water, then thoughts absolutely have a huge impact on our health. This spurred my own growth in the importance of emotional honesty. I share that each of us has the capacity to change our mindset, and empower people with the knowledge that they have options.

✳ **Aging Well: Surprising Guideposts to a Happier Life from the Landmark Harvard Study of Adult Development** - *by George Vaillant*
A social person myself, I enjoyed learning that yes, having fun and connecting with people socially is critical for a healthy longevity. The research reinforces the fact that play and fun and creativity are more important than the typical North American mindset allows. Long living cultures emphasize this, and we can learn from it. I heartily endorse fun as well as hard work!

✳ ✳ ✳

778.555.1212 | sonia@newleaf.com

Stephanie Clark, CRS, CIS — Nanaimo, B.C., Canada

[Date]

TO: Workforce Partnership of Austin; Task Force Selection Committee
      Attention: Joanna Ramirez and Perry Johansen, Co-Chairs

FROM: Edward Hendrix, 936-555-0111

This report outlines the focus I will give to your major areas of concern and expectations for the first three months if you select me to serve as your new Executive Director/President and CEO for the Workforce Partnership of Austin. This plan, subject to revision after hire, is based on the information now available to me.

Action Plan for the First 90 Days

Executive Overview

- Resolve office lease chokehold now draining agency funds.
- Establish strong rapport with staff at all facilities.
- Analyze effectiveness of grant writing function.
- Review entire funding system and auditing protections.
- Visit OneStops; review job- and labor-market reporting systems; review operating contracts; meet with contractors.
- Appoint task force to assess quality of training and job search services to clients, including use of Web 2.0 interactive services to speed hiring rates. Review mechanism for assurance of ongoing implementation of up-to-date best practices.
- Consider appointment of volunteer ambassadors to aid staff in promoting employers' participation in Workforce Partnership activities.
- Revisit mechanism for incoming reports from headquarters staff and OneStop managers.
- Issue concise weekly progress report to Policy Board.
- Make contact with managements of other workforce agencies.

(Note: 10-page report follows the executive summary)

_____

Edward Hendrix, Cell (936) 555-0111

Gregory Lowell, L.D.O.

1956 Alvaston Boulevard • Melbourne, FL 32935 • 321.555.5555
e-mailname@gmail.com

[Date]

RE: Licensed Optician Position

My goal is always 100% accuracy for both vision and looks – a perfect fit the first time. Whether I'm working with customers, or in the lab, or managing a retail store I find my having a knack for sales, finance, and technology comes in handy every single day.

Prior to practicing as a Licensed Optician, I was an Optical Sales Representative. I gained invaluable customer service skills and was honored to receive several National Sales awards.

I recently relocated to this area and I'd like to put my wide-ranging experience as a **Licensed Optician** to work for you. Here's a copy of my résumé and references for your review.

Thank you for your time and consideration, I'd welcome the opportunity to meet with you and will plan on giving you a call to follow-up in a day or so.

Sincerely yours,

Gregory Lowell

Gregory Lowell

Enclosures: Resume, References

Judith L. Gillespie, CPCC, CPRW, CEIP — W. Melbourne, Fla.

SUSAN L. BAKER

123 Hollywood Dr. ◆ Oceanside, CA 92057
Cell: 760-555-0112 ◆ Home: 760-555-0111 ◆ Email: susan500baker@yahoo.com

Mr. Antonio K. Garcia, Director of Service   [Date]
BMW Dealers, Escondido
123 Auto Park Way
Escondido, CA 12345

Dear Mr. Garcia:

Any claim that the grass is greener outside the auto-industry-fence is a myth! At least it is for me.

After 20 years of rock-solid experience in our industry, a series of outside opportunities briefly tempted me to cast eyes elsewhere. But not for long.

My inner voice keeps shouting loud and clear that the auto side is where I belong and that's why I'm selectively contacting you – hopefully, you will see how adding me to your quality operation will be a big win for (name of company).

My progressively responsible experience includes **service management, service consulting,** and **service writing**. *Initiative*, *drive*, and *positive attitude* teamed with *customer satisfaction* and *product know-how* have contributed to my documented success:

★ Service Manager, Star Mercedes Benz, Carlsbad, CA: Managed all customer service operations. Hired, trained and supervised a culturally-diverse workforce of 15. Additionally, as a member of a leadership management quartette, co-managed a separate department of 33 full-time workers. I drove a customer satisfaction winning score in the 90s, up from a failing score in the 70s, when I took responsibility. [dates]

★ Service Manager, Star Honda, Carlsbad, CA: Managed all customer service operations, as well as oversight of equipment purchasing and building maintenance. Hired, trained, and supervised a staff of 44 employees. Initiated cross-skills training, attained State of California "Green Shop" certification. [dates]

★ Service Manager/Service Advisor, Planet Acura, Porsche, & Audi, Carlsbad, CA: Maintained customer satisfaction score of 90% or higher for 10 years with increasing responsibilities, including managing all used-car reconditioning. Promoted to service manager position where I maintained customer service transactions for all three car lines. Utilized manufacturer marketing tools to create customer-satisfaction-measurement mailings, and management of "units in operation" reports. [dates]

What about dealership operation skills? I am up to speed and ready to roll in software skills, including Word, Excel, Outlook, and PowerPoint; as well as Visio, Publisher, and Project.

What about interpersonal skills? How many references shall I provide? I think you'll find that my brand in our industry is this: Susan is a thoroughly competent professional who understands that integrity and fair-dealing are essential to remaining viable in business for the long run. She's liked by bosses, coworkers and direct reports for her ability to deal genuinely and without arrogance, or when things don't go her way, without bias or pettiness.

I will contact you on Tuesday afternoon to see when should meet, and to answer any questions you may have concerning my commitment to again water greener grass on a team providing great customer service and boosting profits.

Sincerely yours,

Susan Baker

Susan L. Baker

Good words for Susan:

"Although I thought I should have been saving money on a lower priced car, I kept returning to the Porsche dealer because I was treated with such respect by Susan Baker. She really understands how to keep customers happy with their service. She once sent a car at four in the morning to pick me up when, rushing to the airport, I had an accident rolling across roadside brush and wound up with flat tires and tumbleweed and little purple flowers growing out of the grill. She's an American treasure."
 — Norma Luna, Porsche owner and customer.

"When Susan was the handling the customer service ops at Honda, she hired me, a woman, giving me a chance to show I could do the work right along with the guys. I'll never forget her fairness in opening an opportunity for me. I'm still here. Thanks, Susan."
 — Leslie Lubinski, service writer.

"Susan Baker is so good that if after 30 days on the job, anyone who hires her isn't satisfied with her work, I'll pay that salary out of my own pocket."
 — Cory Miller, former Mercedes dealership owner.

More Cool Job Letters Ahead

Keep turning pages to discover lots more ways you can use the persuasion of words in letters that make a positive difference in your job search and career plans.

Chapters 4 through 7 offer a treasure chest of sample letters that you've probably already met. These include job ad reply letters, networking letters, job prospecting letters, and after-interview letters.

Chapters 8 through 13 present a raft of less familiar job search letters. These include mobile and social media messages, branding statements, bios, profiles, job interview leave-behind supplements, reference commentaries, and post-hiring letters that grow your career.

Signs of the times

Sandwich boards and street signs are dramatic types of job letters, as the following three true stories illustrate:

Too big to fail. An unemployed Wall Street investment banker decided that nothing else was working for him and that being bold could be the right sauce to perk up his job hunt. The banker devised his own kind of job letter by hanging a sandwich board over his suit that read "Experienced MIT Grad for Hire." Then he hit the streets of New York. The billboard guy landed a job with a major accounting firm.

Will work for job. A young college graduate working in a bike shop had snagged only one interview for a job with management potential in the year since her graduation. The frustrated rookie held a street sign that read "Will work for entry-level position" at one of the busiest corners in Washington, D.C. The right person walked by and later called her for an interview.

She got the quality of entry-level job she sought with a technologies company.

Spinners and winners. When some free-spirited job hunters are desperate, their creative genes light up and they devise ways to set themselves apart — in this case, whirling and twirling signs at busy intersections. Sign spinners find jobs at $9-11 an hour on such websites as Sign Spinners (www.signspinning.org). Although I don't know of a job seeker hunting for a sit-down job who has found one using sign-flipping skills, that could happen as the world turns.

The takeaway

Hiring authorities are split on whether the jumbo outdoor tactics are professional and whether they work out well in the long run. If you decide to try sign messaging, keep the text short enough to read at a glance. You're a big part of the sign, so dress like a businessperson.

Part II

Essential Job Search Letters

The 5th Wave   By Rich Tennant

JOB LETTERS TO AVOID

Scented letters

Origami letters

Frivolous letters

Confusing letters

In this part . . .

Welcome to the main event! Here, you'll find four principal job search letter types: job ad reply letters, networking letters, prospecting letters, and after-interview letters. When you put these power players to work, you put yourself in the lead of other job contenders. Within these chapters is a bevy of samples, written by today's leading document writers, to guide you on your way.

Chapter 4

Job Ad Reply Letters and Notes

* *

In This Chapter

▶ Learning from a treasure trove of more than 50 super replies

▶ Choosing strategies for your specific situation

▶ Viewing interview-magnet approaches anyone can use

* *

Whether it's posted online or printed on paper, a job ad appears because an employer wants to hire someone to do a specific job — now! Not six months from now.

The immediate potential of employment is what makes answering a job ad a nearly universal experience. This chapter of job reply letters and notes contains way more examples of how to do it well than any other chapter in this guide.

All samples were written by successful professional job search letter and resume writers. For your convenience, this book's appendix contains contact information for each writer.

The samples in this chapter hold something for everyone, regardless of occupation — from new graduates, to midcareer professionals, to seasoned executives.

 Read the interesting variety of styles with an eye toward mixing and matching design and marketing elements. Because the samples range from traditional to forward leaning, use your judgment in deciding which style best fits your target industry and your personality. Also think about the sample's eye-candy appeal in attracting your intended readers.

Study all the samples; you'll find a wide range of techniques that snag an employer's interest and hold it all the way to interviews.

Watching for Smooth Moves

The following sections give you the scoop on what's great about the upcoming samples (found at the end of the chapter), as well as ideas for putting them to work in your own reply letters and notes. The samples appear in the order mentioned in the following descriptions.

Magic connectors

Candidates who document point for point their capacity to accomplish what the employer wants accomplished earn interviews. A *T-letter* is a popular way to do this. After an introductory paragraph, the T-letter presents two columns. In the left column, you list the employer's job requirements; in the right column, you list your qualifications as they match the job's requirements.

The following three samples illustrate the visual power of directly connecting job requirements with candidate qualifications:

- A food chain manager (ARMSTRONG) approaches a food company that seeks a category manager. She uses a "T" letter format and emphasizes her key qualifications in bold typeface.

- A satellite operations manager (BELL) jumps right in with a comment that she's a match. The candidate also calls attention to her status of qualified candidate in a vertical treatment. A "You require" list appears on the left side of the page. An "I offer" response appears directly across the page on the right.

- A senior sales specialist (TRIETELMANN) takes a one-two-three bingo! approach to matching the job's requirements with her "been-there-done-that" and "can-do's."

P.S. winners

Observe the use of a postscript to prod contact by directing eyes to a super selling point or a potential benefit to an employer. This old marketing copywriter's trick animates letters and hijacks attention, as you see in the following two samples:

- A marketing executive (REDMOND) uses a postscript that reinforces his headline of "Confidential," to accomplish two aims: (1) to keep his job search under the radar and (2) to position himself in the currently employed candidate category (*translation:* he must be good because someone hired him).

✔ A communications information technology executive (SCHOFIELD) writes a postscript containing the tease of his solution to an unrecognized industry problem.

Fast starters

Opening a letter with pizzazz contributes enormous value to its successful journey through screening activities, as these two samples show:

✔ A transitioning military veteran (FORSYTH) not only saves the employer time by specifying his interest in a specific job opening and where he found it, but follows quickly with related leadership traits in bold type.

✔ A Red Cross emergency manager (HORTON) opens his letter with the intensity of a crime novel — "I don't scare easily." He names his areas of expertise and the skills that make interviewing him essential.

Praise gold

American humorist Will Rogers wrote it right: "Get someone else to blow your horn, and the sound will carry twice as far." When a candidate sets the stage with positive comments by others, employers are impressed. That person is no longer a "nobody that nobody knows."

Note how these two samples presell the candidate by quoting kudos from others at the top of the letter, in the right column, or in the body of the letter:

✔ A direct sales ace seeking a managerial position (W. JONES) headlines impressive praise from a former employer.

✔ A part-time, temporary instructor candidate (YOUNG) uses quotations from previous performance evaluations to great effect.

Design arts

Looks count in attracting favorable notice in all media. To rewrite Steve Jobs, "Design is not just what it looks like. Design is what makes you take a second look."

Even so, some applicant software systems have trouble handling creative formats. (See Chapter 6.) Even so, some designs are so attractive, they're tough to ignore, as these three samples illustrate:

✔ A sales manager (SHIELDS) makes a wise choice of a design that virtually guarantees a stop-what-you're-doing-and-read-this reaction. Using two columns and a vertical rule, the cover letter effectively overviews his value proposition: broad experience, commitment to excellence, skill in communications, and strategic planning.

✔ A sales associate (ROSEN) leads with a tasteful thumbnail list of core competencies and skills at the top of her letter.

✔ A small business owner–turned–job seeker (CLARK) features a branding circle of strengths to call attention to her marketing and creative strengths.

Graph gems

Graphs and charts present information easily and quickly, enabling us to get our points across fast. In job search letters, the can effectively communicate your impressive performance and accomplishments. Notice the high impact of graphs in these three samples:

✔ An operations executive (A. BOTKIN) uses graphs to communicate her success in meeting revenue goals, after she compares the studio operations director's requirements with her own qualifications.

✔ A sales professional (MORRISON) dramatically uses a graph in a business-savvy letter to illustrate how his sales nearly doubled in one quarter.

✔ Another sales professional (D. BOTKIN) embeds a twist: He incorporates the Sales Skills Index, an independent evaluation of skills needed to succeed in the sales environment, into his recounting of a highly successful track record.

Attention grabbers

In the following samples, can you spot the use of bold typefaces, italics, and underscoring to highlight some combination of the following factors?

✔ The position sought

✔ Accomplishments and achievements

✔ Skills and personal characteristics

✔ Special benefits, such as security clearances and fluency in more than one language

Writing quality is another factor that causes employers to pay serious attention to you. Check out the following five samples for inspiration:

- A well-educated researcher (MARTIN) uses eloquent but comfortable language to propose that she join the staff of a prestigious research institute.

- A candidate for a human resource director's position (SCHULTZ) doesn't say that she hasn't yet held an HR director's title, but uses a classically simple design to direct eyes to her professional merit. The candidate's branding statement proclaims a commitment to excellence, followed by a focus on her master's degree in HR management.

- A bilingual senior technology executive (DANFORTH) speaks geek in language a corporate chief can cheer, especially the part about adding 30 percent to company sales for a new technological product.

- An experienced food and beverage server (ROCK) responds to a job ad for a part-time server position with a short, punchy message that can be sent as a letter or an online cover letter note. (Cover note samples appear later in this chapter.)

- A chief executive officer of a firm in the green energy industry (MASSEY) decides he wants to be on someone else's payroll. As a hint that he fits well into the industry's youthful culture, the candidate chooses an informal "business casual" approach when reaching out to the third-party recruiter.

Memorable storytellers

Simply being remembered as a qualified individual among faceless hoards of candidates is a big threshold to cross. A memorable story helps employers recall individuals when deciding who to interview. Notice the humanizing touches that bring readers closer to good feelings about unknown candidates in the two following samples:

- A national health care practitioner (CHERMAINE) weaves a personal history into her letter to a health food products sales manager, suggesting that she is a good fit in the health food culture by closing with "Namaste," a conventional Hindu expression, usually stated while holding the palms together vertically in front of the bosom.

- A new graduate competing for a position as an occupational therapy assistant (YATES) begins her occupational story at the beginning, when she was a candy striper. The reader thinks, "What an empathetic, thoughtful person."

Blue standard bearers

Job search documents, including cover letters and resumes, are increasingly welcomed by employers of installation, maintenance, repair, construction, and production workers. Plenty of people continue to get jobs without self-marketing documents, but why not get an edge for the best jobs by using every available tool? The following two samples illustrate:

✔ A construction estimator (REZENDEZ) nails key job requirements in a short and zippy letter. He precludes the agony of sitting around waiting for a contact by saying he'll call to discuss not an interview, but "your needs and my qualifications." Well played!

✔ An "unretirement" candidate (SIMMONS) responds to an ad for a maintenance technician. He adroitly puts his motto ("You can count on me!") in italics and emphasizes his command of systems and equipment. Inspired! Employers of blue-collar workers seek reliable and able workers, a good selling point for an older worker.

Main points

Look over the following sample that shows the wisdom of getting to the heart of the matter. What is the one factor that, if missing, kills interest in the candidate? Always try to pinpoint the make-or-break factor in a hiring decision and make it work for you:

✔ A personal banking officer relocating from one city to another (APPLEBEE) knows that the ability to offer great customer service is a key essential in selecting personal bankers; she loads her letter with charm and warmth.

Making Contact with Cover Notes

Sometimes there just aren't enough hours in the day. When you need to get your resume or job application out and about quickly, consider using a cover note to introduce it.

You typically send a cover note in text, not as an attachment — although examples shown here are presented in Microsoft Word typeface for easy reading. Your resume may follow in text, but more likely you'll attach it in a Word or PDF document.

When you need to do a more persuasive job of self-marketing than a few brief paragraphs allow, follow a cover note with a cover letter and a resume attached in a single Word or PDF doc, or in separate docs. When you do send two attachments, one for your cover letter and the second for your resume, add a message like this:

> *Two documents are attached — my cover letter and my resume. Please review. Thank you.*

This request, although terse, may put pressure on recruiters to open and look at the e-mail's attachments.

Getting good writing tips

Consider a few tips for writing your cover notes:

- The subject line of your e-mail sparks a reading of your cover note, which sparks a reading of your resume. Power each one with a sales message that causes the reviewer to keep on scrolling.

- Use names of mutual friends or other connections; list matching qualifications to job requirements; and try for fresh, eye-catching phrasing, unless you're applying for seriously serious work.

- Practice writing a long story short until you get the hang of it. Send your finished work to yourself and read it over the next day to judge whether it's as brilliant as it was the day you wrote it.

Ageless models and bell-ringing closes

Be aware of traditional samples that speak softly but carry a big carrot. Lacking graphic bells and whistles, such samples depend solely on strong writing and the market value of the candidate's background.

Don't overlook samples that showcase an action close (see Chapter 17). A promise to follow up positions you to pursue the job on your timetable instead of forcing you to merely bide your time and hope for a call.

Using cover notes for a fast start

The seven sample cover notes in this section are examples of the kind of message you can send online to introduce your digital resume. Generally, cover notes are more informal than cover letters. The names of their writers appear beneath each sample; a directory of all writers appears in this book's appendix. I comment on each cover note:

- **Nurse Uses Top 10 Lure.** Employers are impressed with candidates who are in the top 10 percent of their class. Even in a talent-short category, such as RNs with a Bachelor's degree, the candidate leaves little to chance and mentions other positive points as well.

- **Assistant Headlines Industry Experience.** A candidate for a job on the plant floor adds references from previous employers to establish his ability to do the job that he wants.

- **Retail Manager Covers Key Points.** A manager who has been around long enough to know all the verses in the retail repertoire bags attention with an offer to make money for a new employer, cites frequent promotion to back up his claims, and interjects a smile at the end.

- **Networker Follows Up Job Lead.** The seeker of an office manager position puts the mutual contact in the subject, where it can't be missed.

- **From Friend to Friend: Help!** This cover note is a classic way to tap into a personal network to line up a referral.

- **Transitioning Marine Sells His Skills.** A military service member, who may be at sea or overseas, suggests immediate contact by telephone or online as a means of encouraging the employer not to hire anyone before interviewing him. His subject line identifies the job opening, ending the reader's need to guess what the e-mail discusses.

- **Pharma Executive Shows Enthusiasm.** A well-qualified pharmaceutical professional bubbles with vigor to be placed on the A-list of candidates who will be interviewed.

Feasting Your Eyes

As a last reminder before you read the samples, take note that name is the game in tempting the intended to read your letter. Yes, in some exceptions, you must use a generic title (such as Dear Hiring Manager), either because you simply can't uncover the hiring names in a committee structure or because the name of the hiring authority is guarded like a state secret before Wikileaks.

Maximum message readability is the presentation criterion for each sample letter in this chapter. To save space in some superb but lengthier samples, I had to chop the original boilerplate text leading into the letter — most often deleting the recipient's name, title, company, and address. So when you see a letter leading off with "[Date, inside address, salutation]" or some variation of that, the generic line is merely a reminder that you can't just say "Hey, you, read this!" If you're not sure how to lay out your letter, turn to Chapter 15.

For a collection of some of the most arresting and action-sparking job ad reply letters ever, turn the page and begin checking out samples.

LORI ARMSTRONG

Philadelphia, PA 99999 • H: (444) 444-4444 • M: (555) 555-5555 • loriarmstrong@yahoo.com

[Date, inside address to VP of major food company, salutation]

RE: Your Next Category Manager

With 10 years of category management and merchandising experience for three leading grocery chains, my qualifications are a perfect match for the Category Manager position with your company:

Candidate requirements:	My qualifications:
Minimum 4 years category management/merchandising/buying experience in a related business or brand.	**Ten years of progressively responsible category management and merchandising experience,** including full responsibility for category sales and profitability for supplements and other natural health products.
Self-motivated and action oriented with a sense of urgency and anticipatory qualities.	**Throughout my career, I have been successful in driving sales and margin growth** by anticipating consumer purchasing trends and emerging products, and devising and executing action plans with a sense of urgency.
Experienced with and skilled in negotiation of pricing and marketing support agreements with a broad array of vendors.	Leveraging my vast industry experience, **I negotiate the lowest possible cost of goods and advertising support** using sound judgment of how deep a vendor can discount. I ask for what is necessary to create a successful and profitable partnership for both parties, and ensure the price is competitive in the market while maintaining margin goals.
Superior analytical skills and comprehensive understanding of retail math.	**Thoroughly understanding and analyzing the keys to profitability** is one of my greatest strengths.
Written and verbal communication and presentation skills.	The quantifiable results I produced in every role would not have been possible without **the requisite communication and presentation skills.**

What differentiates me from other candidates is my specialized knowledge in the natural health segment (particularly dietary supplements and body care), combined with proven business acumen and a deep network of contacts with suppliers in the segment. Additionally, I live the healthy natural lifestyle and exude a genuine and contagious passion for the industry. I would like to bring this same energy, drive and experience as your next Category Manager. I look forward to learning more about this interesting opportunity and discussing how my skills can add value to your team.

Sincerely,

Lori Armstrong

Louise Garver, CPBS, JCTC, CMP, CPRW, CEIP — Broad Brook, Conn.

WANDA L. BELL

222 Higgins Lane ~ Palo Alto, CA 23354 ~☎ 915-555-0111 ~ ✉ wanda.bell@comcast.net

[Date]

Dell Advanced Information Systems
Attn: Mr. Dennis Coney, Human Resources Director
12450 Lakeview Circle
Fairfax, VA 22033

SUBJECT: "Satellite Operations Manager" position listed on your company website on [date]

Dear Mr. Coney:

Upon perusal of my résumé, you will find that my previous experiences effectively parallel the skill set required for your position.

You Require	I Offer
• Demonstrated experience installing, maintaining, and repairing satellite communications ground terminals, systems, networks, and associated equipment used to support voice, data, and video transfer.	✓ Demonstrated experience installing, maintaining, and repairing satellite communications ground terminals, systems, networks, and associated equipment used to support voice, data, and video transfer.
• BS, Engineering Management with an emphasis in communication systems.	✓ BS, Engineering Management with an emphasis in communication systems.
• 7 years of experience with satellite and radio frequency systems engineering to include managing personnel and projects.	✓ 14 years of experience with satellite and radio frequency systems engineering to include managing personnel and projects.
• Top Secret Single Scope Background Investigation Security Clearance.	✓ Top Secret Single Scope Background Investigation Security Clearance.

I thrive in an atmosphere of challenge and excitement that I envision accompanies employment with your agency. I welcome the opportunity to meet with you or your designated agency representative to discuss my qualifications and your objectives further. I will follow up with your office early next week to discuss interviewing possibilities. Thank you in advance for both your time and consideration.

Respectfully Yours,

Wanda L. Bell

Wanda L. Bell

Encl: Résumé

Phyllis G. Houston — Upper Marlboro, Md.

GLORIA J. TRIETELMANN, RN, BSN
Lawrenceville, NJ 08648
609.771.9999
gloriajtrietelmann@njmail.com

[Date, inside address, salutation]   Code Job ID #: XXXXXXXX

PharmaSol's job posting for a **Pharmaceutical Sales Territory Manager** immediately
appealed to me because of your focus on excellence ("Recruiting only the Sales Elite").

So, why should you consider me?

First, I am a **high–performance producer**. As a Senior Sales Specialist with a Fortune 10 pharma, I
turned around a bottom–performing territory (achievement level 1 out of 12) to rank at level 3 in less than
one year and level 9 within three years. My team picked up 30 back–to–back quarterly sales awards for
sales volume and market share in 8 years.

Second, my team orientation and strategic sales planning skills mean I can fit in and deliver
profitable results immediately. Whether spearheading new sales programs that target key–influencer
physicians or motivating and training other team members who became top producers, I am determined
to do what is best for the company.

Third, my qualifications meet all your stated requirements (see resume enclosed):

- ☑ **Bachelor of Science Degree in Nursing (BSN) + RN License in New Jersey**

- ☑ **Eight+ years of pharmaceutical sales experience,** including hospital sales. Practice / Product
  Consultant to targeted customer base of medical specialists.

- ☑ **Performance mindset:** Recognized by regional and national management for sales leadership.
  Named National Sales Call Champion and National Trend Setter.

A recent 360degree anonymous feedback survey cited my "can–do" attitude, passionate enthusiasm,
loyalty, and motivational sales leadership as enduring personal brand themes. That is a good fit with
PharmaSol's expectations of delivering "client–focused personalized services" and "excellence in
execution and customer satisfaction."

May we speak soon? I will follow–up within the week. Thank you for your consideration.

Eager to join your team,

Gloria J. Trietelmann

Susan Guarneri, MRW, CERW, CPRW, CPBS, NCCC, DCC — Three Lakes, Wis.

SHAWN J. REDMOND
GLOBAL BUSINESS DEVELOPMENT

Global Marketing

S J R

Sales Leader

Las Vegas, NV 55555 • Ph: 555.555.5555 • sjr@hotmail.com • @SJ_Redmond

[Date]

Ms. Laura Bell
Human Resources Manager
TNT Corporation
55 Swan Road
Las Vegas, NV 55555

Confidential

Re: **Global Marketing Director**

Dear Ms. Bell,

"Invite the best and ditch the rest!" is what I hope you'll do by penciling me in on your calendar to interview as a candidate for your new global marketing director.

My current position carries global accountability — International Marketing Manager, Retail & Food Services — for a Fortune 1000 company. It brings me front and center in leading marketing initiatives across the world by drawing on my proven talents as a marketing and sales strategist.

My director has credited me for major contributions in skyrocketing profit by 17% in Latin & Central America, 12% in Europe, and 11% in Japan over the past five years. My professional secret? I consistently drive sales by combining solid marketing expertise with motivational leadership. As I detail in the attached resume, my accomplishments in the following areas have resulted in impressive revenue-generating KPI:

- Marketing, Sales & Advertising
- Global Market Development
- P&L Management
- Brand Building & Positioning
- Product Launch
- Competitive Market Analysis
- Consumer Research
- Team Development & Leadership
- Business Intelligence

If you don't beat me to it and call me (mobile: 555-555-5555) before early next week, I'll contact your office to circle my calendar for your best day to meet. One of my competencies is tenacious follow-up. I don't give up because marketing aces never fold.

Sincerely,

Shawn J. Redmond

**P.S. My interest in exploring a new opportunity with TNT is confidential;
I'm sure you will respect my interest in keeping it confidential. Thank you.**

Resume Enclosed

Tanya Sinclair, CHRP, MCRS — Pickering, Ontario, Canada

GEORGE SCHOFIELD

Austin, TX | (C) 512-555-4655 | Geo2Schofield@gmail.com

[Date]

Mr. Rob Strickland
Chief Information Officer
T-Mobile USA, Inc.
12920 SE 38th Street
Bellevue, WA 98006

Re: Opening for Executive Vice President of Information Systems

Dear Mr. Strickland,

Does your IT organization drive business growth or get in the way?

For more than twenty years I have developed integrated IT strategies and architectures, aligned technology and business goals, led large-scale integration projects that kept pace with 35% annual growth, and generated IT solutions that directly impacted business productivity, customer service, and profit for leading telecom companies.

In fact, over the past fifteen years I have:

- ❖ *Consolidated nine regional information systems* into a single, enterprise-level Point of Sale, Inventory, and Accounts Receivable system supporting 900 Verizon retail stores.

- ❖ *Executed customized ERP and CRM systems* generating 13% global manpower reduction for Sprint.

- ❖ *Developed an enterprise architecture strategy* that enabled Alltel to increase profit 47% and nearly double in size over six years.

When a telecom's IT organization aligns with and supports its overall business goals, growth and profitability follow.

I have spent solid, successful years driving growth and profitability for rapidly expanding US telecoms like T-mobile. Let's sit down and explore the value I can bring to your technology leadership team.

Sincerely,

David Bergh

Enclosure: Resume

P.S. I found your article on "Six Trends CIOs Need to Focus On in the Year Ahead" to be a very insightful read. However, there is a seventh trend not mentioned in the article that T-Mobile must consider as you launch into the coming year. I would love to discuss at your earliest convenience the seventh trend and how I could help implement a solution.

Mark Forsyth

19 Lewiston St., Boulder, CO. ◆ Cell: 555.555.5555 ◆ Home: 555.555.5555 ◆ E-mail: name@comcast.net

[Date]

[Name of Hiring Manager]
[Title]   **RE: Store Manager Position**
[Company]   **Advertised in Colorado Reader**
[Address]

Dear [Name of Hiring Manager]:

As a former member of the United States Army, the **9 Cs of Leadership** became instilled in me: **Curious, Creative, Communicate, Character, Courage, Conviction, Charisma, Competent, and Common Sense.** And there's more I would bring to the job of *Store Manager*: the ability to think on my feet, the mindset to provide excellent customer service with diverse populations, and the talent to increase sales through promotional events.

As a *Customer Service Manager*, my experience has taught me how to meet and exceed each customer's expectations with service that sells. I have assisted all types of customers in all types of settings. I realize the importance of acquiring and maintaining loyal repeat business. Positioning a company for better exposure and greater marketability is a function that I have performed with success many times.

As a human resource specialist, I am an exceptional trainer who achieves ongoing success with his teams by building morale, maintaining teams' self-confidence, and training team members to build the sale by improving their people skills.

I look forward to meeting with you to discuss in greater detail your requirements and my qualifications. In the meantime, if you have any questions, please feel free to contact me at 555.555.5555 or e-mail me at name@comcast.net.

Thank you for your consideration.

Sincerely,

Mark Forsyth

Enclosure: Resume

Deborah Barnes, CPRW, JCTC— Nahant, Mass.

Joseph T. Horton

51 Siver Road   Residence: (999) 555-0111
Troy, NY 12000   Office: (999) 555-0112
joseph.horton@us.army.mil   Office Voice Mail: (999) 555-0113

[Date]

Mr. Justin Martin, Hiring Coordinator
123 Madison Avenue
American Red Cross
Albany, NY, 12222

RE: Red Cross Program Manager, State Emergency; Organization Job ID: 5517BR

Dear Mr. Martin:

I don't scare easily. Nor do I own a panic button. Instead, when the wheels come off, I remain alert and act calmly to deal intelligently with a crisis. My skills, experience and professional credentials make me confident that I am the ideal match for your Program Manager, State Emergency position advertised on New York's Job Bank. My skills, experience, and professional credentials makes me confident that I am an ideal candidate.

I offer over 19 years of *Emergency Management*, *Security / Surveillance*, *Logistics*, and *Operations Management* experience in positions of progressive responsibility and duties. My areas of expertise include

✓ Emergency Response   ✓ Staff Training And Development
✓ Disaster Planning And Response   ✓ Intelligence / Operations Analysis
✓ Emergency Preparedness   ✓ Information Collection / Analysis
✓ Homeland Security   ✓ Event Planning, Interagency Coordination
✓ Program / Project Management   ✓ Sensitive Information Management
✓ Team Building / Management

I possess an active Top Secret / SCI security clearance with a current background investigation. With strong leadership and organizational skills, I have a track record of designing and implementing emergency / disaster response programs and leading large-scale emergency / disaster response and security / surveillance operations in high-risk situations.

With strong technical / computer abilities, I am skilled at utilizing technology, databases, and computerized systems to manage emergencies and disasters. As a seasoned instructor with excellent communication skills, I am talented at training and coordinating the efforts of multiple teams of professionals. My professional credentials include a Bachelor's degree, comprehensive FEMA and security / surveillance training, Six Sigma Lean Manufacturing Certification, and IS100, IS200, ICS300, and ICS400 Certifications.

With the track record and leadership abilities that I offer, you can be assured that I will make an immediate and positive contribution to the American Red Cross. I would like to further discuss my background in a meeting with you. Thank you for your time and consideration. I look forward to your reply.

Sincerely,

Joseph T. Horton

Enc. Resume

John Femia, CPRW — Schenectady, N.Y.

J *Wiley Jones*

8 Winding Road, Houston, TX 77023 wiley.jones@hmail.com

Date

John H. Bentley
Senior Vice President of
Sales Reeling Distribution, Inc.
55 Rocket Center
Dallas, TX 75203

Dear Mr. Bentley:

Please let your assistant, Jennifer Lewis, know how much I appreciate the link she forwarded to me at your request. I have carefully reviewed your criteria for the Territory Account Manager role and am delighted to submit my career management materials. Per your suggestion, I am sending the information directly to you.

> "Wiley Jones is a first-class act. His drive, tenacity, and investment in our company's success have had an immense impact on our sales revenues. When he speaks, I listen."
> Ben Dwyer, CEO, AirGo Products, Inc., Houston, TX 773-345-7890

Briefly stated, my credentials include:

- Ten years of direct sales success and achievement in diverse, competitive industries.
- MBA with territory management experience in multi-state areas of the South and Southwest.
- Knowledgeable of distributor networks and key partnerships to drive business success.
- Trusted relationship-building skills in generating sales calls on both new and existing clientele.
- Willing to travel to meet employer expectations; attentive sales documentation and follow-through abilities to support employer's vision, mission and business goals; technical savvy.
- Valued for delivering consistent sales revenue and profit growth in volatile markets.

In perusing your literature, I read with interest your organization's values: Interest. Integrity. Intention. Inspiration. Innovation and Involvement. I, too, share those same values and am desirous of discovering an employer who is strongly committed to developing talent and rewarding achievement. The attached resume provides a more in-depth overview of my sales and territory management experience.

Feel free to contact me by email at < Wiley.Jones@gmail.com > or at my mobile, 532.555.8234 to schedule a time to meet when I'm in Dallas next week. I so look forward to learning more about your operation. Thank you for your thoughtful consideration.

Sincerely,

Wiley Jones

Enclosure

Billie R. Sucher, CTMS, CTSB, JCTC, CCM — Urbandale, Iowa

GRETCHEN YOUNG, *MS*

20 S. Main Street, Columbus, New Jersey 08505 • (555) 555-0111 • gretchenyoung@email.net

[Date]

Charter University
Adjunct Search Committee
Department of Business Administration/LN0622
P.O. Box 1002
Charter, Pennsylvania 17551-0302

RE: *Business Administration Adjunct Instructors*

Dear Adjunct Search Committee Members:

I hope to join the Charter University faculty as a part-time, temporary Instructor. As a resident of Charter County, I am very familiar with your University and your commitment to education and community outreach. Here are highlights of my relevant qualifications and accomplishments:

Expertise / Experience I Offer

Six years of teaching experience in higher-education environments. **Focus on Corporate Communications, Marketing, and Business Writing.**

Ten years of experience in both corporate and non-profit settings; held various management positions in Marketing and Internal Communication departments.

Graduated with a Master's Degree in Marketing from the University of Kansas. Certified as a Business Communication Professional (CBP).

My passion is providing an engaging and productive learning experience to all students. My style is participatory and one that involves all students. I look forward to discussing with you how I can use my experience and knowledge to further the mission of Charter University.

Sincerely,

Gretchen Young

Gretchen Young
Enclosure

Professional instructor with academic credentials and real-world corporate experience;
engage students in an active learning environment and encourage new ideas about traditional subjects.

Comments from Past Evaluations

-Professor Young takes the time to get to know her students. She wants us to succeed and it shows.

-I truly enjoyed the learning environment Ms. Young created. She doesn't stand and lecture for hours – instead she challenges us to think for ourselves and be involved.

-Professor Young cares about her students. I felt that I could always approach her with a concern. She took me seriously.

-I was nervous about taking Managerial Communications, but Professor Young made the experience enjoyable. She gave us the tools to prepare our presentations and it was a positive learning experience.

Milton W. Shields
479 Niles Road
New Reading, Pennsylvania 90000

(H) 222-555-0111   shields@hotmail.com   (M) 222-555-0112

[Date]

Ms. Lorraine Lutz
Senior Director of Sales
Global Technologies Company, Inc.
4446 A-Street SW
New Reading, Pennsylvania 80000

Re: Field Sales Management

Dear Ms. Lutz:

Your job posting for an experienced, top level field sales manager is right on target for my current job search. With years of successful hands-on customer service, sales, and management with a global leader in construction related products and services, I believe that I can very comfortably meet your requirements as the ideal candidate for this position.

As my accompanying résumé clearly indicates, my professional qualifications and personal strengths reveal high-end management qualities, such as commitment, integrity, trust, and insight when dealing with personnel under my supervision. I have motivated my sales staffs to work at earning high commissions and praise for reaching targeted productivity while maintaining customer satisfaction, retaining loyal client base, and expanding new business.

Below is a brief overview of the value I can bring if hired by your firm:

Broad Experience	Fifteen years of competent, reliable, trustworthy service to clients and employees in a highly respected multinational firm that employs over 14,000 in 122 nations.
Commitment to Excellence	High energy leader with a proven record of superior team-building qualities that inspire sales personnel to attain top performance while exhibiting professional standards.
Articulate, Precise, and Confident	Excellent communications abilities that facilitate the work of recruiting, training, coaching, team-building, motivating, and creative problem-solving.
Strategic Planning	Reached profitability target of 9 million dollars through meticulous staffing and in-depth scheduling of 17 Pro Shops.

If you need a strategic sales manager with impressive business acumen and out-of-the-box problem-solving talent blended with proactive team leadership and the ability to execute tactically, then I am your candidate. I would welcome the opportunity to demonstrate how I could benefit your organization. I will call to arrange a meeting convenient to your calendar. Thank you for your time and interest in considering my application for this position.

Sincerely,

Milton W. Shields

Enclosure

Edward Turilli, CPRW — North Kingstown, R.I., and Bonita Springs, Fla.

MICHELLE ROSEN

Seminole, FL 33776 • MRosen@gmail.com
(M) 727.123.4444 • twitter.com/mrosen591

SALES & MARKETING PROFESSIONAL

Core Competencies / Skills

✓ Account Management
✓ Client Relationship Development
✓ Telephone Skills
✓ Collaborative Team Player
✓ Client Advocate
✓ Resource Management

[Date]

Ms. Anne Hutten
Director of Sales
Verizon
2402 West Busch Boulevard
Tampa, FL 33602

Dear Ms. Hutten:

I want your **Residential Sales Associate** position! Sales is the theme of my successful career and I have close-up experience in working with customers one-on-one to cross-sell and up-sell.

My résumé details my professional background, including marketing and customer service experience across a variety of environments. Highlights of my qualifications include:

- **Strong Work Ethic.** Committed to going the extra mile to complete the job accurately and thoroughly to not only meet—but exceed—management and customer expectations.
- **Skilled in Building Connections.** Adept at determining the customer's needs and motivation and adapting sales presentation to those interests, with a track record of utilizing a soft sales approach to make effective one-on-one connections with clients and close more sales.
- **Effective Communicator.** Always communicate with diplomacy, discretion, and tact when handling confidential or sensitive information and as primary contact on contracts or projects. Reputation for being the trusted 'go to' person to assist with critical issues.

Based on these strengths and more, I am confident that the talent and experience I can bring to your company will make an immediate and lasting contribution. I'll be keeping track of the days until you call me for an interview!

Sincerely with enthusiastic anticipation,

Michelle Rosen

Enclosure: Resume

Laurie Berenson, CPRW, CEIC— Franklin Lakes, N.J.

Caitlin Clark

111 West 10th Street
Chicago Illinois 60623

777.555.1111
cclark@newleaf.ca

Marketing | Business Administration Degree

Top Strengths:
Ideation
Social Media
Prospecting
Branding
Research

[Date]

City of Chicago
Applied via online submission

Re: Manager of Strategic Marketing & Creative Services

As I read through the job description for the position of Manager of Strategic Marketing & Creative Services, the phrase "they get excited about exploring new ideas" leapt out. I am an idea person, high-energy, a natural relationship builder and leader, and I am confident of my abilities to manage the creative process of articulating customers' objectives into influential marketing and communication strategies.

In 20xx I launched a business, which I've now entrusted to new owners, and my focus has been redefined to a marketing management role. Here are highlights of how I fit the needs of the City:

- I created and developed a brand, steered the art direction of all marketing collateral and wrote the marketing copy. It was recognized as clear and succinct.
- Recognizing a valuable partnership opportunity, I approached retirement homes and developed a lucrative relationship with five local homes. I am recognized for building quick rapport.
- With energy to spare, I volunteered with strategic fundraisers and not-for-profits, and sought out media opportunities in print and radio. I've been told I am articulate and informative.
- Very much a *hands on* leader, I coached staff and contracted on-site help, ensuring that standards of communication and service matched the brand.
- I managed my business with an eye on savings and outsourced services. I negotiated terms and pricing, and ensured that the level of service was in line with my expectations. This is a testament to my business, marketing, and staff management abilities

Past roles include Market Researcher, Fundraiser Coordinator, and Client Service Representative with Market Sales Communications Inc. A lifelong resident of Chicago, I am enthused about supporting worthwhile initiatives with strategic communications and marketing, as well as with fiscally sound management. I look forward to hearing from you. Thank you for your time.

Sincerely,

Caitlin

Caitlin Clark
Encl: resume

Stephanie Clark, CRS, CIS — Nanaimo, B.C., Canada

AILEEN BOTKIN

Phone: 555-234-1456 ■ Fax: 555-234-1457
Email: aileen_botkin@lycos.com ■ LinkedIn: linkedin.com/in/aileenbotkin745

[Date]

Digital Arts Center
San Diego, CA

RE: Director of Studio Operations position

Dear Hiring Manager Name:

I am writing to express my interest in your current opening for a Director of Studio Operations; therefore, please allow me to submit my resume for your review. With executive-level, P&L leadership experience, demonstrating success in meeting a broad range of goals, I am confident that I can make a valuable contribution to your organization's future initiatives.

In reviewing the position description and requirements, I noted numerous connections with my experience and skills. Because it is important that you find the most qualified candidate, one who can both meet requirements and exceed expectations, I have developed a chart below to illustrate my background relevant to key areas:

Position Responsibilities	My Qualifications
▪ Track hiring plans; assist with staffing; point person for cross-training.	➢ **Built an entire HR department from scratch**; hired and trained employees; created employee recognition and training programs.
▪ Oversee all operations; streamline processes; manage space planning.	➢ **Directed all operational functions for Industries, Inc.**; streamlined inventory from manual to automated process; arranged all logistics.
▪ Demonstrate background in technology production services and procedures.	➢ **Coordinate all IT and online activities for current company**; managed video production; currently leading efforts to Cloud transition.
▪ Manage and optimize intra- and inter-organizational relationships.	➢ **Built and maintained superb relationships** with employees, vendors, suppliers, and customers from multiple industries.

In addition, I hold full responsibility for meeting all revenue goals; over a 1-year period, I drove an exceptional increase in revenues, including **record-breaking 147% and 150% above-goal results** for Q3 and Q4 2011:

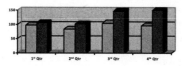

My resume contains additional details regarding my career accomplishments, including my recently-awarded Executive MBA. I would welcome an opportunity for a personal interview to discuss your organization's needs and the leadership results you can expect from me. Thank you in advance for your time and review of my qualifications.

Sincerely,

Aileen Botkin

Enclosure

Dan Dorotik, NCRW — Lubbock, Texas

sales professional   *Will consider relocation*

Allen P. Morrison
100 Markwell Lane — Montgomery, Alabama 36100
☎ 334.555.0111 — 334.555.0112 (cellular) — ✉ apmorrison@charter.net

[Date]

Ms. Laura Worth
Sales Manager
TopLine, Inc.
320 Sun Parkway
Suite 17
Montgomery, Alabama 36100

Dear Ms. Worth:

I want you to get the credit for adding ROI to the TopLine sales team. Specifically, I'd like to become your newest sales professional. And, perhaps the best way to link those two ideas is with this graph that shows how I'm performing right now.

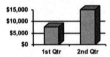

What I do isn't magic. I just work harder and smarter than my competition by finding some profitable way to say "yes" to every customer and potential customer.

My focus on your sales needs starts on the next pages. I wanted you to see a résumé that offers more than the usual recitations of job titles and responsibilities. That's why you'll find six capabilities I want to put at TopLine's disposal at once. Backing them up are a dozen examples of sales those capabilities in action.

My company values what I do. And, if I thought our market was growing as fast as yours, I would stay with them. While I cannot control market conditions, I am interested in making even greater contributions to my employer. That's why I'm "testing the waters" with this confidential application.

I do best using the consultative approach to sales. So, as a first step, I'd like to hear about TopLine's sales needs in your own words. May I call in a few days to arrange time to do that?

Sincerely,

Allen P. Morrison

Encl.: Resume

Don Orlando, CPRW, JCTC, CCM, CCMC, CJSS, MCD — Montgomery, Ala.

DAN J. BOTKIN
9803 Clifton Street ▪ Lubbock, TX 79432
806-555-0111 ▪ danjbotkin@door.com

[Date]

Mr. John Rockford, Sales Director
XYZ Company
123 Main Street
Lubbock, TX 79423

Dear Mr. Rockford:

It is with great enthusiasm that I apply for your advertised position of **Sales Representative.** Count me in because my skills are a finely tuned match for your requirements!

In fact, my combination of sales experience and relationship selling skills has given me the opportunity to exceed sales expectations, grow market share, outdistance the competition, and establish a strong foundation for future revenue growth. Two selected accomplishments documenting my qualifications are:

- **Trusting, win-win relationships with customers and suppliers,** including Coca-Cola, Pepsi, McLane, Wal-Mart, Owens-Corning, and other partner companies;

- **Consistent, year-over-year pattern of increasing revenues** through robust and downturn economies, from $50,000 to $1.2 million as illustrated below:

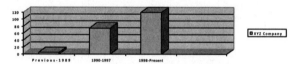

Sales is about making connections – between customer and product, between product and its benefits, and between sales associates and customers. Because I position myself as a consultant to my customers, I am able to gain their trust, make these connections, and pave the way for increased sales as a result.

My resume provides you with specific details of my qualifications but a personal interview will more fully reveal my positive attitude and potential to assist you in making your numbers – make that *exceed* your numbers!

You may want to reach me first on my cell phone, 806-555-0112, but I plan to call you on Thursday afternoon to see if we can set a time to sit down and chat. I've done my research on your company and it's a beacon in the industry. Thank you, Mr. Rockford, for considering adding me to your sales wish team.

Sincerely,

Dan J. Botkin

Enclosure

Dan Dorotik, NCRW — Lubbock, Texas

Julia Martin, Ph.D.
12 Cranwell Road St. Geneve, ON L5R 6P7 ✉ jm2002@gmail.com ☎ 905.555.555

[Date]

Mr. Ken Courton
President
Provincial Institute for Social Policy
1354 Wellington Street, West
3rd Floor
Ottawa, ON K1Y 3C3

Dear Mr. Courton:

I want to make it as easy as possible for the Provincial Institute to add me to your team as your newest Research Associate. This letter and the attached résumé are my first steps in that process.

My resume may not look like others you have seen. I thought you deserved to read, right at the top of the first page, my pledge of value: capabilities you will see me demonstrate from the first day.

Backing them up are more than a half dozen examples of research that cuts through distractions to focus on the right problem, increase program sustainability, and boost productivity. Most important of all, they illustrate my talent for giving clients powerful tools they can use with confidence.

I loved my work teaching at a university. But something was missing: the chance to harness my love of research to help people champion powerful ideas well.

If my track record and philosophy appeal to you, I'd like to hear about the Provincial Institute's specific research-related requirements from the person with the biggest stake in the outcome. May I call in a few days to get on your calendar to do that?

Sincerely,

Julia Martin, Ph.D.

Encl.: Resume

Don Orlando, CPRW, JCTC, CCM, CCMC, CJSS, MCD — Montgomery, Ala.

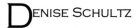

DENISE SCHULTZ

47262 18th St. ✧ Denver, CO 80002
303-467-0001 ✧ schultzdee@.gmail.com

*Provide vision and operational leadership through a
variety of human resource skills and a commitment to
organizational excellence.*

[Date]

[Mr. / Ms.]
[Title]
[Company]   RE: HR DIRECTOR
[Address]
[City, State, Zip]

Dear [Name],

With superior education and solid training in human resource development, benefits and compensation, employee performance and employment law, I see a potential perfect fit for me in your quest for a new HR director.

My background includes 15 years of office administration and management, customer service strategies, employee training, and revenue increases. Additionally, I've gained a tremendous amount of hands-on experience in social responsibility and diversity with my current position at Ball Corporation. I have expertise in managing multiple tasks, confidently training large groups of people, and providing support to management and colleagues alike. Highlights of my experience and accomplishments include:

- Hands-on project management experience, performance management and team leadership.
- Outstanding leadership skills focused on resolving key issues, facilitating customer–focused training, and promoting positive culture change.
- Developed and maintained standard practices of communication to ensure all staff were on the 'same page'.
- Performed annual reviews, career counseling, team building, corrective action and conflict management.
- Master's in Human Resource Management from the University of Colorado.

I'm eager to leverage my graduate education with my skills in management, office administration, human resources and staffing for your advertised position of HR Director. The enclosed resume briefly spells out my experience and accomplishments. I'll contact you next week to see when your calendar is open for an interview.

Sincerely,

Denise Schultz
Enclosure

Erin Kennedy, MCD, CMRW, CPRW — Lapeer, Mich.

JAMES DANFORTH

28 Sutton Lane   M: 713-555-1212
Houston, TX 77003   E: danforth@email.com

[Date, name, inside address, salutation]

With this letter and enclosed resume, I wish to be considered for the position of **TITLE,** as posted on **JOB BOARD,** as well as other positions within your company that can utilize the skills of a **highly accomplished, bilingual Senior Technology Executive** with a broad knowledge base, modern skill set, and **track record of transforming companies into industry leaders.**

Combining an **Electrical Engineering degree** with strong **Organizational Development and Leadership** skills, I have catapulted early-stage IT, Networking, and Telecommunications companies to award-winning success. **As VP of Technical Operations for a leading Data Networking Technology Solutions provider named by Forbes as one of the 10 fastest-growing technology, media, networking, and telecommunications companies in Houston and honored with over 40 top industry awards,** my capacity to promote your organizational goals is well-developed. A more in-depth overview of my qualifications includes a background of

Transformational Leadership:

- In my current role as VP of Technical Operations, **I turned the organization around** by building vital teams, processes and procedures. This led to a 50% improvement in deployment time and 40% increase in subscriber revenues while simultaneously doubling its customer base within 3 years.

- As Director of R&D for a global leader in FDDI communication solutions, **I reengineered the QC process,** saving the company millions of dollars by streamlining the procedure, reducing labor hours, and virtually eliminating downtime.

Technology Leadership:

- As CTO for a manufacturer-distributor of advanced technology solutions, I conceived a way to connect and consolidate 2 product offerings to develop a third line. Result was a new product line engineered for the Healthcare vertical-Optimal Technology — **that added 30% to company sales its first year.**

The above is a brief overview of my background, strengths, and ability to drive (Company Name)'s success now and into the future. I look forward to an opportunity to meet with you to discuss my qualifications and candidacy in further detail. Thank you.

Sincerely,

James Danforth
Enclosure

Karen Bartell, CPRW — Massapequa Park, N.Y.

SAMANTHA ROCK

sammy13@gmail.com
(702) 887-3404

[Date]

Jamie Wilson
Administrative Manager
Downtown Café
8745 Tropicana
Las Vegas, NV 89044

Re: Part-time Server Position Advertised in *The Las Vegas Chronicle*

Dear Ms. Wilson:

My experiences as a barista for Starbucks and a server at Wilson Country Club in Austin, Texas, while I was a student were both extremely positive and I learned a great deal about providing quality customer service to the guests. I enjoy working with the public very much and would appreciate the opportunity to interview for a server position at the Downtown Café.

My supervisors will confirm that I am extremely professional and responsible in all situations, always have a smile on my face, and am an accomplished multitasker.

I will be available to start work at the end of July and can be contacted before then at (702) 887-3404 or by e-mail at sammy13@gmail.com. If I have not heard from you by early July, I will contact your office to arrange an interview.

Thank you for your consideration.

Sincerely,

SamanthaRock

Samantha Rock

Gay Anne Himebaugh — Corona del Mar, Calif.

Jonathan Massey

215.555.5555   9999 Niagara Road • Philadelphia, PA 19999   JMassey55555@aol.com

[date]

Kevin Smith
Retained Recruiting International
[address]

Dear Kevin:

While researching CEO opportunities in the Green Energy sector, I came across your announcement for Luca Technologies, and noticed that it emphasizes the identification of emerging technologies. Assessment of "green" technologies and trends – and intense analysis of every related bit of information I can get my hands on – is a hallmark of my management methodology.

I think my operational and financial achievements – and management style – as CEO of Bristol Industries might be an excellent fit for Luca, because both our companies are developing new technologies that address the global availability of clean energy.

My top skill – and a secret of my success in the volatile world of emerging green technologies – is my ability to devise real-time strategies that consistently succeed in high-pressure situations. Here are three additional attributes that your client can tap into:

- **Decisive Leadership** – No matter how bad the competitive dynamics, I have a knack for turning around impossible situations and making money for investors. When Bristol's Board challenged me to double sales within three years, I delivered 210%.

- **Combined Financial and Operational Expertise** – In addition to an MBA in finance (Wharton), I leverage eight years as a top consultant – Arthur Andersen and McKinsey – to streamline manufacturing and squeeze the maximum ROI from R&D.

- **Media and PR Savvy** – During the past five years, I've orchestrated some very favorable media buzz for LED lighting in general and Bristol Industries in particular.

I've led Bristol through five years of fierce competition for technological primacy, market share, sales, investment capital, media coverage, and human talent. And your client, Luca Technologies, is probably facing similar challenges. My ability to harness chaotic market conditions and guide a company to success is the #1 reason why Luca should hire me as its next CEO.

I would like to learn more about this position, which sounds like a great and mutually beneficial opportunity. Please review my resume and contact me anytime next week to discuss the next steps. Thank you very much for your time and consideration, Kevin, and I look forward to hearing from you!

Sincerely,

Jonathan Massey

Donald Burns — New York, N.Y.

Catherine Chermaine

charismatic ❧ dynamic ❧ driven ❧ energetic ❧ motivated ❧ passionate

Account Manager

[Date]

Mr. Peter LeSage
National Sales Manager
Natural Health Food Products

Re: Account Manager Position

Dear Mr. LeSage,

Challenge to most means hardship or tackling difficulties, but to me it means excitement and it generates motivation. Cold-calling, establishing almost instant rapport, and building relationships through truly outstanding service, is what I do best and thrive on. I admit that you will have a challenge with me, and it will be to hold me back! Boundless enthusiasm, creative ideas and a love of natural, high quality products rounds out what I offer Natural Health Food Products.

I met Foster Spears, who works in your head office, while with Mushroom Naturals, where I was working with Sam Smith, and they both brought this opportunity to my attention. I am grateful that they did so. As a natural health care practitioner I recommend Health Sure, Vegan Food and Smoothie Delight to many, both in individual consultations and when delivering group seminars. I love the convenience that these Natural Health products provide to healthy eating. The next logical step would be for me to promote your products on an even larger scale.

Sales is something for which I have an innate ability. I am one of those people who could talk a Cadillac owner into a Smart Car! I must believe in the product, and the rest comes naturally. I welcome the opportunity to meet with you and sell you on me!

I thank you for your time, and look forward to building this relationship.

Namaste,

Catherine

Catherine Chermaine
Encl: resume, two pages

❧ ✿ ❧

City, State 999-999-9999 (cell)

Stephanie Clark, CRS, CIS — Nanaimo, B.C., Canada

JULIE E. YATES

2990 Rocky Point Road ♦ W. Melbourne, FL 32904 ♦ 321.555.0111 ♦ email@email.com

[Date]

Mr. Jonathan Burgess, HR Director   **Occupational Therapy Assistant**
Wellness, Inc.
1333 Business Place
Melbourne, FL 32901

Dear Mr. Burgess:

From the time I was a Candy Striper back in high school, I've always been passionate about helping people. Just two years ago, I realized I could best be of service by pursuing a career in occupational therapy.

I was awarded my Occupational Therapist Assistant degree this May at Keiser University where I was an "A" student, and on the honor role and dean's list each quarter.

Additionally, I gained valuable experience while interning at Medical South, LLC and Health Consultants, Inc.

Working my way through my occupational therapy training, I enjoyed my experiences as a swim instructor, waitress, and teacher. Whether someone is pre-school age, senior citizen, or somewhere in between, I find I'm easily able to find common ground.

Working with patients, I've learned the special importance of bringing someone out of a shell because "spirit equals outcome."

I'm very excited about starting my new career in occupational therapy and am completely focused on providing the best possible patient service. I'm known for being organized and always eager to learn.

If you believe, like I do, that my qualifications and experiences are of value to Wellness Inc., I would welcome the opportunity to meet with you. I'm enclosing my résumé and references for your review.

Thank you very much for your time and consideration. I will follow-up next week.

Sincerely yours,

Julie E. Yates

Julie E. Yates
Enclosures: Resume; References

Judith L. Gillespie, CPCC, CPRW, CEIP — W. Melbourne, Fla.

Matthew J. Robertson

36 Park Circle • Indian Harbor Beach, FL 35555 • name@cfl.rr.com
321.555.5555 (home) or 850.555.5555 (cell)

[Date]

Name
Title   **RE: Information Services Position**
NEWIT Corporation   *"Smart Service with Sunshine!"*
Street Address
City, ST Zip

Dear [Name]:

I appreciate that your time is valuable so I won't rehash my enclosed resume. Instead, let me just say that I bring to the table 20 plus years of exceptional customer service, administrative, and technical expertise and a **"Can Do Spirit."** A strong suit of mine is the management of complex data bases, accounts receivable, and refined office management systems.

Currently, I am an entrepreneur providing small businesses with cyber or on-site office services. Prior to this I managed an extensive client database for a privately owned company providing national and international client support for medical, trade, and scientific associations.

I have also worked in a wide variety of areas for a multi-million dollar direct mail company. And, I was requested by Executive Management to assist with the training of new employees when the company made a strategic business decision to move a majority of the operations off-shore.

[Name], the opportunity to work for a leader in virtual communications is exciting. If you believe, as I do, that I have the experience and expertise that will serve ABC's operational needs well, I'd welcome the opportunity to meet with you.

Thank you for your time and consideration. I'll follow up with a call later this week.

Sincerely yours,

Matthew J. Robertson

Matthew J. Robertson

Enclosure: Resume

Robert Rezendez

Saddle River, AZ 55555
Tel: 555.555.5555 • Email: name@comcast.net

[Date]

[Name]
[Title]   **RE: Estimator / Project Manager**
[Company]
[Address]

Dear [Hiring Manager Name]:

You asked for an <u>Estimator / Project Manager</u> who can meet project deadlines, maintain quality, troubleshoot and solve problems, and keep clients happy. That's what you get when you hire me.

My 12-year track record in the heavy construction industry demonstrates my ability to:

- Thrive on challenges and meet difficult situations head on, and lead by example
- Prioritize projects and establish timelines, resulting in project completion on time and within budget
- Propose, design, and supervise innovations to streamline efficiency and communication, advance company's mission, boost productivity, and grow the bottom line
- Wear many hats, including training and motivating employees to roll up their sleeves to get the job done

My track record gives me the assurance to predict I can make an immediate cost-effective and valuable contribution to your company. I will call you next week to see when your calendar is open to meet and discuss your needs and my qualifications.

Thank you for your consideration.

Sincerely,

Robert Rezendez

Enclosure: Resume

Deborah Barnes, CPRW, JCTC — Nahant, Mass.

Calvin Simmons
300 Burgundy Lane
Turners Falls, MA 98889
Home: (413) 555-0111 • Cell: (413) 555-0112
E-mail: calvinsimmons@aol.com

[Date]

Mr. John Deming   My Motto:
Director of Facility Maintenance   *"You can count on me!"*
Southwork Manufacturing
Turner Falls, MA 98889

Dear Mr. Deming:

Although I decided to retire at a young age, I have come to realize that I have too much
energy and many skills that I still enjoy using. Retirement is definitely not for me.
Therefore, your ad for a **maintenance technician** caught my attention as I offer the key
qualifications your company needs.

Specifically, I have an excellent performance record in the operation and maintenance of
building systems and equipment, including *electrical, HVAC, telecommunications,
pneumatic, electro-mechanical, hydraulics.* I am also knowledgeable of *state building
codes, safety* and *other regulatory guidelines.*

My expertise encompasses multi-site facilities oversight, staff supervision, project
management and vendor relations. Examples of relevant accomplishments include
reduction in annual maintenance costs and improved functional capabilities while
consistently delivering quality service.

Equally important are my planning, organization and communication strengths. Despite
the challenges that can often be encountered, I have completed projects on time and
under budget on a consistent basis. I would welcome a personal interview to discuss
the value I would add to your company. My resume is enclosed.

Sincerely,

Calvin Simmons

Calvin Simmons

Louise Garver, CPBS, JCTC, CMP, CPRW, CEIP — Broad Brook, Conn.

Noreen Applebee

Satellite Beach, FL 32555 ★ 321.555.5555 ★ apples@ cfl.rr.com

[Date]

Ms. Teresa Michel Forrest
Human Capitol Manager
Smart and Friendly Bank
13 Downtown Street
Satellite Beach, FL 32500

RE: Personal Banking Officer
Experience with a smile

Dear Ms. Forrest:

After recently relocating from the Gulf Coast to Satellite Beach and spotting your opening for a Personal Banking Officer, I'm tossing my best hat into your ring of candidates.

> ♦ *Why am I a superb and amply qualified match for your job? Here are three*
> *highlights of why you should hire me:*

1) I have significant banking experience having worn many hats from Teller to my most recent position as a Personal Banking Officer at the Community First Bank in Sarasota.

2) I put the customer first. I profile customers so I can best determine what their needs are and I always follow-up with them on a regular basis.

3) I am cheerful, careful, punctual, and a team player — and I can prove it with references. For example, co-workers feel comfortable asking me questions. If I don't know the answer, I don't pretend that I do, but follow through by finding out the correct answer.

Ms. Forrest, I've heard good things about Smart and Friendly Bank from friends and colleagues on both sides of the coast. If you believe, as do I, that my commitment to community banking will be of value to Smart and Friendly going forward, I welcome the opportunity to meet with you — hopefully, next week.

I'll call your office on Monday to check your availability for a sit-down to discuss how I fit into your planning for the best Personal Banking Officer ever to hang her professional hat at Smart and Friendly Bank. Thank you.

Sincerely yours,

Noreen Applebee

Enclosures: Resume, References

Judith L. Gillespie, CPCC, CPRW, CEIP — W. Melbourne, Fla.

Nurse Uses Top 10 Lure

Subject: Top 10% of Class Nurse Candidate

Dear Ms. Johnson:

Having recently graduated from The Ohio State University, my enthusiasm and desire to assist others is deep and authentic. I graduated in the top 10% of my class and received numerous awards of achievement for my volunteer work in the community and a local hospital.

Please consider the following resume for the Pediatric Unit Registered Nurse position I found posted on your website on June 12. I hope you will be as happy about my credentials as I am about the prospect of working in such a renowned facility.

Standing by,

Kathy Lloyd
(123) 555-0111

Haley Richardson, CPRW, JCTC — Minneapolis, Minn.

Assistant Headlines Industry Experience

Subject: Experienced Joe Smith for Manufacturing Assistant position

Dear Mr. Paul:

With more than five years of experience in our industry, with great interest I submit my résumé for consideration as a Manufacturing Assistant with TRU Manufacturing. While browsing job postings on HiringBoard.com, I was delighted to see an opportunity that so closely pairs with my qualifications.

In addition to my résumé you will find letters of recommendation from past employers who will testify to my quality of work managing staff and production lines.

Additionally, I look forward to hearing from you to schedule an interview. I will be contacting you early next week to ensure you've personally received my application materials and to answer any questions you may have.

Sincerely,

Joe Smith
(123) 555-0111

Haley Richardson, CPRW, JCTC — Minneapolis, Minn.

**Retail Manager
Covers Key Points**

Subject: Store Manager Racks Up Profits - For You?

Hello Ms. Harrison:

As an experienced store manager, I have a big-numbers track record in operations management, merchandising, and customer service. I would like to parlay my expertise into assisting your company in exceeding its revenue goals at the Huntington location.

My leadership skills are best demonstrated by my frequent promotions. As the attached resume indicates, I also have significant experience in sales analysis and expense control. And finally, I'm a hard worker. Anyone who's been in retail for more than 30 minutes has got to be!

The opportunity to interview would be most welcome. I'll check back with you very soon. I hope we can profitably connect.

All the best,
Mary Jane Farrell
mjfarrell@mail.com
(204) 555-0111

M. J. Feld, CPRW — Huntington, N.Y.

**Networker Follows
Up Job Lead**

Subject: Office Manager: Paul Gold refers Betty Larson

Dear Ms. Carlson:

Your colleague Paul Gold, whom I met at a recent networking event, informed me of the opening within your organization for a competent Office Manager. He spoke briefly about the qualifications and requirements but couldn't provide a lot of detail. He asked that I contact you for more information.

I am attaching my resume to this e-mail in an effort to see if we have a match concerning the requirements of the position and my qualifications. Please contact me if you have questions and to schedule a time to talk in person.

As you probably know, Paul Gold thinks your organization is special and that you are a wonder. I'm fired up about exploring this opportunity with you.

All best,
Betty Larson
B_larson@yahoo.com
(123) 555-0111

Haley Richardson, CPRW, JCTC — Minneapolis, Minn.

Subject: Will you do your pal Steve a favor?

Hey Bob!

I was checking out some job openings online and noticed there is a position listed for a sales rep at EFG Corporation. Didn't you mention that company is one of your vendors? From the description given in the posting, I'm sure I have the necessary qualifications they are looking for. I would greatly appreciate any help you can give me in making a connection with the person who is doing the hiring.

I'm attaching a copy of my resume with the hope that you will forward it to your contact at EFG. I'm assuming you have a good relationship with him. Be sure to tell him you've known me for 12 years and can vouch for my character, so that he would be more likely to pass my resume along to the hiring manager.

I'll call you in a few days to see how things are going.

Thanks a lot!

Steve

Melanie Noonan — Woodland Park, N.J.

Transitioning Marine Sells His Skills

Subject: Delivery facility operations; supervising skills; Navy trained

After reading your online job posting for an EXPRESS DELIVERY FACILITY OPERATIONS COORDINATOR, my qualifications would like to introduce themselves to your requirements. I will leave the U.S. Marine Corps in two months after a ten-year assignment [identify persuasive civilian matching points — such as overseeing high-volume unloading operations and redistributing urgent materials]. These duties demanded team leadership skills, strong communications ability and careful time management. My resume is just a quick click away.

I will relocate to Louisville in June. I'd appreciate a telephone or online interview before then if you'd like to have a sharper picture of how I could meet the needs of your firm. Please reach me at (826) 555-0111.

Kathryn Kraemer Troutman — Catonsville, Md.

**Pharma Executive
Shows Enthusiasm**

Subject: Associate Director, Business Development (Req: 5867)

Ben Bolt, HR Director, Clear Pharmaceuticals, Inc.
Dear Mr. Bolt,

From your company's website, I learned of the job opening for **Associate Director, Business Development (Req: 5867).** I'm chomping at the bit to tackle this position with Clear Pharmaceuticals because my skills and experience are custom made for your requirements!

Work History Snapshot: At BZY Pharmaceuticals I worked collaboratively with high-level and mid-level government officials, public and private sector stakeholders, and international organizations. At Tosata HealthCare Systems, I established and brought to scale the sustainable supply chain systems which captured 18% growth in market opportunities with local businesses. I can make similar profitable contributions to your team at Clear Pharmaceuticals.

Former managers will tell you that I am very creative, productive, and work effectively in a large team environment. My resume is embedded (click here) for your review.

I'm fascinated with Clear Pharmaceuticals and its impressive R&D pipeline! I truly look forward to talking with you regarding this challenging opening.

Sincerely,
Dhruv Patel
(555) 428-1111 | Skype: dhruvp | Email dhruvp@gmail.com

Divya Gupta, ACPEC, CCC, PCC — Herndon, Va.

Classy models and bell-ringing closes

Be aware of traditional samples that speak softly but carry a big carrot. Lacking graphic bells and whistles, such samples depend solely on persuasive writing and the market value of the candidate's background.

Pay special attention to samples that showcase an *action close* (See Chapter 16). A promise to take the initiative by following up with an employer allows you to pursue the job on your timetable, rather than forcing you to merely bide your time and hope you get a call.

Chapter 5

Getting Help: Networking Letters

. . . .

In This Chapter

▶ Tuning into networking letters that turn up job leads

▶ Looking beyond who you know to who you *can* know

▶ Avoiding detours and heading straight for the hire

. . . .

*U*sing personal relationships and human contacts to your advantage is the essence of *networking*. Successful job search networking pulls back the curtain on what's known as the "hidden job market" — that is, the jobs that aren't advertised publicly through print ads or online posts, or mentioned in social media for the entire world to see.

Networking techniques also score hits when a job *is* advertised but attracts a tidal wave of resumes. Smart networkers shop for an edge by finding human links to the people who call the hiring shots.

Today's networking concept reinvents the "who you know" school of job finding by extending it to "who you can meet and convince to help you."

In this chapter, I concentrate on identifying connections that matter most to your career path, pinpointing networking spots, and presenting excellent letter samples that help others know you and clear roadblocks for you.

Zooming In on Purposeful Networking

Executive talent agent Debra Feldman (JobWhiz.com) personally conducts job searches for professionals and is widely respected as a master networker. Feldman advises you to ditch lottery-ticket-like networking habits and head for the people who are most likely to give you a good return on your time. She calls her method "networking purposefully."

When you pursue new contacts too casually and without focus, Feldman explains that you not only waste your time, but you become frustrated. And when you become frustrated, you may give up. Instead, follow her eminently practical strategy of networking purposefully:

Aim to find targeted connections to hiring decision makers.

It's a logical idea, but how does it work in practice? Here are two baseline tactics Feldman recommends to make her strategy pay off for you.

Advance scouting

Before heading out to a live event such as a group meeting or industry conference, identify the people who are going to be there who you want to get to know — and ones who need to know how *you* can help *them*. Just call event producers and ask when a list of attendees will be available online or in print.

After obtaining the list of invited guests and presenters, do some research to see if you share mutual interests with your target connections. "Going in ready to talk about things your target likes to talk about changes you from a forgettable person with a pulse, to a memorable individual with obvious good judgment," Feldman observes. Research makes building new relationships much easier.

Selective aim

The quality of your connections is a far more important factor than their number, Feldman explains. "Set a goal for each event to get at least one strong new contact with a potential job lead, or with an individual who can refer you to a job lead, or with someone who can refer you to a hiring authority."

Examples of people Feldman identifies as being able to make referrals include employees of your target company, as well as its former employees and retirees. Others are vendors, suppliers, partners, consultants, bankers, auditors, customers, investors, advertisers, board members, and neighbors of employees.

Finding the Best Places to Network

Whether pressing the flesh the traditional way on land or meeting new people the 21st-century online way (see Chapters 2, 8, and 9), putting together a personal network is a work project highly recommended by virtually every career adviser I know.

When networking Feldman's way — purposefully for jobs without wasting time — consider the following suggestions of places to build your personal network:

- ✔ **Industry events.** Here's where you meet compatible people who speak your language and understand what you're selling. You may even be able to impress several employers and recruiters.

- ✔ **Trade or professional associations.** They offer a giant office grapevine where, as a member, you can find out from fellow members which companies are hiring and which are firing, and who inside the hiring companies will pitch for you and who won't.

- ✔ **Relevant conferences and trade shows.** These turfs make it easy to walk up to strangers and make a favorable impression that you can later parlay into a contact or link to a job.

- ✔ **Online networking websites.** Know-everybody groups like LinkedIn or Facebook can help establish contacts in various ways. For instance, check out LinkedIn's group membership rosters for individual employment affiliations that may become helpful inside connections.

  Visit discussion boards like the job search forums on About.com, Monster, and Indeed to network with professionals and other job seekers.

  Check out Twitter's feature that allows you to see a list of who the target is following, and a list of who is following the target, which collectively may suggest others whom you'll want to contact for job leads.

  Many colleges and universities maintain online career networks where you can spot alumni you may convince to help with your job search.

- ✔ **Job fairs.** Booths, tables, and people are natural ingredients for nonstop networking and follow-up.

- ✔ **Schools.** Classes where you're learning along with others make for a natural turf to strike up conversations. Similarly, an alumni event is an open sesame to super networking opportunities.

- ✔ **Local chamber of commerce.** Here's a jellybean jar where you can meet lots of different kinds of people and hand out your business card with your branding statement and a scannable QR code (see Chapter 3) that pulls up your resume on a smartphone. But merely exchanging cards is unlikely to generate a relationship that will reward your effort. Step up your networking game by volunteering to help with a chamber effort.

- ✔ **Volunteer work.** Contributing your time to causes and events is likely to cement strong support for your job-finding efforts among like-minded, empathetic people.

- ✔ **Associations.** From hobby clubs and exercise teams to ethnic groups and improv comedy troupes, associations offer promise in the common bond of membership. Belonging to any association can pay career dividends as long as you remember the purpose for which you joined.

Networking Letters to Note

The 12 sample messages that follow in this chapter demonstrate the potential ripple effect in tapping into the networks of others — or into the networks that you create. All the samples make it easy for a letter's recipient to help the job seeker. Some have angles that may surprise you.

My comments about each sample call your attention to one or more specific features that have a strong chance of capturing the reader's attention. The samples are displayed in the order mentioned in the following descriptions.

Door openers

Many of the most effective networking letters from job seekers prominently display a referral from someone whose name the recipient either recognizes or, better still, knows personally. The following five samples illustrate:

- ✔ An educational technology and course design expert (MAGNOLIA) opens her networking letter with the name of a mutual friend, lays out her expertise, and retains the initiative by saying that she'll follow up soon.

- ✔ A pharmaceutical sales professional (MITCHELL) gets his letter in the door by identifying himself as an employee referral. He emphasizes that he is searching confidentially before irresistibly describing his number one status in sales for his current employer.

- ✔ A financial executive (HANKERD) with exceptional government contracting expertise breaks out on his own with a networking letter after originally being filtered through a network contact.

- ✔ A business technology consultant (FOSTER) seeks to find a larger job opportunity by bringing into the loop the implied recommendation of his former professor. Because professors are swamped with requests from current grads, the candidate may be perceived as A-list when a professor reaches back in time to endorse an alum.

- ✔ An aerospace professional (SLOAN) seeks an executive job in a large corporation. The first two words of his self-introductory letter to a recruiter are the first and second names of a mutual acquaintance, followed up with a flattering compliment.

Event connections

Connecting or reconnecting with someone you met at an event is an artful open to a networking letter. Professional and community events are made to order when launching your letter. Even an opening line as simple as "When we talked at my granddad's birthday party" facilitates getting your message off and running. These two samples demonstrate:

> ✔ A graphic designer (CALL) follows up a possible job lead with an employer she met at a design trade meeting. She makes it easy for her talent to be noticed by linking to her resume, her career portfolio, and a news story about her recent award in web design.

> ✔ A vocational rehabilitation counselor (SMITH) reconnects with a fellow professional at a conference and follows up with a cut-to-the-chase but graphically appealing networking letter and resume. Industry and career field insiders can supply breaking news of job openings.

Self-starters

Sometimes the network you want a piece of doesn't exist. When you can't find off-the-rack connections, don't give up: Start your own custom network. The two samples that follow illuminate ideas you may be able to use:

> ✔ A small business owner (LOBLOCK) asks a public official to appoint her to a county supervisor post that she ran for — creating a network of supporters — but lost to a competitor who now has vacated the position. Note her inclusion of a QR code that links to her web page, making it easy for the official to remind himself of her abilities in detail.

> ✔ A high-earning executive (SAXENA) launches a confidential job search by e-mailing her objective and status to an executive search recruiter. The candidate hopes to benefit through the recruiter's network. (*Tip:* Keeping a job hunt quiet is tricky; browse online for "confidential job search.")

Digital circuits

Message is everything when sending a no-frills networking e-mail that you hope will be a stopover on your way to a job. The next three samples display an up-to-date outlook:

- ✔ A confident food service executive (McDONALD) networks his way into the decider's attention span with an employee referral. He delivers an irresistible message by offering to resolve the employer's chief business challenge.

- ✔ A high-earning executive (SAXENA) whom you just met in his letter to a recruiter refuses to rest on his laurels. Instead, he taps into a LinkedIn network by asking a fellow member of his industry group to share Intel for his confidential job search.

- ✔ A new chemical engineer (MEEK) asks an industry headliner to share wisdom with her. Who could refuse a rookie with an impressive new credential, asking so nicely and letting the headliner know that she reads his professional articles and appreciates him as a source of top advice?

Help on the Way — Samples Ahead

Conventional advice suggests that, in networking letters, you ask for advice and help — not for a job. A direct request for employment puts people on the spot, and most of us hate to say "no" to a friend or colleague.

But as with most practices in job search, this advice is not chiseled in stone. Exceptions will arise. In approaching staffing agencies or people who hire contract workers, asking for a job makes sense. Use common sense.

Reflecting on the following samples puts you steps ahead of others who haven't learned to write enticing networking letters.

Steele Magnolia
3 Peachtree Drive
Savannah, GA 00000
(h) 555-555-1212
(m) 222-222-1220

[Date, inside address, salutation]

Our mutual friend Rob Davenport suggested that I contact you regarding the potential for opportunities to provide **consulting in educational technology and course design for university business and finance departments.** My aim is to combine my boardroom savvy with my expertise in classroom management and curriculum development.

I am an MBA graduate with solid experience in business development, marketing and organizational management. I have developed and executed market and distribution strategies for a diverse range of businesses in the financial services industry.

My expertise in establishing strategic direction is especially welcomed by my start-up clients, for whom I develop business plans and engage in other pre-launch activities such as raising capital and managing development of technology project plans.

Energized by my business and technological background, I have had the privilege of providing best-in-class educational programming to students throughout my county's school districts, helping to prepare the next generation for the technological and managerial challenges that lie ahead.

I have attached my resume with the hope that we can have a conversation about my qualifications and where I might best fit in. I would greatly appreciate your perspective and will follow up in the coming days to see if a mutually convenient meeting can be arranged.

Sincerely,

Steele Magnolia

Steele Magnolia
Attachment

Linda Tancs — Hillsborough, N.J.

Mark R. Mitchell
Orlando, Florida 32211
(770) 555-1212   mrmitchell@email.com

[Date]

Mr. Sam Hennegar
Executive Vice President
Global Elder Care
316 Colonial Ave.
Orlando, Florida 32222

Dear Mr. Hennegar:

A friend who works for your company, David Richardson, told me about the possibility of an opening in your organization in the near future. Reflecting on my experience in the pharmaceutical industry with GlaxoSmithKline, I've decided it is time to *confidentially* pursue additional challenges.

My primary interest is aimed at a corporation such as Global Elder Care, well respected in the medical industry and a leader in caring for the elderly – an expanding demographic.

Over the past 4 years, I have learned much about the medical community in Orlando and the surrounding areas of North Florida and have made some wonderful friendships. My greatest strength is my ability to work with people and build strong client relationships. Consequently, the doctors and their associates ask me from time to time to participate in their Community Health Fairs. This is a great opportunity to speak with people first-hand and to better understand what they want and need from the healthcare industry.

As for me personally, my accomplishments as a pharmaceutical sales representative are evidenced in my enclosed resume, but here are two highlights:

- Received "Top Sales Rep Award" for outstanding sales in the past two years; member of the $10K Club and the Number 1 Ranked Team in Florida

- Recognized in 20xx as my company's Number 1 Sales Representative in the Region (Florida, Alabama, and Mississippi)

With my qualifications, experience, and professional network, I can be a positive contributor to the further success of Global Elder Care. Thank you in advance for your consideration, and I look forward to hearing from you soon.

Sincerely interested,

Mark R. Mitchell

Mark R. Mitchell

Enclosure: Resume

Sharon M. Bowden, CPRW, CEIP — Atlanta, Ga.

GRIFFIN M. HANKERD

1732 Resort Rd.   gmhankerd1@aol.com   Home: 313-555-0111
Utica, MI 48233   Cell: 787-555-0112

[Date]

Mr. Jim Edwards
Chief Executive Officer
US Connect, Inc.
8750 W. Pleasant Ave.
Jackson, MI 49272

Dear Jim:

Since we've been unable to connect personally and have been speaking through Tony Mancini for the past week or so, I wanted to get my resume to you before our July 7th meeting for your review.

With over 25 years of success in linking finance to business operations, the value I bring to US Connect extends far beyond that of a typical **Chief Financial Officer**. Not only am I effective in developing strategic plans, budgets, and forecasts, but I know what it takes for operations, marketing, and sales to successfully execute them to deliver strong and sustainable revenue, profit, and performance results.

My career has included CFO roles in $140 million base operations, with over 2,000 personnel. I provide a unique combination of tools and direction to continuously navigate financial, market, and operational success as measured by:

- **Best Practices Implementation** to boost the value of employee productivity and process improvements.

- **Payroll and Travel Expense Management** for U.S. Army personnel and Joint Task Force in Baghdad, Iraq.

- **Project Management** for Air Force Defense Team. As project manager, completed 135 sites on time and $750,000 under budget.

I have built financial teams from the ground up, implementing financial systems and facilitating merger integration and change management initiatives that have directly impacted the top and bottom lines.

Aware of the caliber and reputation US Connect holds in the marketplace, I look forward to our continued discussion next week as the first of many positive communications.

Sincerely,

Griffin M. Hankerd

Griffin M. Hankerd

Enclosure

Erin Kennedy, MCD, CMRW, CPRW — Lapeer, Mich.

KEVIN S. FOSTER

44-64 70th Road ▪ Forest Hills, NY 11375 ▪ 718-555-0111 ▪ kevinfoster@gmail.com

[Date]

Mr. Leonard Clemmons, CEO
Infosource Inc.
34 West 47th Street
New York, NY 10036

Dear Mr. Clemmons:

My former professor, John Severnis, recommends that I contact you regarding your current opportunities for **Business Solutions Consultants**. With **over five years of experience in IT business solutions roles**, I strongly believe that my background meshes well with the needs of your organization.

In my current role at Compusource Limited, I conduct extensive IT audits and needs assessments to optimize the operations infrastructure and improve customer servicing.

✔ In just one year I created a ticket tracking system to minimize problem resolution time, built operational scripts and flowcharts to streamline product delivery, and wrote inaugural company policies and procedures.

Prior to my position at Compusource, I was a technology consultant for IBM where I project managed an Exchange migration program for 25,000 users.

✔ At IBM I rolled out a 7,000-seat NT/Exchange and Outlook initiative, authored a "how to" repository for users, and significantly trimmed server down time and crashes by auditing server logs.

Excited by your opportunity and impressed by your company's services, I would welcome the chance to meet with you in person. My resume is attached for your review. Thank you.

Sincerely,

Kevin S. Foster

Kevin S. Foster

Attachment

Barbara Safani, CERW, NCRW, CCM — New York, N.Y.

Thomas R. Sloan
700 West Paces Ferry Drive
Jacksonville, Florida 32211
(904) 555-0111
email@email.com

[Date]

Mr. Arnold Williams, Recruiter
Global Executive Search
253 Arlington Expressway, Suite 300
Orlando, Florida 32216

Dear Mr. Williams:

Gerry Maronni says you're the go-to recruiterfor aerospace aces ready to fly in new directions. Reflecting on my highly successful professional experience within the aerospace industry, I've decided it's time to pursue new challenges.

My primary interest is in working for a large corporation, possibly in a division-level capacity, or for a small company that's poised for growth as its chief executive. Yes, I pledge to relocate for the right job.

Why can I transition easily to another industry? My ability to quickly identify *areas of concern, evaluate potential solutions* and, most importantly, *make the changes necessary to turnaround situations* are my greatest strengths.

I'm savvy in the business world: My aerospace industry experience has tuned me into the relationship between sales, government regulations and overall production and productivity. These areas are evidenced in my resume but here is a sampling of my notable accomplishments:

- ☑ Reorganized/restructured departments, processes and operations resulting in annual sales growth from $5 million in [date] to $200 million today

- ☑ Maximized knowledge of and experience with government regulations resulting in the procurement of funds for training and tax exemption for capital expenses totaling almost $200,000

- ☑ Developed and implemented daily performance reporting techniques that led to a 25% increase in production

Thank you for your consideration of my resume and I look forward to talking soon. I'll follow up within 10 days.

Sincerely,

Thomas R. Sloan
Enclosure

Sharon M. Bowden, CPRW, CEIP — Atlanta, Ga.

CINDY A. CALL

Raleigh, NC 11111 • (123) 456-7890 • cindy.call@anyemail.com

[Date]

Ms. Louise Lutz
Owner, Graphic Design Solutions
456 Best Company Avenue
Raleigh, NC 11111

Dear Ms. Lutz:

What a pleasure it was to meet you at the AIGA, Professional Association of Design event last evening. I am excited to increase my involvement in the organization by volunteering for various committees and feel that I am better prepared to take on this challenge because of your guidance.

Moreover, it was wonderful to learn about the accomplishments of your firm over the last five years. Congratulations to you and your team!

During our conversation you mentioned your need to hire an additional graphic designer to assist with the increased workload this success has brought. Per our discussion, I link my resume and my career portfolio for your review. You'll see that I've been very involved in our profession since the completion of my graphic design degree. I have volunteered 200+ hours with local non-profit organizations to assist them with marketing objectives and further hone my skills in software programs such as Illustrator, InDesign, and Photoshop.

I realize that when we spoke I failed to mention my recent award in web design, which would be an asset to your firm considering your current project. You will find additional information here concerning this award, as well as the web article that announced this distinction attached to this letter.

Please be sure to let me know if you have any questions about my experience or professional development. I sincerely look forward to hearing from you to talk further about this exciting opportunity.

All the best,

Cindy

Cindy A. Call

Haley Richardson, CPRW, JCTC — Minneapolis, Minn.

SALLY SMITH

123 ABCD Circle • Anywhere, SC 29666
(864) 555-0111 • name@bellsouth.net

[Date]

Mr. Charles Jackson Washington
American Vocational Rehabilitation Association
9906 Causeway Blvd.
Charleston, SC 40000

Dear Charlie:

It was good to see you at the last conference. Since then, I've learned that change is in the air in my agency and I've decided to check out my options sooner rather than later. Can you help me by letting me know of any attractive job openings you hear about that you think I'm qualified to fill? Here's a capsule of my background:

> As a quality-driven, visionary team member with more than 9 years of experience providing rehabilitation services and managing caseloads in multiple locations in the southern part of Alabama, I feel confident in my abilities to generate winning results. I have 9 years of combined experience in providing career counseling and job placement assistance to persons in career transition: displaced from disasters, high school students, college students, retirees, and persons who were being laid off/downsized or losing jobs that were being off-shored.
>
> My past roles ranged from Senior Vocational Rehabilitation Counselor, to District Supervisor, to Disaster Relief Counselor. A sample of my accomplishments:
>
> - **Honored with the Employee of Year** distinction by the Department of Rehabilitation
> - **Wrote a successful grant proposal** that received funding to implement a technology showcase for persons with mild to severe hearing impairments to be able to test products to ascertain the effectiveness for their personal needs.
> - **Co-authored legislation** with Senator Doe for Senate Joint Resolution No. 123 that acknowledges American Sign Language as a true, complete, and rich language to be recognized in all American states by public schools, colleges, and universities.
> - **Quantifiable successes in job placements** by placing over 40 clients in competitive employment each fiscal year.

Charlie, my resume is attached. I'd like to stay in the South. Please give me a call if you hear about something, and I'll get right back to your lead's hiring authority. You know I appreciate your efforts. Thanks so very much.

All best,

Sally Smith

Sally Smith

Kristen Jacoway, CRC, CPRW, CCC, CPBS — Auburn, Ala.

JANET LOBLOCK

505 Rangel Road | Bethel, PA 55050 | 555-505-5055 | jtloblock@live.net

Service- and People-oriented Leader

[Date]

Mr. Mitch Smegel
New Chelefont Township Municipal Building
5555 Masury-Warren Road
Bethel, PA 55050

Dear Mr. Smegel:

Please accept this letter of interest for the appointment to fill the position of **New Chelefont Township Supervisor** vacated by Delbert Jones. I offer strong qualifications including **business ownership, dedicated community service**, and an active **interest in the direction of our township.** Highlights of my experience and the leadership and communication skills include:

Proven interest in a public servant role: I ran for the position of Supervisor against Mr. Jones in 2012, acquiring the most votes as a write-in candidate for the position.

16 years as an owner and operator of a successful janitorial service: I established and grew a successful operation, building a base of many satisfied business clients.

Executive-level directorship capabilities from my business experience, through my involvement with Littleton Nature Watchers since 2005, as administrator of a local Celiac Disease support group since 2009, and three years as President of Butler Regional Mixed Bowling League: Representative examples of the value I bring to the Township:

- ✓ Administer organizational budgets and financial activities. I know funding, cost control, and record keeping.
- ✓ Preside over boards and committees. Establish committee/departmental missions.
- ✓ Communicate with the public, the Township, and outside organizations.
- ✓ Negotiate contracts with suppliers, distributors, and federal and state agencies.
- ✓ Review and analyze Township Code and other pertinent legislation, laws, and public policy.

I bring **enthusiasm, new ideas, and a dedication to attracting new businesses and residents to our Township.** You can also count on my ability to quickly **build close and productive relationships** with the other Supervisors. A professional behavioral assessment of my management style indicates: *I am motivated by teamwork; excel at gathering information and making fact-based decisions; and a leader who looks for productive compromises.*

I look forward to the opportunity to meet with you. Thank you for your time and consideration.

Sincerely,

Janet Loblock

Janet Loblock

Scan to visit my webpage!

Jane Roqueplot, CPBA, CWDP, CECC — West Middlesex, Pa.

Subject: Confidential digital media marketing search

Hello Ms. Barnett,

My name is Hershell Saxena, and I am currently the Vice President of Digital Media Marketing for PenTel Consulting in Houston, TX. Although I am fully engaged at PenTel, I've decided that it's time to consider a highly confidential job search.

I am selectively introducing myself to top executive search professionals. Because you specialize and are highly successful in placing executives in the energy sector, you are at the top of my list. It is my hope that you have a search in process for a high-value communications, public affairs, or marketing professional that would leverage my talents and experience to the benefit of your client.

To help you understand the details of my experience and contributions, my full resume is attached for your review. As an overview, my expertise is centered around developing and executing high impact marketing initiatives that deliver on even the most aggressive organizational objectives.

Specifically, I specialize in the design and implementation of brand positioning and digital media communications programming. On a daily basis I am responsible for managing direct-report teams of up to 40, news releases, corporate and media relations projects, marketing publications and web communications for oil and gas, electric, solar, wind, and alternative green energy suppliers.

I am willing to relocate and open to exploring possibilities requiring a significant amount of travel. As a frame for reference, my current base salary is $165,000. I would appreciate the chance to speak with you directly to learn about the candidate preferences and current hiring needs of your clients. Would this be possible? Thank you for your time and consideration.

Sincerely,

Hershell Saxena
hershell.saxena@gmail.com
www.linkedin.com/in/saxena
(C) 123-456-7890
@hershellsaxena

Debbie Ellis, MRW, Phoenix Career Group — Houston, Texas

Subject: Referred by Janet Bezos for General Manager, East Region opening

Dear Ms. Rosani,

Your executive director and my lifelong friend, Janet Bezos, tells me your #1 business challenge is building employee teams in a high-turnover industry that can deliver memorable culinary experiences day-after-day across every restaurant in the Eastern Region.

That's where I can help.

No stranger to high-turnover environments, I built the most cohesive, stable culinary teams in Boston by breathing energy and creativity into the workplace, incentivizing employees, and reducing turnover to 5% against a 25% industry standard.

Does this sound like the kind of leadership that can help resolve your #1 business challenge? If so, then let's plan to talk after you have had the chance to review my attached resume.

I am in the area and available at your convenience.

Sincerely, Mitch McDonald
Mitch.Mc.Donald@gmail.com
917-555-8749

Kevin R. Morris — Naples, Fla.

LinkedIn: Confidential search

Hello Ms. Rigby,

My name is Hershell Saxena, and I am currently the Vice President of Digital Media Marketing for PenTel Consulting in Houston, TX. I've just begun a highly **confidential** job search and am writing to ask if you would consider talking with me for a few minutes by phone.

In my endeavor to find the right position and fit in an energy-sector organization, I am reaching out to a very small group of professionals to gather information. I found your profile on LinkedIn, and notice that we belong to the same group (International Wind Energy). Your posts have been exceptionally interesting (thank you!), and so your insights into current industry trends and challenges would be both valuable and much appreciated.

Should you be open to speaking with me, please let me know what day and time is most convenient, as well as the number you prefer that I call. Thank you so much, Ms. Rigby.

My best,

HershellSaxena@gmail.com
www.linkedin.com/in/hsaxena
(C) 123-456-7890
@hershellsaxena

Debbie Ellis, MRW, Phoenix Career Group — Houston, Texas

Subject: New chemical engineering grad needs career advice

Hello Bob,

My name is Margaret Meek, and I've just graduated from Purdue University with a Master's Degree in Chemical Engineering.

While looking for opportunities to professionally network, I read with great interest your article in last month's AEE newsletter. Your background and information immediately caught my attention, so I am reaching out to ask if you would consider speaking with me by phone about your experience in the oil and gas business. As I am about to initiate a job search, I am certain that your thoughts and insights will be extremely helpful.

There seem to be opportunities "out there", but more than a job, I am looking for a position in an organizational culture that I can endorse. For me, the right fit is key. As you've had experience with several big-player energy companies around the world, I'm hoping that you'll have some good advice to share. Would it be possible to schedule a time to talk at your convenience?

Thank you Bob. My best wishes for your continued success,

Margaret Meek
m&m@gmail.com
www.linkedin.com/in/mmeek
(C) 123-456-7890
@margaretmeek

Debbie Ellis, MRW, Phoenix Career Group — Houston, Texas

6 Tips to reap networking rewards

Impatient job seekers think networking takes too long and is too much work. Others chalk up networking to being merely a buzzword, or they've heard tales of networking fatigue and growing resentment toward would-be networkers. Still others are introverts who utterly detest the thought of putting themselves out there to leverage a network of people to find jobs.

If you're in one of these groups, are you game for a rethink?

The fact is that networking can be a top tool for people who are looking for a job or trying to advance their career. Here's a blend of best tips I've collected from an A-team of career advisors:

1. Dig a well before you're thirsty. Networking is a mutual support system. You help other people and they help you back. Start not by asking for anything when you first meet, but instead by offering a brief compliment, or to make an introduction or connection to another member of your network. At all costs, avoid coming across as pushy, needy, or self-serving. Your motto: How can I help you? Mean it.

2. Make a plan. When you get an offer to help, know what you specifically want. Think about what you want from your network. And keep records. Maintain an e-database of everyone you speak to, and their names, addresses, job title, phone numbers and summaries of what you discussed and any promises made by either of you. Sometimes it really is better to be lucky than organized, but you can't count on it.

3. Be thrifty with time. We live busy lives. When someone new approaches, an immediate reaction is "How much time is this going to cost me?" Set limits with your opening request: "I'd like to briefly discuss one item — no more than five minutes. Do you have time now?" This approach shows you are considerate, not a time waster, and leaves the door open to talk later if this isn't a good time.

4. Be selective in choosing events. Attend fewer events ad be more astute about who you spend time with. If you good-soldier-it to every business event, you could become a weary and pale imitation of your best self.

5. Use a phone and social networking to land face-to-face meetings. A large number of connections on social websites are great assets, but the payoff is in sit-down meetings where you can build budding interpersonal relationships, rather than rely on technology connections.

Use your social contacts to grow your network. When you learn about someone you'd like to network with, send a brief message asking if the person could spare 20 minutes for a networking conversation in person or over the phone.

6. Give your contacts VIP treatment. Send each new contact a thank-you note (and your resume if you haven't already provided it). Never reveal your contact's private phone number or e-mail address without permission. Most importantly, do not bug your contacts daily or weekly. It's a good idea to keep your name in front of them every several weeks to let them know how you're doing, but keep it brief!

Chapter 6

Prospecting Letters

In This Chapter

▶ Taking initiative with sales letters to potential employers

▶ Learning the techniques that make your letters stand out

▶ Choosing when to e-mail, postal-mail, or hand-deliver

*P*rospecting letters are self-marketing documents designed to discover an opportunity in the hidden (unadvertised) job market. They're sent to individuals singly or in small batches. The best ones are customized — tailored to the recipient's needs and interests.

When you use prospecting letters to turn the job market inside out for opportunities that you want and can do well, you waste your time and resources if you take the easy way and send letters that are garden-variety bombs — boring, trite, too familiar, mediocre, outmoded: They'll simply be treated as spam or junk mail. Go for the win!

Pitch with Immediate Promise

Prospecting letters done right can hit the jackpot, says John Lucht, career management guru, author of *Rites of Passage at $100,000 to $1 Million+* (Viceroy Press), and chief executive officer of RiteSite.com: "If you send a highly persuasive letter that arrives with perfect (though accidental) timing, the decision maker *will* pay attention. Why would he or she not? But if what you send is unpersuasive, even the neediest decision maker will pass."

Successful prospecting letters must pique interest with a striking opening and quickly move on to persuade the recipient that you offer an enriching employment relationship for the price of an interview. This chapter helps you write effective sales letters to strangers.

Bonus: The samples in this chapter can also serve as models you can use in writing job reply letters (see Chapter 4).

Send Digital Mail or Postal Mail?

Deciding which medium is most likely to get results for your letters is a toss-up. Here are a few important considerations in addition to those discussed in Chapter 1:

- ✔ E-mail is cheaper and quicker than postal mail. The medium is growing rapidly and producing similar results in many circumstances, particularly with recruiters.

- ✔ Third-party recruiters like e-mail because they can punch a button and send your materials to clients with ease.

- ✔ Conducting an e-mail campaign addressed to employers is risky even if you can find the decider's personal e-mail address. Why? Your letter and resume may disappear into the spam version of the Bermuda Triangle. Unless a company has advertised an HR (human resources) address, you have no assurance that your campaign will get to the right people.

- ✔ A persuasive mailing on quality paper is still the best way to forward an unsolicited letter and resume to top-level executives and other prominent deciders. Delivery is assured, your letter will arrive looking the same as when you sent it, and you signal that you are management quality.

When you're facing an uphill search in a thin job market, a direct postal mail or e-mail campaign comprised of prospecting letters riding herd on your resume can produce leads you may otherwise miss.

Techniques to Tap

Good ideas are revealed in each of the letters presented in this chapter. Any single sample may suggest several winning strategies and tactics that you can use in stepping up your job search. To launch your learning experience, I've organized the letters into groups that highlight a specific winning factor.

Eye catchers

The not-so-hot news is that some older applicant software systems have trouble handling formats with graphic designs.

But the great news is that recruiters take notice of creative letters much like teenagers lock eyes on new shiny sports cars. Both viewing groups are interested in finding out what's under the hood. Feast your eyes on these five samples:

✔ A technical professional (CLARK) displays his 21st-century skills in a fresh-looking letter that focuses on accomplishments and skills. The arresting figure zeros in on what he seeks; the letter can be created with standard computer options.

✔ A nurse (STEIN) uses a designer letter to highlight her professionalism in emergency care. Her versatile document appears here as a stand-alone approach to a health employer, but it is easily modified to create a cover letter for a resume or an after-interview "bio-blurb" to remind employers how special she is. (See more document ideas in Chapter 3.)

✔ A rookie graduate (SMITH) who hopes to break into marketing or advertising uses screens to display her job search focus, talents, and experience.

✔ A software development professional (MICHAELSON) also leads with a tasteful but traffic-stopping screen to proclaim that he's worth interviewing.

✔ A sales executive (BORDEN) attracts attention with five well-aimed bullet points framed in a dotted-line rule like a theater marquee. Don't miss his appealing closer.

Class acts

Job search letters are a specialized niche of sales letters. The best are written by professionals who know how to use words that influence people you want to work for and with. Draw inspiration from the following sample:

✔ An academic with impressive credentials in health physics (GREGSON) forgoes the formality of a CV in favor of a bio that illuminates his special worth as a subject matter expert and an educator. Clearly, the academic speaks the university nuclear power chief's language.

Rave reviews

Getting others to verbally clap hands for your accomplishments rings truer to employers than inserting your own best-crafted brags. The following sample illustrates the savvy incorporation of quotes in job search letters:

✔ A marketing executive (ANDERSON) combines a rousing endorsement from two former employers with an attractive design, targeted positions, and accomplishment-based text with a result that's both persuasive and stylish.

Important words

Treating everyone like a VIP was an operating business principle for a famous American entrepreneur named Mary Kay Ash. The multimarketing icon knew what she was doing as she built a billion-dollar world-famous cosmetics business from a $5,000 start-up.

When Mary Kay retired, her company had 800,000 beauty consultants. She urged all of them to pretend that every single customer had a sign around his or her neck that said, "Make me feel important." It's great advice for job seekers, too.

Making job search letter readers feel important is the underlying theme of the two following samples:

- An engineer who specializes in the engineering and analysis of bridge structures (LIVINGSTON) helps the hiring authority to feel like a big shot by immediately congratulating him on the company's big new contract to upgrade bridges in the state. Using a bulleted format, she quickly follows with qualifications that rank her as a top pick to join his team.

- A seasoned sales professional (NEWBURY) welcomes and congratulates a corporate vice president to her neck of the woods with his company's expansion into new markets. Her recognition of putting the reader first makes him feel important. And when you feel important, you read the whole letter.

High flyers

Whether you believe that the "career ladder" is dead and gone or merely updated to a multiprong approach for "rising above" in the 21st-century economy, the next sample gives you an idea for communicating your desire to move on up:

- A business executive (DEAN) swings for a homerun seeking a position as a Fortune 100 information systems architect and executive vice president. Note the killer postscript. Targeting the high-tech industry, he chooses the digital delivery of his letter.

Storylines

A good story almost always outshines dry facts in gaining a reader's awareness. As *Alice's Adventures in Wonderland* author Lewis Carroll exclaimed, "No, no! The adventures first, explanations take such a dreadful time."

The next sample shows how storytelling can be very effective in cementing reader interest:

> ✔ A medical doctor (KILLIAM) is more interested in running a free clinic than in earning high financial compensation. He writes the modest but inspiring story of how his professional and volunteer history has led toward a public service job with his name on it.

Business boosters

Most prospecting messages are aimed at increasing the quality of an organization's business performance — boosting profits by turning problems into opportunities. The next sample illustrates the appeal of commercial success:

> ✔ A sales professional (DUVAL) aims to climb even higher mountains in the money market industry. He shouts what he can do for the reader in the upper-right quadrant; the letter's the prime real estate. The topper: He tantalizes by writing that he can raise "even larger amounts of investment capital." Who doesn't want more money?

Durable styles

Like navy blazers or black pantsuits, well-presented classic constructions are always in style. They serve as models of excellence to offer recognized value. The final sample illustrates an interesting treatment of a tried-and-true approach:

> ✔ An executive (ARMSTRONG) takes aim at a high-level job in the consumer products industry. Following a masterful accomplishment statement in bold type at the top, he legitimizes his eye-popping claim with bulleted details, ending with an action close (see Chapter 17).

On with the Letters!

The 13 samples that follow are a spectacular collection of prospecting letters written by professional job search document writers. As in other chapters, the name of the writer of each letter appears beneath it. For more information about the writers, turn to the appendix. Start reading and get ready for a treat!

Maximum message readability is the presentation criterion for each sample cover letter in this chapter. To save space in some superb but lengthier samples, I had to chop the original boilerplate text leading into the letter — most often deleting the recipient's name, title, company, and address. So when you see a letter leading off with "[Date, inside address, salutation]," or some variation of that, the generic line is merely a reminder that you can't just say, "Hey, you, read this!" (If you're not sure how to lay out your cover letter, turn to Chapter 15.)

RALPH R. CLARK

999.555.1111   102 Tech Crescent, New York NY 10001   ralph@newleaf.ca

[Date]

Ms. Sarah Cole
Recruitment Specialist
Advanced Technologies
301 Bloor Street
New York, NY 10002

Software Development Director / Manager

Maximizing resources, productivity, and quality
with new "best practice" processes.

Dear Ms. Sarah Cole,

Advanced Technologies' reputation for technological innovation has prompted me to forward my resume for consideration for suitable openings that may come up in 20xx. Along with exceptional professional qualifications, you will find that I also have those intangible personal qualities that fit your culture, and will enable me to make a positive impact.

My career has evolved with two principal employers: Office Technology Systems, and currently, Interpersonal Communications Inc. Within each I have held progressively senior and more demanding roles, and my focus - and passion - is always with cutting edge technology. I have had the privilege of leading, growing, and evolving innovative teams, and currently I lead a team of 40+ as Director of Handheld Media applications. My teams continue to file several patents annually.

Highlights of my career:

- ☑ Masters of Mathematics, Honours Computer Science, extensive technical skills, and leadership training. My expertise is sought out as dependable guidance.

- ☑ A record of building high performance teams through good hires and *hands-on* mentoring. Performance is all in the details and I am noted for my focus on the details. I encourage collaboration, grow trust, and have seen several staff move into their own management positions.

- ☑ Many examples of effectiveness in increasing productivity; drastically reducing quality debt; taking on added accountabilities; growing staff numbers while enhancing morale; unifying, reorganizing, changing team dynamics and culture — all to support the delivery of corporate goals.

My methodology is process-driven. Standardizing processes improves time management and organization, establishes expectations, and eliminates the need to recreate, or make ad-hoc (and often misguided) decisions. In short, processes are efficient. Several of the release train model processes that I established have been accepted as best practice and have subsequently been rolled out to additional teams. You will find details on my enclosed resume.

It is time for new challenges and I am launching a <u>confidential search</u>. I welcome your call for an exploratory meeting. Thank you for your time and consideration.

Yours truly,

Ralph R. Clark
Ralph R. Clark

Stephanie Clark, CRS, CIS — Nanaimo, B.C., Canada

BRISEYDA STEIN, RN

Terry Brook Drive, Clifton, NJ 07307

303-600-8603   *brn@mail.com*

REGISTERED NURSE ◆ EMERGENCY DEPARTMENT

[Date, inside address, salutation]

Providing comprehensive nursing care, stabilizing acutely-ill patients, and volunteering to increase the quality of healthcare services has comprised my nursing career for the past 15 years. Having passionately and deliberately well-managed my nursing career to amass advanced patient care experience - I am confident in my qualifications to implement excellence in nursing care. Please review my resume for consideration as an ER nurse on your staff.

Prior to my tenure as a **Pain Management Specialist** at Memorial Health Hospital, I served in a variety of healthcare and leadership roles which will be advantageous as I assume the role of ER nurse at your facility. Please refer to my resume for a detailed account of my career chronology. Additionally, below I have summarized noteworthy achievements...

CAREER SNAPSHOT

ER Nurse 12+ Years
Unit's First Pain Specialist
Inaugural Triage Team RN
EMT Volunteer & Educator
Mentor to New RNs
Revered Patient Advocate

ACCOMPLISHMENT HIGHLIGHTS:

Earned a reputation as *"The Good Nurse"* based on consistently demonstrating genuine empathy and in-depth knowledge of emergency care and EMT services.

Contributed to the proper care of patients, requiring a wide-range of advanced acute and emergency care, ranging from infants to elderly patients.

Nurtured deep medical knowledge, including advanced triage, complex assessments, critical interventions, IV therapy, IV drips, pushes, cardiac monitoring, and competence in all central line care.

My dedication to patient care is matched by advanced clinical techniques—I can insert anIV line in 0.2 seconds! I remain confident I will be an exceptional **ER Travel Nurse** as I adapt quickly and react immediately with preciseness.

Allow me to share the following story as evidence of my spontaneous critical thinking: I accompanied a relative to the ER. While there, a high-level emergency occurred and I quickly joined the ER team to care for a family of burned victims. I earned praise from physicians for "jumping to action" with a calm demeanor.

Thank you in advance for your consideration. I will follow up next week to set a time that will be conveinient for us to meet and discuss your clients' needs in more detail. I look forward to meeting you in person.

Sincerely,

Briseyda Stein

Rosa Elizabeth Vargas, MRW, CERW, NCRW, ACRW — Orlando, Fla.

SARAH M. SMITH

50 Henry Lane, Matawan, NJ 07747
(732) 995-1846 ♦ sarahsmith@montclairstate.edu

ENTRY-LEVEL MARKETING AND ADVERTISING PROFESSIONAL
Creative with a positive and professional demeanor and a strong work ethic.

Experience includes:
- Sales & Marketing Support
- New Product Launches
- Trade Show Demos
- Social Media Marketing
- Customer Service

[Date]

Mr. Michael Thomas
Director of Corporate Marketing
Highland Beverage Company, Inc.
1100 Hilltop Avenue
Summit, NJ 07901

Dear Mr. Thomas,

I have identified your firm as one for which I would be honored to work and would like to see if my strengths and experience could fill your need for a Marketing Assistant. Graduating this May with a double major in Marketing and Advertising, I am focused on **joining a corporate marketing team in the food and beverage industry.** Project management and organizational skills developed during my internships complement my academics.

With a demonstrated strong work ethic, articulate communication skills, and the ability to switch gears often and quickly, I would like to be considered for employment. Three specific reasons to consider hiring me:

- **Strong Problem Solving & Research Skills.** Experience in small, hands-on environments has taught me to think outside of the box, anticipate needs in advance, and prioritize multiple assignments and requests for information while remaining flexible to changing priorities.
- **Social Media Savvy.** My last summer internship involved blogging about current industry news and trends, building brand recognition through Facebook Twitter activity, and updating websites for both content and retail sales.
- **On-Campus Practicum in Addition to Academics.** For additional course credit, elected to participate in a team effort to create a new brand, marketing plan logo, and advertising for Collegiate Prints, an on-campus printing company servicing students and faculty. This real-world activity applies and tested the theories we had learned in the classroom.

For these reasons and more, I would very much appreciate the opportunity to meet with you to discuss my competencies and skills and how I could make an immediate and lasting contribution to your organization.

I will call your office next week to follow up. Thank you for your time and consideration.

Sincerely,

Sarah M. Smith

Attachment: Resume

Laurie Berenson, CPRW, CEIC — Franklin Lakes, N.J.

JAMES E. MICHAELSON

Provide cost effective technology solutions ... improving business processes, functionality, and development teams.

[Date]

[Inside address, salutation]

If your organization is in need of a technically competent **Software Development** leader for enterprise-wide projects, we should talk. My resume is enclosed for your review and consideration.

My value to Viacom lies in the foundation of my experience in people, process and performance leadership. What sets me apart from others is my core understanding of how to break things down, simplify it for all groups and identify the most effective solution. Along with these strengths, I have been instrumental in:

- Project estimations, business analysis for technical requirements, and definition of new services, transactions and communication layers.
- Business process engineering including business objective identification, goals and needs, gathering, documenting and analyzing business requirements and translating those requirements into technical specifications.
- Training, mentoring and leading staff through the Software Development Lifecycle (SDLC) and OOAD.
- As a Technical Lead, provided solutions to issues/problems and brought them to a speedy resolution.

While my core competencies lie in software design and development for a wide variety of systems, undoubtedly my greatest strengths can be found in my ability to incorporate software processes into business analysis, convincing management and staff alike of the corporate value to be gained through speedy resolutions to application issues uncovered during testing.

Confident that I would add immense value to Viacom, I would welcome the opportunity to discuss opportunities to join your IT department where insights in designing and developing software solutions will result in significant top- and bottom-line growth. To that end, I have taken the liberty of enclosing a copy of my resume, which highlights key successes throughout my career history.

Sincerely,

Jim Michaelson

Enclosure

Erin Kennedy, MCD, CMRW, CPRW — Lapeer, Mich.

CHARLES T. BORDEN

7733 Lionheart Lane, Alexandria, VA 22315
703-555-0111 ▪ charlestborden15@yahoo.com

[Date]

Name
Title
Organization
Street Address
City, ST Zip

I increased sales 300% for my last employer.
Can I do it again for my next employer?
The answer is a resounding yes!

Dear [Name]:

I'm looking for a new boss, but you need look no further for a **sales executive** with a track record of hitting quota challenges out of the ballpark.

Excelling with turnaround sales management challenges, I've paid my dues by orchestrating company first's for sales performance and by lighting fires beneath mediocre territories and regions.

My résumé reveals nitty-gritty details, but here's food for thought: **five fast reasons why you should consider hiring me.** These are results attained in turnaround sales management at the regional and national levels — all verifiable.

- ▪ **National Director of Sales:** Reorganized turnaround of struggling 3-year-old start-up to attain national sales quotas within 3 months for Eastern US region (PharmaSystem).

- ▪ **Regional VP:** Achieved company record for hitting regional revenue quotas in first year for long-sales-cycle, high-ticket medical equipment and devices sold to hospitals in 15-state region (MediEquipMore).

- ▪ **Regional Director of Sales:** Outperformed other regions to capture top sales ranking for capital equipment and software in four consecutive years with previously underperforming 20-state region. Won President's Club Regional Manager of the Year award (National Medical Processing & Systems Automated).

- ▪ **Regional Business Director:** Boosted historically sluggish sales record for Southern US region to near-quota (99.5%) levels within 6 months (Corp500Care).

- ▪ **Director of Marketing:** Requested by CEO to step into interim national marketing role for one year and devise winning market strategy. Achieved highest lead generation rate in company history and top-notch sales for new product launch (Corp500Care).

Are you my next employer? Let's plan on talking soon. I'll call you next week to set up a meeting. But if you need action sooner rather than later, you can reach me on my cell phone: 703-555-0111.

Sincerely,

Charles T. Borden

Susan Guarneri, MRW, CERW, CPRW, CPBS, NCCC, DCC — Three Lakes, Wis.

Stanley A. Gregson, Ph.D.
Center for Disease Control and Prevention
National Center for Environmental Health
Agency for Toxic Substances and Disease Registry
✉ stanley.a.gregson@gmail.com – ☎ 770.555.5555 (office)

[Date]

Mr. Tony Marlston, PE
Director
Center for Nuclear Power Generation
National Polytechnic State University
4100 South Sandy Springs Parkway
Marietta, Georgia 30000

Dear Mr. Marlston:

The opportunity to join the team developing the new health physics curriculum appeals to me greatly. My goal is to put my 22 years as a health physicist, subject matter expert, and educator at your disposal as soon as I can. The bio I've attached is my first step toward that goal.

I rejected condensing my CV at once. You deserve more than sterile lists of credentials, job titles, presentations, and publications. Rather, I focused on two capabilities I hope will offer National Polytechnic the most value: a subject matter expert and an educator.

The words "subject matter expert," by themselves, have never told the full story. My rewards come not just from pulling together important information quickly and efficiently, but in helping others find new and better ways to use that commodity. I am happiest when informed leaders hold me to those standards.

That philosophy also directs my work as teacher and facilitator. I must transcend subject knowledge if people are to use it to think better. This personal code directs my actions:

- ❑ Critical listening is the first step toward critical thinking
- ❑ Knowing the best questions can produce compelling, durable learning
- ❑ Knowledge is only powerful when it is shared, not hoarded
- ❑ Efficiency and consensus are no substitutes for quality

As a next step, I'd like to explore how helping mitigate any obstacles standing between National Polytechnic's goals and the curriculum it will be proud to field. May I call in a few days to do that?

Sincerely,

Stanley A. Gregson

Stanley A. Gregson, Ph.D.

Encl.: Brief bio

Don Orlando, CPRW, JCTC, CCM, CCMC, CJSS, MCD — Montgomery, Ala.

John Anderson

458 River Road • Tarrytown, NY 96880 • Home: 914.555.0111 • Mobile: 914.555.0112 • johnanderson@aol.com

"Having worked with John in a very dynamic and fast-past environment, I was always impressed with his ability to look straight at the goal and help guide the team to the objectives. This ability was invaluable to the group when working with various organizations, people, and processes, to build cohesive business and marketing plans spanning our worldwide organization."

Vice President of Marketing
Remintar Technology, Inc.

"John can be counted on to take an assignment, project, complex problem and pull the right resources together (people and funding) to drive to success. He works to understand the customer needs, requirements and pain points and then addresses those in creative new ways. One of the most talented individuals I have had the pleasure to work with in my 18 years."

Worldwide Vice President of Marketing
Remintar Technology, Inc.

[Date]

Name
Title
Company Name
Address
City, State, Zip

Dear Mr. or Ms. [Name]:

As a business and marketing leader in program management and process improvements that have increased revenues and reduced costs, I offer a combination of knowledge and skill sets that will benefit your company. My expertise in leading companies through periods of growth and change have prepared me for any number of challenges that your company may be facing.

Highlights of my achievements during my rapid growth at Center Technology Inc. include:

As Marketing Manager for the global business unit:

- Led a global team of marketing and product managers to redefine the program scope, which increased storage revenue by more than $50 million incrementally in 6 months.

As Marketing Manager for the hardware program:

- Directed the reduction of over 120 marketing programs with a $13 million quarterly budget down to 8 marketing programs with an $8 million budget.
- Implemented promotions and extensive training programs to increase cross-sell of PCs and support services by over 25% and server.

As Business Planning Manager:

- Leveraged the company's global account organization and sales force to increase global accounts revenue by more than 12%.
- Improved relationships between the Americas' regional business and marketing teams through the implementation of best practices.

If you need a strategic marketing executive with strong business acumen and out-of-the-box problem-solving talent blended with extraordinary team leadership and the ability to execute tactically, then I am your candidate. I would welcome the opportunity to discuss how my vision, creativity and skill sets could benefit your organization. May we meet?

All Best,

John Anderson

John Anderson

Louise Garver, CPBS, JCTC, CMP, CPRW, CEIP — Broad Brook, Conn.

To: JS Prescott@gbsenterprises.com
From: emlivingston@yahoo.com

Subject: Congratulations on new contract – I can help

Dear Mr. Prescott:

When I read on CentralValleyBizBlog.com that GBS Enterprises won the Caltrans contract, I was excited that a local business will be leading the $16 million project. Congratulations! With wide experience in the engineering of bridges across California, I am the ideal candidate for your company. Having planned, led, and contributed to similar projects, I am very familiar with the existing 1930s-era infrastructure and the seismic retrofitting implications. Please see my resume here.

Highlights of my career:

- Earned **2007 Master Design Award** from the American Engineering Institute for the design of a 240-foot arch bridge over the Montgomery River in Clarke County, California.
- As member of the senior design team, I **engineered one of the first suspension bridges in the U.S. with an aerodynamic steel deck** in an area of high seismic activity.
- Performed a **seismic susceptibility assessment of an historic 1933 suspension bridge** over the Meade River in Farrugia, California for the California Department of Transportation.
- **Led the investigation of the highly-traveled J. Thomas Marlow Bridge**. Delivered an analysis of potential modernization to accommodate rail service, created a modernization strategy, and completed a risk assessment regarding seismic vulnerability.
- **Delivered the opening address at the National Seismic Conference on Bridges and Highways** in 2008. Also served as a panelist at the same conference, four of the last six years.

As you launch this vital major initiative, you'll be building a team upon which you can rely. Based on my accomplishments, engineering acumen, and ability to collaborate with team members, I believe it would be mutually beneficial for us to talk. I will call next week to inquire about the possibility of meeting to discuss your company's goals and how I can help you achieve them. Thank you for your time and consideration.

Sincerely,

Elizabeth M. Livingston, P.E.
emlivingston@yahoo.com
777.123.5555 (mobile)

Tamara Dowling, CPRW — Valencia, Calif.

Elaine Newbury

Fairfield, CT 99999 ■ (555) 555-5555 ■ ElaineNewbury@aol.com ■ @ElaineNewbury

[Date]

Mr. Jose Martins
Regional Vice President
Karma Corporation
3333 Mullen Lane
Woodbridge, NY 99999

**Westward Ho Welcome
To Karma Corporation!**

Dear Mr. Martins:

Congratulations on your company's recent successful new market entry in the Southwest. Perhaps you have a need to expand your sales team. If so, I'd be happy to help.

Throughout my sales career, I've **delivered double-, triple-, and quadruple-digit sales and profit increases**. In addition, I've ranked **as a consistent Top Producer in sales nationally** 7 consecutive years. A few highlights of my results include:

- **Managed a profitable business, producing 50% sales growth ($12 million) in just 3.5 years.**
- **Built and managed a profitable book of business from zero to $13.5 million** in recurring annual revenue over 10 years as a national account executive.
- **In first 6 months as a sales territory manager, led a nonperforming region (7 branches) to jump from #9 in monthly sales to rank #1** in all 9 regions throughout Texas. My region consistently ranked among top 3 sales winners.
- **Within 30 days, turned around an underperforming region from last to rank #3** out of 8 regions as a senior sales consultant.

I've also achieved annual membership in the Million Dollar Round Table "Top of the Table" for 5 consecutive years; only 4.6% of 38,000 members globally qualify for the "Top of the Table" distinction. I can be a valuable addition to your team. May we schedule a call to discuss your company's needs?

Sincerely,

Elaine Newbury

Elaine Newbury

Louise Garver, CPBS, JCTC, CMP, CPRW, CEIP — Broad Brook, Conn.

TRAVIS DEAN

San Francisco, CA | (C) 765-555-5622 | travis.Dean04@gmail.com

[Date]

Nathan Pritchett
Chief Information Officer
Hewlett-Packard Company
3000 Hanover Street
Palo Alto, CA 94304-1185

Dear Mr. Pritchett,

Could HP be a more efficient, agile, high-performance company?

I have spent the past 20 years helping three of the world's largest companies become more responsive to customers and more competitive market players through technology. In fact, the architecture and infrastructure solutions I have defined and executed:

- *Created new business capabilities for GM helping propel it back to world's #1 automaker.*

- *Virtually eliminated forecast variance for GE Financial Services starting an upward stock price trend.*

- *Introduced cloud-based services to IBM reducing product development costs and time-to-market; these cloud-based solutions evolved into IBM's multibillion-dollar SmartCloud services division.*

As [number] on the Fortune 100 land a rapidly evolving company, HP knows the value of innovation and agility. As CIO of a global technology leader, you know the value of building a leadership team that drives innovation and growth.

Could you use the services of a Fortune 100 Information Systems Architect and Executive Vice President who has steered technology innovations and impacted profit and growth at three of the world's largest companies?

I would enjoy the opportunity to hear your vision for HP and to discuss how my experience and expertise could play a significant role in achieving your vision. I am located right here in the Silicon Valley area and available for face-to-face discussions.

Sincerely,

Travis Dean

Travis Dean
Enclosure

P.S. Ask me about the game-changing recommendation I made to former IBM CIO Mark Hennessy in initial discussions leading up to HP's groundbreaking partnership with IBM.

Kevin R. Morris — Naples, Fla.

RONALD C. KILLAM, M.D.

444 Snowball Drive
P.O. Box 1158
Mammoth Lakes, CA 93546

(760) 633-8478 Land
(760) 633-8449 Mobile
skirunner777@yahoo.com

[Date]

Deepak Pirham, M.D.
Mammoth Lakes Free Clinic
4789 Grand Lake Road
Mammoth Lakes, CA 93546

RE: Clinic Executive Director

Dear Dr. Pirham:

As a citizen of Mammoth Lakes for more than 13 years and former clinic volunteer, I am aware of the importance of the free clinic in our town and am now in a position to become more involved.

Meeting the healthcare needs of a community as diverse as that of Mammoth Lakes is an ongoing challenge, and one that I am prepared to meet. Your consideration of the attached resume for the position of **Executive Director** of the Mammoth Lakes Free Clinic would be greatly appreciated.

I have a background in emergency medicine, hospital department management, and business ownership. This experience, combined with my ability to build strategic partnerships with community, business, and government while managing resources in a businesslike, conscientious, and ethical manner, would be an extremely valuable contribution to the clinic and its future growth.

Highlights of my career include:

- As a business owner, successfully negotiating and directing all aspects of business management, including staffing, salary negotiation, financial planning, cash flow management, collections, staff training and development, regulatory compliance, marketing, and advertising.

- Negotiating additional funds from the county to meet the needs of an underfunded and understaffed community clinic

- Managing a $15 million emergency department budget for a major California hospital without ever exceeding it.

At a time in my life where money is not my primary motivator, I would consider it a privilege to use my knowledge and experience for the benefit of the citizens of Mammoth Lakes.

I welcome the opportunity to meet with you to discuss the many ways that my background and qualifications can benefit the clinic and will follow up with you later this week.

Sincerely yours,

Ronald C. Killam, M.D.

P.S. My attached resume notes that I am a Fellow of the American College of Emergency Physicians.

R. Killam

Prospecting

Gay Anne Himebaugh — Corona del Mar, Calif.

THOMAS R. DUVAL

19875 Washington Blvd.
Fredericksburg, VA 22401

(555) 999-4487
trduval555@Mail.com

[Date]

Mr. Roger Cummins
President
Capital Investments
24458 Freedom Way
Washington, DC 20001

Three reasons to talk: Raising investment capital, building customer relationships, and driving profitable sales. That's what I do. And do well.

Dear Mr. Cummins:

For most of my career, my sales performance has consistently ranked in the top 5% of more than 200 brokers.

When I began working in the organization, I was challenged with building a book of profitable clients while at the same time contributing to the ROI of my employer. As the book grew, so did my employer's profits. I knew then that I had found my niche and my passion – trading – and I have been doing it successfully ever since.

I'm now at a point in my life when I seek new professional challenges to scale even higher mountains. I intend to branch out and raise even larger amounts of investment capital, while continuing to focus on trading commodities and financials.

Yes, my closing skills are above the industry average. I build genuine rapport quickly and easily with clients, provide them with reliable information, and ultimately close the sale.

My experience, track record of performance, and dedication to servicing the client can add measurable value to your operations. I'll contact your office next week to arrange an appointment for us to meet at your convenience.

With sincerity,

Thomas R. Duval

Thomas R. Duval

Enclosure

T. Duval   Prospecting

Gay Anne Himebaugh — Corona del Mar, Calif.

TONY L. ARMSTRONG

970 Dunmore Circle
Chicago, IL 60693

Cell: 947.555.0111
tlarmstrong@aol.com

[Date]

Mr. Peyton Diamond, Jr.
President & CEO
Excalibur Products, Inc.
1444 Murray Boulevard
Chicago, IL 60631

Dear Mr. Diamond:

Building high-performance, high-profit consumer products companies is my expertise. Whether challenged to launch a new venture, facilitate a complete business transformation, or accelerate growth throughout markets worldwide, I have consistently delivered multimillion-dollar gains in revenues and bottom-line profits. Most notably, I:

- **Led development and launch of more than 800 new products throughout my career that have generated combined revenues in excess of $2 billion for major consumer products companies.**

My career can be briefly summarized as follows:

- Currently, as **COO/EVP** with GXT Products, orchestrated integration of two consumer products companies into one organization with 28% revenue and 20% margin growth in year one. These achievements were realized through operational changes (third-party manufacturing), new product development (6 patents pending), and massive upgrade of internal IT and e-commerce capabilities (53% increase in web traffic).

- As **Founder/President** of **Crestar Consumer Products,** built new global venture and brought to profitability in first year. Developed and patented four new products, negotiated strategic alliances with distributors worldwide, and penetrated new B2C and B2B markets in the U.S., Europe, and Asia.

- As **VP** with **Newman Consumer Products** and **Director** with **Reynolds Products,** led the sale of some of the most recognizable consumer brands in the US. In total, facilitated development of hundreds of new products and product line extensions that generated more than $200 million in new product revenues.

These achievements are indicative of the quality and caliber of my entire professional career - identify and capture opportunities to build revenues, reduce costs, eliminate unprofitable products, streamline operations, leverage IT resources, and penetrate global markets.

Currently, I am managing a complex due diligence process for the sale of GXT Products and, as such, am exploring new executive-level opportunities within the consumer products industry. I would welcome the opportunity to meet with you to discuss your needs for a top-level leader who can, and will, deliver positive results. I'll follow up with you next week to schedule an interview, and I appreciate both your time and your consideration.

Sincerely,

Tony L. Armstrong

Enclosure

Wendy S. Enelow, CCM, MRW, JCTC — Coleman Falls, Va.

Chapter 7

After-Interview Letters

In This Chapter

▶ Turning thank-you letters into powerful self-marketing messages

▶ Reviewing a dozen good reasons to step up your post-interview game

▶ Analyzing sample letter tactics to decide which work best for you

*D*oes the letter you normally write to an employer following an interview read pretty much like one you may send to a grandparent saying thanks for a graduation gift? If so, you're missing golden opportunities.

The old single-purpose thank-you format shows good manners. It's polite. But manners and politeness aren't nearly enough to make sure you cross the finish line first. The solution? Burn your old-fashioned thank-you-for-the-graduation-gift format and step lively into to a 21st-century sales mind-set.

Learn to write *job clincher letters,* as superstar professional writer Don Orlando terms them. Learn to write persuasive after-interview messages that are sales letters at heart.

In your resume and during your interview, you sold yourself on being a great match for the job — superb qualifications, competencies, skills, experience, and interest — all brought to life with true and lively tales of accomplishments. Why stop the winning streak that brought you this far? Use what happened during the interview to build on your worth, as this chapter illustrates.

Great Reasons to Write After Interview

Here are a dozen reasons to put after-interview letters to work for you:

✔ **Sell your talents one more time.** The blur of brutal competition means interviewers may develop memories like Swiss cheese; it never hurts to remind hiring authorities that you're running hard to win. Your letter is your last easy chance to cement a "best of the bunch" image, especially if you are interviewed early in the selection process and are followed by equally strong competitors.

- ✔ **Contribute to top-of-mind awareness (TOMA).** TOMA is a marketing term describing a product or brand that pops into a customer's head first when thinking of an industry. Your letter is another reminder of your interest.

- ✔ **Reprise perfection for the job.** Here's your opportunity to again remind the interviewer of what you specifically can do for a company, not what a company can do for you. Draw verbal links between a company's immediate needs and your qualifications: You want A, I offer A; you want B, I offer B.

- ✔ **Delve deeper into your abilities.** Elaborate on your experience in handling concerns discussed during the interview. Prove your claims with brief, fact-based paragraphs describing how you solved problems of interest to the hiring company.

- ✔ **Contribute freebie research.** After looking into an issue facing the company that was mentioned during the interview, if you've got the creds for serious research skills, include a brief but pertinent statement of your findings, perhaps even enclosing relevant reports, surveys, and news clips.

- ✔ **Flesh out a point that escaped you.** Add information to a question you didn't fully answer during the interview. Say that, upon reflection about (topic), you want to add a follow-up comment.

- ✔ **Demonstrate your communications skills.** A number of researchers charge that texting and e-mail have contributed to a drastic decrease in effective communication skills of this generation, even in the corporate world. Here's another chance to show the texting slam ain't u.

- ✔ **Confirm your grasp of business etiquette.** Putting other people at ease through the way we behave is the essence of etiquette. Sending a letter after meeting with an interviewer shows that you know the rules for conducting yourself in a professional manner.

- ✔ **Substitute equivalent competencies and skills.** When your work history shows that you are not a look-alike for the job — or that you are trying to dramatically change careers — your follow-up letter has some chance to narrow the yawning gap. Give it a whirl!

- ✔ **Overcome various unspoken objections.** You may come away from an interview feeling that there was an elephant in the room — such as relocation or childcare or age. For legal reasons, the interviewer didn't exactly mention the objection, but you could feel its presence and you're fairly sure it's a job killer for you. Even if you dealt with the hidden objection in the interview, a letter allows you to affirm that the employer need not worry — you like new places and faces, you have solid childcare arrangements, you walk 2 miles every day.

✔ **Demonstrate your soft skills.** By establishing at least a modicum of rapport with a hiring authority, you create the perception of someone who isn't a pain to work with. And that's worth plenty in today's world.

✔ **Reaffirm your interest in the position.** In professing respect for the company, you need not dish enthusiasm with a shovel. But including a couple statements about your zest for the position is a basic requirement.

Tackling the Mechanics of Your Letter

What's your timeframe? Try to transmit your follow-up letter within 24 to 48 hours. But when you're in a swarm of candidates for an easy-to-fill job, recruiter Jenny Foss (jobjenny.com) suggests that if you really want to wow them, send your letter immediately after the interview: "Same day. From your laptop in the parking lot."

So, what's the best method for sending your letter? Check out the whys and hows of the three basic ways:

✔ **E-mail:** In this digital age, so many people send after-interview letters by e-mail that it's no longer unusual. If the company's workforce uses e-mail heavily, your e-mailed follow-up will be a fine cultural fit, with the subtext that you're one of them.

E-mail's also a good choice when you know the hiring decision is going to be made quickly. But hiring timelines are growing longer; today's job seekers understandably complain about long, drawn-out hiring decisions.

✔ **Typed and mailed:** For high-end jobs, consider responding with a typed, dead-tree-industry letter. You can send it by postal mail or, if time is short, via an overnight delivery service. The letter can run two, even three pages if it is flush with white space and easy to read.

✔ **Handwritten:** Some people swear by handwritten notes. But even when the penmanship is good, a handwritten social note doesn't readily lend itself to the requirements of a sales tool when you're up against tough competition in a crowded labor market.

Letters to Lift You Above the Crowd

A typical way to begin a follow-up letter is by expressing appreciation for the interviewer's time and for giving you a fresh-from-the-front-lines update on the particulars of the position.

Pay attention to the finer points in the following samples from professional writers who are credited at the bottom of each letter. For more information about the writers, turn to the appendix.

After-interview samples are displayed at the end of the chapter in the order mentioned in the following descriptions.

Extra helpings

You may have purposely held back an accomplishment or two for your after-interview letter to keep selling your value. Or perhaps you genuinely realized only after the interview that you have more promise to offer than you've already mentioned, and you want to be on record when the hiring decision is made. Check out how the following samples handled sending on the additional information:

✔ A potential new pastor (CONNOLLY) writes an extremely thoughtful message to the chair of the Pastor Search Committee. He describes insights gained from the meeting and explains how he would pursue his approach to the position now that he has talked with representatives of the people he would serve if selected.

✔ A workforce expert (JOHNSON) learns of a CEO's progressive view of human resources influence on change, and shares two additional experiences in health care negotiation and training.

People pleasers

A hard skill (technical skill) is the ability to do the job. A soft skill (people skill) is the ability to harmoniously do the job by working effectively with others. Soft skills are a big positive factor that includes a host of personality traits, including friendliness, optimism, and enthusiasm. Sometimes the best approach to an after-interview letter is to show your soft skills:

✔ An aspirant for an executive assistant post (GREENE) gently reminds an HR director that the announced hiring decision date has come and gone, explains that she won't wait forever, and sets a deadline to hear back. A good move well played when you've got marketable talent.

✔ A prospect for a teaching assistant position working with preschoolers (BYERS) doesn't position her qualifications behind a hard-fact blackboard, which her resume would illustrate. Instead, the candidate fills her after-interview letter with soft skills, which makes her memorable for both words and warmth.

✔ An experienced office manager (HARRIS) seeks a change of scenery at another company doing the same job. He manages to inject enthusiasm into his follow-up as he pairs his software skills and efficient work habits, reinforcing his image as a pleasant individual with common sense who gets things done.

Crossover sellers

Crossover skills are mobile — like apps on a smartphone. You may be able to cart them from your previous job to a wholly different type of job. (Find more on crossover skills in Chapter 17.) When the interview reveals that you're short on certain skills, fill in the experience blanks and gaps with crossovers in your follow-up letter:

✔ An executive (HENDERSON) seeking a job with less responsibility senses that he is about to be turned down with an "Overqualified" objection — too much education, too much pay, too rigid with demands, or too rusted with obsolete skills. His after-interview letter asks for a second interview to explain why his skills are current and will transfer well.

✔ A dealmaker and marketer (ANDERSON) writes to a Chicago equity company president a rationale he hopes will overcome objections that he has never worked in the Windy City. He refers to his extensive financial contacts nationwide, many of whom are connected to the Chicago area and who will help him start his own regional network of contacts.

✔ A sales ace (PATEL) seeks to become an information technology solutions analyst, but isn't the preferred IT engineer. In his last shot to make the sale, he compensates with a reference to having produced similar engineering reports and uses a postscript to call attention to his certification in IT architecture and project management.

Matching sets

Zeroing in on important requirements of the job — the ones that your qualifications specifically match — makes a persuasive case for winning the offer:

✔ Choosing a classic two-column "you want/I deliver" T-letter format, a contender for a new position emphasizing emergency control management in the facilities and events industry (SCOTT) skillfully reminds the interviewer that she's a stand-out candidate in every way.

Wrong way to follow up

Writing about his experiences with interview follow-up letters, funnyman Tim Sackett, who in real life is executive vice president of HRU Technical Resources, has a definite viewpoint about *where* to send your letters. Here's what he wrote about following up, on his website, www.timsackett.com.

"Do not send a thank-you letter to me at my home. Yes, this has happened to me — and yes, it was way creepy. The last thing I want to deal with when I walk in the door of my home is some crazy candidate from work. No, it does not show initiative — it shows your propensity to be a stalker."

✔ In an alternative version of matching employer requirements to candidate qualifications, a prospect for a human resources position (CARY) leaves no doubt of his ability to handle big jobs by repeatedly introducing accomplishments with "I have met the challenges of —." Why it works: Memorable and consistent chants carry conviction.

✔ A seasoned numbers professional (WOODS) dives into the requirements for a senior budget analyst, noting that the screening interviewer rated him as "among those best qualified." A subtlety, but a convenient technique to jog an interviewer's memory that he's too good to forget.

See Samples That Jell the Sell!

Few people these days receive immediate job offers during a job interview. That's why it's a mistake to assume that the interview process is over once you leave a one-on-one meeting.

Is it a smart move to send an after-interview letter to all interviewers? You bet! Multiple interviewers may have dissimilar interests in who is chosen to fill the open position. For instance, a peer hopes for a new hire who will be compatible in work activities and perhaps socializing after work on Friday nights; a manager hopes a new hire's work performance will put a halo around the her or his head. When you've met with multiple audiences, write multiple persuasive after-interview letters.

In the samples that follow, you find thoughtful ways to market yourself with an after-interview letter. As in other chapters, the name of the professional writer of each letter appears beneath it. To obtain contact information for the writers, turn to the appendix.

CONFIDENTIAL   *Will relocate to Baltimore*

John Connolly
35934 County Road 81 Valley Grande, AL 36703
📧 JohnConnolly4144@bellsouth.net ☎ 334.555.5555 – 334.555.6666

[Date]

Jonathan R. Killey
Chair, Pastor Search Committee
The Central Baptist Church
P.O. Box 555555
Centerville, Maryland, 21200

Dear Mr. Killey:

After my time with you, your committee, and your church, my first thought was to write to convey my thanks immediately. But that wouldn't have been fully satisfying to either of us.

Even before our conversation, I bound myself to a single goal: to listen, *really listen*, to what's on the hearts and minds of your church. Since my return, there has rarely been a moment when I haven't been in prayerful reflection about how I might do the Lord's bidding in serving and supporting Central Baptist Church.

Your members have devoted a lifetime of service to build a strong congregation, one that will continue doing the Great Commission. It heartens me to see them seeking ways to accommodate change.

And so, if there was just one thing I could do for Central Baptist, it would be to support our church by helping all of us turn away from the secular view of change as threat, toward the Christian ideal of change as opportunity.

I have some familiarity with that, using the Nehemiah Principal to guide others facing those same challenges to success. It works so well because it rises above blame and personal interest to help us do our work better than even we might imagine.

If I were fortunate enough to serve as your next pastor, I would devote my first year to learning, reaching out, building relationships based on trust with every member of our congregation.

"Servant leader" has become a cliché because the concept is true. I would apply both of those words with complete commitment—and in precisely that order. The leader can only lead if he is first the listening servant of the Master.

I want to keep our conversation going. May I call in a few days to benefit from your reactions to what you have just read? Looking forward to that time,

Yours in Christ,

John Connolly

CONFIDENTIAL

Don Orlando, CPRW, JCTC, CCM, CCMC, CJSS, MCD — Montgomery, Ala.

GREG JOHNSON

3801 Grand Avenue South • Minneapolis, MN 55402 • (612) 555-9445• gregjohnsonhrexec

[Date]

Mr. Patrick Trowel
President
Beecham, Inc.
5000 Zenith Avenue
Minneapolis, MN 55402

Dear Mr. Trowel:

I thoroughly enjoyed our meeting this morning, and hope you agree that it was time well spent, as I sensed we connected on every major point discussed.

Your insight on human resources' influence on change was intriguing. I told you that I was recognized by Boston University for implementing one of the first Integrative Bargaining training sessions in the U.S. (with Union and Company representatives). I failed to say that I also

- Served on the Massachusetts Health Association Board and Negotiation Team, representing over 60,000 eligible members on healthcare and other benefits – very timely expertise in today's healthcare reform climate.

- Acquired a Ford grant supporting a training program with innovative, unique components that partnered the Unemployment and Training Council with Michigan State University.

I think I was clear that my hat's in the ring. To use the brand given to me long ago by colleagues, I can be Beecham's CPO – Chief People Officer. I'll equip your talent for the "What now?" questions. What's next to make this happen?

Warmly,

Greg Johnson

Greg Johnson

Barb Poole, CCMC, CLTMC, CMRW, CPRW, PHR — Maple Grove, Minn.

Kirsten Ann Greene
42 Kinney Road ▪ Worcester, MA 01602
Kirsten_green@anyisp.com
Home Phone: 555-555-0111

November 1, 2011

Ms. Vivian Miller, Director of Human Resources
Burns and Company, Inc.
89 Milton Street
Auburn, MA 01500

Dear Ms. Miller:

Thank you again for the opportunity to interview for the position of Executive
Administrative Assistant for Burns and Company, on October 5.

As we agreed, I've followed up with you by phone on October 15; then twice after that and
still haven't heard back from you. I'm assuming your hiring process may be taking longer
than expected, which is totally understandable.

I would really, really love to work for Burns and Company. Please let me know if you can
give me a status update by November 10.

Once again, thanks for your time and consideration up to this point. I look forward to
hearing from you soon!

Sincerely,

Kirsten

Kirsten Ann Greene

Joellyn Wittenstein Schwerdlin, CCMC, JCTC — Worcester, Mass.

KIMBERLY ANN BYERS

1773 Circle Drive, Dallas, TX 75211
(214) 555-0111 ◆ kimabyers1@aol.com

[Date]

Dr. Catherine McKennick, Director
Ms. Janet Carlys, Co-Principal
Pine Grove Speech School
1225 Middletown Avenue
Dallas, TX 75211

Dear Dr. McKennick and Ms. Carlys:

Thank you for taking time from your busy schedules to meet with me yesterday regarding the position of **Teaching Assistant**. Your passion for what is best for your students was evident, as was your genuine warmth and contagious enthusiasm.

I am confident that I can meet your performance expectations as a member of the Pine Grove Speech School team. The desired attributes you mentioned most often in our meeting follow, along with my matching qualifications and teaching philosophy.

Team player — Just as I took the initiative to refill your water cooler without being asked, I will pitch in to help in any way needed. My maturity and proven teaching ability will be an immediate asset in this position. In addition, I will gladly contribute to cultural and artistic enrichment functions through my own activities and the guest artists I can secure.

Nurturing personality — Feeling empathy and relating well to others are in my DNA. My belief that every child should have a fair shake is a strong draw for me in fulfilling this developmentally critical role for your students.

Focus on mainstreaming — Your goal of educational mainstreaming indicates the high value you place on having your pre-scholars master independence. My career and life values resonate with this philosophy of encouraging and supporting independence and learning as tools for attaining happy and well-developed lives.

I enjoyed our meeting and believe that personality–wise I can be a good fit on your team. As an experienced teacher, substitute teacher (Texas certification), and arts and recreation program facilitator, I have successfully dealt with difficult and emergency situations. You can count on me!

My references will enthusiastically confirm that I am a dependable and flexible team player with a gift for nurturing and teaching children. Will you give me the opportunity to prove that I can deliver the exceptional results that your pre-schoolers deserve? I'm counting on you!

Sincerely,

Kim Byers

Kimberly Ann Byers

Susan Guarneri, MRW, CERW, CPRW, CPBS, NCCC, DCC — Three Lakes, Wis.

BARNEY L. HARRIS

500 North 42nd Street ~ Salt Lake City, Utah 84101

555-706-0111   **harrisb@gmail.com**

[Date]

Ms. Bridgette Parsons
Director: Human Resources
Borland Financial
123 Golden Street
Salt Lake City, UT 84404

Dear Ms. Parsons:

Thank you for taking the time to meet with me on [Date] about the Office Manager position at Borland Financial. I enjoyed learning about your company and the services you provide. Having learned about your operation and processes, trust me — I can quickly become a productive member of your team.

During our discussion, I mentioned that I am proficient with every component in the Microsoft Office Suite. I am also highly organized as proven through five years of managing the office staff at CDE Insurance.

Let there be no doubt that I am very excited about your employment opportunity! I have worked hard to establish myself in this industry and I believe that Borland Financial can benefit from my skills and experience.

If I can be of further assistance in the decision process, please feel free to contact me. I look forward to hearing from you shortly.

Sincerely,

Barney L. Harris

Barney L. Harris

David J. Jensen, CEIP — Salt Lake City, Utah

Gary Henderson

30 Marshall Street ■ Hamilton, AL 35570 ■ (205) 555-0111 ■ gary@henderson.com

[Date]

Mr. Thomas Zachery
Human Resources Director
GHI Corporation
2100 Capital Highway
Huntsville, AL 35804

Dear Mr. Zachery,

Following our initial interview, some thoughts came to my mind that I would like to share with you. I got the distinct impression that you felt I was overqualified for the position of security manager at GHI Corporation. While that might be true since I come from an executive background, I am certainly not under-motivated. If your fear is that I will leave when something better comes along, rest assured that at this stage of my career, my financial goals are not top priority.

Even though you think I am qualified for a higher level position, taking charge of your security staff is exactly the kind of job that I am looking for. In addition, by putting me into this job now, should an opportunity to move up within your organization become available in the future, I will have already proven myself capable of filling that opening. If such is the case, I can mentor the person who follows me in this job. Hopefully, you will agree this makes good business sense.

Please give some serious consideration to my suggestions. I want you to know that I am extremely interested in contributing to your company's success in any way that I can. I would welcome a second interview so that I may convince you and your Vice President of Operations that I am a far better choice for hire than taking a risk on a lower quality candidate.

Thank you for your time and the courtesies you have extended to me thus far. I will eagerly await your call to continue the interview process.

Very truly yours,

Gary Henderson

Gary Henderson

Melanie Noonan — Woodland Park, N.J.

QUINCY ANDERSON

♦ 946 Cedar Lane ♦ Nashua, New Hampshire 14532 ♦ 619-555-0111 ♦ qanderson@gmail.com ♦

[Date]

Mr. Steven Wexler, President
Princeton Equity Services
190 Wabash Avenue, Suite 120
Chicago, IL 60661

Dear Steve:

Since leaving our meeting on Thursday, I have thought at great length about our discussion, the tremendous opportunity in the Chicago market, and the value I bring to your organization.

First and foremost, I am a dealmaker and marketer, able to identify and capture opportunities that drive strong revenue and asset performance. I tackle each new project with a two-pronged focus: (1) negotiate the best possible transaction for all partners; and (2) create strategic and tactical marketing programs that consistently create value, dominate and catapult earnings.

My efforts can easily be measured by gains in real estate value and improved project cash flows. Full financial documentation can be disclosed (without conceding the confidentiality of Dover Properties). I have maximized the value of each asset under management and transitioned average properties into top performers.

You're right. I have never worked in the Chicago market. However, I have demonstrated my ability to build presence within other new markets nationwide (e.g., Atlanta, Southern California). Further, I have an extensive network of contacts across the country, many of whom are well connected in Chicago and will be of significant value in facilitating the start of my own regional network.

I have always been fortunate in that networking is a natural process for me. I am able to quickly ascertain who it is that I must establish a relationship with, identify the appropriate channels to do so, and quickly begin the process. In turn, despite often unfamiliar territories and personalities, I have quickly established myself in key markets nationwide. I am not daunted by challenge, but rather motivated to succeed and beat the odds.

I hope that we have the opportunity to continue our discussions and certainly appreciate the amount of time you spent with me last week. I guarantee that I can not only meet your expectations, but exceed them.

Sincerely,

Quincy

Quincy Anderson

Enclosure

Wendy Enelow, CCM, MRW, JCTC — Coleman Falls, Va.

DEV PATEL

123 Lake Drive ◆ Arlington, MA 01933
Telephone/Fax: 617.555.0111 ◆ Mobile: 617.555.0112
E-mail: email@email.com

[Date]

ISMIBC Corporation
320-B Scenic Road
Boston, MA 01772

Attn: Don Smith, Principal Engineer

Dear Don:

I enjoyed meeting you and the team on June 13th and 21st and want to reiterate my strong interest in the <u>Solutions Analyst</u> position. I understand that you are looking at additional candidates and I'd like to take this opportunity to review what I can bring to this role for the ISMIBC Corporation.

My experience has been a combination of pre- and post-sales, always centered on the business aspects of IT. My roles have involved exchanging knowledge between Sales/Marketing and Engineering/Services departments, with a strong customer focus.

I enjoy change and look forward to a role that constantly challenges me with something new. I have successfully worked independently and in groups. More specifically, I've gathered requirements from various experts and stakeholders, analyzed and synthesized the information and written functional, product, and technical specifications, in addition to being the primary responder to RFIs and RFPs.

While not an engineer from the information storage and management industry, I believe my years of varied experience in pre- and post-sales, customer focus, and people skills will bring the fresh perspective ISMIBC Corporation is seeking.

I look forward to hearing back from you.

Regards and best wishes,

Dev Patel

Dev Patel

P.S. Did I mention that last week I received my certification in IT architecture / project management?

Judith L. Gillespie, CPCC, CPRW, CEIP — W. Melbourne, Fla.

MARY SCOTT

142 Centre Blvd ● Dale, TX 78616 ● (512) 555-0111 ● mary.scott@email.com

[Date, name, inside address, salutation]

Thank you for your time and courtesy during our meeting on Wednesday. I was pleased to learn more about your organization's history and current requirements. The more I learned, the more enthusiastic and eager I became to take on this exciting new position, as I feel totally confident that your needs and my qualifications go together like salt and pepper.

Your Needs	My Qualifications
A proactive individual with both Facilities *and* Event Management expertise.	✓ Solid history delivering facilities and event coordination and management across diverse industries and sectors.
Emergency Control Management to ensure campus safety and security including evacuation planning, building security, and access control.	✓ Administration of company Emergency Response Program , along with oversight of 70-member Emergency Control Force Team to plan and conduct a full range of safety and emergency evacuations and procedures.
Individual to provide leadership in short and long-range space planning and renovation management.	✓ Solid, award-winning experience in long-range building and space planning to promote development, reorganization, and renovation of company facilities.

I appreciate your consideration and am excited by the prospect of leveraging my award-winning skill in Facilities and Event Management to facilitate your organization's immediate and long-term success. An additional copy of my resume is enclosed for your convenience. I look forward to speaking with you again soon.

Sincerely,

Mary Scott

Mary Scott
Enclosure

Karen Bartell, CPRW — Massapequa Park, N.Y.

BOYD CARY

10293 Cedar Street
New Orleans, LA 78874

(661) 555-0111
bcary@aol.com

[Date]

Charles Taylor, President
PYD Technologies
120 Robert Trent Avenue
Columbia, SC 27104

Dear Charles:

First of all, thank you. I really enjoyed our conversation the other day and am completely enamored with the success you have brought to PYD. There are but a handful of companies that have experienced such aggressive growth and can predict strong and sustained profitability over the years to come.

I would like to be a part of the PYD team — in whatever capacity you feel most appropriate and of most value. I realize, of course, that you already have an HR Director who has successfully managed the function throughout the course of the company's development. It is <u>not</u> my intention to compete with Leslie Smith, but rather to complement her efforts and bring new HR leadership to the organization.

Let me highlight what I consider to be my most valuable assets:

<u>**I have met the challenges of accelerated recruitment:**</u>

- In [date], I launched a recruitment initiative to replace 50% of the total workforce in a 900-person organization. This was accomplished within just six months and was the key driver in that organization's successful repositioning.

- In [date], when hired as the first HR executive for an emerging growth company, I created the entire recruitment, selection, and HR management function. Over the next two years, I hired more than 50 employees to staff all core operating departments.

- Between [date] and [date], I spearheaded the recruitment and selection of technical, professional, and management personnel. This was a massive effort during which time I interviewed over 300 prospective candidates throughout the U.S. and Europe.

<u>**I have met the challenges of employee retention:**</u>

- During my employment with Helms Financial, we were staffing at an unprecedented rate. The faster an organization grows, the more critical the focus must become. Costs associated with recruitment can be significant and must be controlled. Following implementation of a market-based research study, I was able to reduce Helm's turnover 35%, saving over $350,000 in annual costs.

PYD Technologies, Boyd Cary
[Date]
Page Two

I have met the challenges of international human resource leadership:

- Throughout my tenure with Laxton Data, I led the organization's International Employment & Employee Relations function. During this time, I developed strong qualifications in domestic and expatriate recruitment, compensation and benefits. Further, I demonstrated proficiency in cross-cultural communications. I traveled extensively and am comfortable in diverse situations.

I have met the challenges of organizational change through development and acquisition:

- Each of the organizations in which I have been employed has faced unique operating and leadership challenges, and focused on improved performance and growth through development of HR and management competencies. To meet these challenges, I created innovative organizational structures and pioneered strategies in competency-based recruitment.

- Most recently, I orchestrated workforce integration of two acquisitions into core operations. This required comprehensive analysis of staffing requirements, evaluation of skills and competencies of acquired employees, and accurate placement throughout the organization. The integration was successful and all personnel are now fully acclimated and at peak performance.

I hope that the above information demonstrates the value I bring to PYD — today and in the future. You will also find that my abilities to lead and motivate are strong and have always been the foundation for my personal and professional success.

I look forward to speaking with you and would welcome the opportunity to meet Mr. Williams. Again, thank you for your time and your interest. I wish you continued success in your efforts.

Sincerely,

Boyd Cary

Boyd Cary

Wendy Enelow, CCM, MRW, JCTC — Coleman Falls, Va.

MICHAEL D. WOODS

8857 Sherman Ave > Brandywine, MD 20613 > ☎ 301-555-0111 (H) > 301-555-0112 (M)
woodsmd@aol.com

[Date]

Sampson Accounting Solutions, Inc.
Attn: Stephen Stone, Chief, Financial Management Division
1234 Rush Mount Blvd.
Falls Church, VA 22665

SUBJ: Senior Budget Analyst Interview

Dear Mr. Stone:

Thank you so much for taking the time to interview me on [date] for the Senior Budget Analyst position. I consider it a privilege to have been considered among those best qualified. To wit:

- **Subject matter expert in budget procedures, reports, and related requirements to compile, organize, and submit budget requests**

- **Familiarity with Treasury Department appropriation accounts, elements of resource, and subsidiary accounts utilized in order to review budget estimates, adjust and reconcile accounts, and research/extract/compile data for reports**

- **Capacity to fully grasp accounting/budgetary terminology, codes, and procedures to ensure that obligations and expenditures are properly recorded**

- **Ability to apply the principles and practices of budget formulation to review, edit, and consolidate budget estimates, and to adjust data on related forms and schedules**

- **Insight to apply administrative budget regulations and procedures associated with the preparation and maintenance of Internal Operating Budgets**

- **Comprehensive knowledge of all phases of the planning, programming, budgeting, and execution system (PPBS) as it is implemented and executed**

I hope that once the matrix is done for all the applicants I will be among those recommended for selection. I look forward to hearing from you in regard to your decision.

All Best,

Michael D. Woods

Michael D. Woods

Phyllis Houston — Upper Marlboro, Md.

Part III
Creative Fresh Messages

The 5th Wave   By Rich Tennant

"Oh yeah, I think we've found our man."

In this part . . .

Ready for even more job search letter know-how and samples? Look to the six chapters in this part to give you the goods on preparing creative messages to win you the job, from social messages to branding statements to professional profiles. This part leaves no job search stone left unturned with added information covering online work portfolios, prezis, and videos. The final chapter offers the lowdown on after-hiring messages to seal your image as a superstar employee.

Chapter 8

Social Media Messages

*D*ecades come and go, but the last ten years was a game changer as Facebook, LinkedIn, Twitter, and an entire new genus of Internet-based communication instruments showed the world how billions of people can connect.

The new kind of connectivity, social media, provides fresh and fertile areas for job finding as the technology continues to evolve.

A dictionary definition of *social media* (the term was first used in 2004) describes it as "forms of electronic communication (as websites for social networking and microblogging) through which users create online communities to share information, ideas, personal messages, and such other content as videos."

Many forecasters expect the magnitude of increased social connectivity to spark a cosmic shift in the way job seekers and employers find each other.

At the very least, going social is a rapidly growing concept. Lucky for you and other job seekers, it showed up at this time in history when talented people are scrambling for jobs in a much changed marketplace.

This chapter highlights the types of messages you can write for a social media job search campaign. But first, here's more about the framework of how to actually use social channels.

Social Media Is a Tool You Can Learn

If the mechanics of social communication are still a mystery, you can master its routines in any of several ways:

- ✔ Identify your preferred social media websites and practice using them on your own.
- ✔ Engage a neighborhood teenager to show you the geek ropes (my fave).
- ✔ Enroll in a social media seminar or class at a high school, community college, neighborhood center, or senior center. (Calling all tech and engineering types who can instruct!)

Meet Three Big Social Players

The dominant social sites for finding jobs are making news with views, as the sum of each site's user base explodes to six, even eight zeros. At least one site has more than a billion users and is still growing as my fingers fly across a keyboard.

(Because the exact numbers of users and other facts about social channels continue to change faster than greased lightening, hop online when you want definitive user statistics, target audiences, and site ownership data.)

This section identifies a trio of leading websites as examples of where you can seed your social job messages.

LinkedIn

LinkedIn (LI) is the career-oriented service that makes it easy to connect with people you know who can help you find professional and managerial jobs. It's the website of choice by professionals, colleagues, recruiters, alumni, industry organizations, and corporations. LinkedIn is free or a fee, depending on your level of membership.

You can see profiles of other people on LI and connect with them in several ways. Among LI's many rich features for social search, targeting a specific company is easy. You may be able to find people who are connected to or inside the companies you select. Check out the following approach to benefit from LI connectivity:

Dear Jackson Harvey: A public relations job is coming open at the American Wildlife Federation, where your LI profile says you work in fundraising. I have an intense interest in the Federation's admirable work with animals.

As a fellow alum of UCSD, any help you can give me will be enormously appreciated. My LI profile summarizes my relevant background.

Sincerely, Martha Price, Class of '08

P.S. Will the selection for the PR post be made by the public relations director, by the executive director, or by a committee? Hopefully I can apply before the floodgates open.

You can also ask your connection to move you forward to a company's hiring authority or to its human resources department.

Facebook

The planet's biggest social media site ever, this one's for friends, family, and either people you know currently or ones from your past you want to get back in touch with. Facebook is also a favorite social conduit for small businesses and entrepreneurs.

The service is free. You can send messages for job help, such as this one:

Hey Cliff! Need your help to get a job. I'm moving to Tucson. Didn't you tell me your uncle Mario in Tucson owns a construction company? Can you get me a meet with him anytime after June 1? Banks of thanks. Sam Nash

Graph Search, a search engine launched in 2013, is Facebook's newest feature. Early reviewers say Graph makes it easier to find contacts in companies by allowing users to comb their groups of friends for business connections.

A *New York Times* review observes that Graph Search changes the nature of Facebook in a way that's good for job seekers: "It converts it from a virtual coffeehouse, where you come to hang out with people you know, into a zone of discovery. For the first time, the vast universe of your non-friends feels as real and accessible . . . as your little galaxy of friends."

Twitter

What most job searchers like best about this free public forum is that Twitter allows you to contact people you haven't met but want to network with. This benefit assumes that you can say what you need to say in a 140-character message.

You make your first connecting move by sending a message (a "tweet") to someone with whom you share a common interest. Your tweet says that you're now following the tweeted one. (In other words, you're reading the person's tweets.) The tweeted one may — or may not— want to "follow" you back.

What you gain from using Twitter — and its offshoot programs like Twellow — is a real-time ability to stay current in your field and find out about available jobs. You can reach out with a tweet that more or less says you need a hand:

> *Hi Tom, I'm a new grad now, hockey teammate. Hoping to land a job in smartphone sales. Can you refer me to anyone? Herb Hops*

Twitter is instant, to the point, and used heavily by a relatively young audience.

More sizzling social sites

Search giant Google+, technology favorite Dice.com's Open Web, video-sharing YouTube, and a number of other sites are among the American ranks of social channels that you can morph into employment channels.

This guide spotlights job search letters and other career messages — not the specific and ever-changing details of navigating social media websites. Please visit each website you want to use for up-to-date and specific ways to light its fire.

For a fairly comprehensive list of social media sites, browse for "How Many People Use the Top Social Media, Apps & Services," by Craig Smith.

Suggestions for Social Searching

If you'd rather apply for a job through a personal connection than make a cold call on a job board, review the following how-to nuggets for accomplishing your mission.

Conducting a LinkedIn search

Social media is a crucial component of the modern job search, says Joshua Waldman, author of the popular *Job Searching with Social Media For Dummies, 2nd Edition*. Waldman's book covers the social media essentials, including these starter pointers for your LinkedIn profile:

- ✔ If you include a photo of yourself, make it a professional-quality head-shot that shows you to best advantage.

- ✔ Update your status at least once per week year-round, to seem more passionate about your career — and to avoid setting off alarm bells with your boss that you're seeking greener pastures.

✔ Join and participate in at least three career-useful industry groups.

✔ Get 10 or more recommendations, to ensure that you look like a top candidate, especially recs from executives, managers, clients, or suppliers. Scratch-my-back recommendations are easily spotted and don't carry as much impact.

✔ Line up at least 150 connections, to increase your chances of having first-degree connections in places you want to work.

Incorporating your e-mail address book

After creating your online profile, upload all your e-mail contacts to your social media website so that when you're targeting a company or position, you can quickly check to see who in your network can introduce you to the appropriate hiring manager.

Becoming a critic and an admirer

Spend a few hours looking over your competition's profiles and portfolios on social media websites. What are your overall impressions of each individual? Good, bad, so-so? What changes would make each person more appealing? Keep a list of pros and cons to guide you in preparing your own checklist for social presentation. (If you're unsure of your judgment talent, ask a business friend to help look you over.)

Some job seekers go social with an online work portfolio. (See Chapter 12 for more information about work portfolios.) You can also view sample portfolios on myefolio.com, a service that offers handsome free templates to display your employment history, educational background, certifications and licensure, and talents.

Floating like a cloud

CareerCloud (careercloud.com) is a free web service that gathers all your social media platforms on one site, creating a "social resume." Your CareerCloud page automatically syncs with LinkedIn, Twitter, Facebook, Google+, and more.

The tool also offers an app that guides job hunters to employers who are hiring.

Social history can kill your job offer

Some companies now require job candidates to pass a social media background check. Companies that conduct social history background checks scrape the Internet for everything prospective employees may have said or done online in the past seven years — both good and bad.

Fortunately, not a big chunk of data comes from such major social platforms as Facebook and Twitter. Much of the negative information comes from *deep web* searches on blogs and posts on smaller social sites, like Tumblr and

Yahoo! user groups. Photos can hurt, too — including such websites as YouTube and Flickr.

(Standard search engines can't index the deep web, also called the *invisible web* or the *hidden web*. That's why a standard web search on your name may come back spotless, giving you a false sense of acceptance.)

Examples of things that can sink applicants include evidence of racially insensitive remarks, sexually explicit materials, clearly illegal activity, and flagrant displays of weaponry.

Sharing with Facebook friends

Your Facebook buddies may be more energetic than LinkedIn or Twitter connections when you send out calls for helping hands. If you're making a stealth search, go to Account, click Privacy Settings, and choose Friends Only. Additionally, create other lists that are based only on information that you want to share with members of each specific type of list.

Including people outside your industry

Enroll as many same-industry professionals as possible in your social spaces, preferably well-connected managers and executives. But also encourage job seekers active in various other industries. Why? As outsiders, they're not in your echo chamber. The outsiders may experience and share a diversity of current recruitment practices and opportunities that you may otherwise miss.

Short and Sweet Social Messages

Attention spans are shrinking as more of us interact with an expanding army of devices that offer touchscreens, swipes, bumps, and instant apps. Short communications is especially popular with Millennials because they grew up texting short messages. And most eyes with a few miles on them don't welcome page-long paragraphs.

When you want people to come to your aid in social job finding, keep your words as brief as you graciously can. Try this formula:

- ✔ **Make it personal.** Address each recipient by name, and mention your connection.

  If you've seen your connection fairly recently, you can begin with an affable comment:

  It was a pleasant surprise to run into you at the farmer's market last month.

  If it's been light-years since you've been in contact with your connection, open your message by reminding the person of who you are and how you know one another.

  You and I met at the Hobsons' anniversary party in May and spoke about our mutual interest in Pinterest. We're also both soccer fans.

- ✔ **State your reason for connecting.** Be clear that you're in the market for new opportunities; mention the position and industry of interest.

  I'm a 25-year applications developer seeking a contract job where I can work remotely. I'm open to most industries, especially transit, polling, and product marketing.

- ✔ **Ask for inside info.** When you already know that your connection has openings you qualify for, but the public information is incomplete, ask your connection to flesh out the job's data for you.

  I see that your company is currently recruiting for a sales assistant. Can you snag me more information about the position than I'm able to get online?

- ✔ **Switch gears.** If your connection's company has no open positions for which you qualify, ask about open jobs outside the connection's company.

  As your company has no open positions at present, do you happen to know of any openings elsewhere that fit my qualifications and criteria?

When the answer to your reaching out for help is radio silence, try again in a week or so. When you don't get a message or a phone call, assume that you made a good effort but struck out. Move on.

The key to using social media to activate your own personal job scouting team is to keep your messaging low-key, friendly, and grateful. Always say thank you.

The following samples illustrate.

Reaching out to right person

Hello Ms. Clark, my name is Debbie Ellis. I found your profile on LinkedIn. Your company is of great interest to me because you specialize in placing senior human resource managers in the manufacturing sector. With nearly 20 years of niche-industry experience, I am a perfect fit for a Director of Human Resources position in a small to mid-sized plastics or injection molding facility. May I send you my resume? Thank you, I'm standing by, Debbie (281-123-4567)

Debbie Ellis, MRW — Houston, Texas

Who do you know?

Hi there! I'm looking for a job and here are six companies I'm interested in. If you have a relationship or connection that could help me in my search, I'd really appreciate your help. Thanks in advance.

Writer: Staff

Your friend and mine, Sonja Hinkle

Sonja Hinkle suggested that I contact you. Currently, and for the last three years, I have been employed by EverythingHome as the manager of the accessories department. A career move is on my mind and given my experience with accessories, Wise Choice Selections comes to mind. Sonja recommends me as a strong candidate if you have not yet filled the open position of director of accessories. Can we meet this week? Thank you.

Writer: Staff

Names, names and more names sought

James, It was great seeing you again last March at the annual meeting of the American Society of TechSavvy System Operators. Hope you're still delighted with your career choice. I'm thinking of using my newly minted associate degree in chemical engineering to relocate to your city. Can you suggest a few people I might contact to determine the state of the job market there? Forever grateful, Tony

PS - I enclose a link to my work portfolio, which may suggest to you people I should contact.

Writer: Staff

From yesterday to tomorrow

Subject: Greetings from your former co-worker

It's been quite a while, Sarah, since we've been in touch, and I hope things are going well for you. As you've probably heard, SunTech has closed its doors permanently since we've both moved on. The last five years have been filled with much change for me, namely earning my Associate's degree in Business Administration from Spartan Community College while working full time at Triboro Construction.

Promoted twice, I am now Sr. Administrative Assistant with a myriad of accountabilities I could never have imagined I would excel at doing. However, cash flow has been slow and so I've been looking for a new opportunity.

Should you become aware of any of your associates or friendswho mightbe interested in my abilities, as shown on the attached resume, I would appreciate your sending them a copy or letting me have their names so I can contact them personally.

Even if you're not aware of any looming opportunity, I'd like to hear from you again. Perhaps we could soon meet for lunch to catch up on what's been going on in our lives.

Best regards, Katy DeAngelo, 555-555-0111.

Melanie Noonan — Woodland Park, N.J.

"If You Don't Ask, You Don't Get"

India's famed political and spiritual leader Mahatma Gandhi is credited with this classic quote. Gandhi asked the British for his nation's independence in the 1920s. Although it took a quarter of a century to happen, Gandhi got his request.

The lesson for job seekers in this digital age: To get, ask. Plug in. Reboot. Go social.

Infographics for social media

An infographic is a communication that visualizes data. It includes words, images, photos, charts, and graphs to convey information. The photo-based instagram is one type of infographic.

Using a visual format, a job seeker can present a resume as an infographic. As About.com's job search guide Alison Doyle says, "A job seeker can use an infographic resume to display previous work experience in an illustrated timeline rather than listing it traditionally in reverse chronological order. An infographic's unique blend of text and images can help job seekers stand out from other applicants."

To see lots of examples of infographics, search for "Data Visualization and Infographics," at SmashingMagazine.com.

How many other job search letters and documents in this guidebook do you think are prospects for an infographic presentation? The short academic answer: lots of them.

Chapter 9

Branding Statements, Bios, Profiles, and Speeches

. . . .

In This Chapter

▶ Branding yourself a winner (even when you're not famous)

▶ Writing a brief bio that can go anywhere, online and off

▶ Constructing a high-impact new style bio flyer

▶ Penning an online profile that showcases you worldwide

▶ Reflecting your brand in an effective elevator speech

. . . .

*A*n online world's impressions and opinions about you get around. You had to be a celebrity in bygone days to quickly reap rewards of recognition and admiration. Today you can grab the planet by its lapels and tell a virtually unlimited number of people who you are, what you're good at, what good you're doing, and what good you can do for them.

In this chapter, I blueprint ways to amp up the power of your recognition and visibility — online and off — by adopting a coordinated self-marketing strategy that begins with a well-thought-out branding statement.

Your professional branding statement communicates the essence of who you are in the workplace. Branding is a marketing concept and tool. Your brand reflects your professional reputation — what you're known for (or would like to be known for). When your reputation is a good one, it includes marketable distinctions like positive characteristics and accomplishments. It's a way to stand out from the teeming masses of competition for the best jobs.

When you've got your branding statement down pat, use it as a compass to write a supporting team of job search documents — *bio, bio flyer, online profile, elevator speech, business card*, and any other doc that grows your prospects for being hired or promoted.

When you visually "connect the docs," the reinforcement of your theme helps employers to mentally "connect the dots" of why you offer superior benefits and excellent value.

Differing Points of View

In an ancient legend found in various cultures, blind men who had never seen an elephant decide that each will examine one small part by touch and, based on their own individual experience, figure out what an elephant looks like. Unsurprisingly, they each came up with a different perception. The man who feels the elephant's leg says an elephant is like a pillar, but the man who touches the elephant's tail says an elephant is like a rope. News flash:

Different people can have distinctly different but equally valid perceptions of the same thing.

The elephant story perfectly describes what I found when I went looking for examples of personal branding statements, bios, bio flyers, online profiles, and elevator speeches. Opinions among experts vary about everything from the length of the documents to whether they should be written in the first or third person. What one professional calls a bio, another terms a profile. Those differing opinions explain why this chapter presents an assortment of sample styles that may surprise you.

Buttoning Down Your Brand

Professional branding (also called personal branding) has become a popular self-marketing concept in job search and career management. It's a strategy to rise above teeming masses of competition for the best jobs.

In a nutshell, your professional brand is the core of how you are perceived in the job market and the workplace. Your brand reflects your professional reputation — what you're known for (or want to be known for). When your reputation soars, it includes distinctions like positive characteristics and genuine accomplishments.

Professional branding begins with self-searching to develop a branding statement, from which the connected documents described in this chapter evolve.

No slacking on your brand's time

Warren Buffett, the American business magnate widely considered the most successful investor of the 20th century, lays branding stakes on the line:

Your premium brand had better be delivering something special, or it's not going to get the business.

Ingredients for a branding message

Keep it simple. Break the concept into five easy pieces to explain your brand in a branding statement:

- ✔ Your specialty — who you are
- ✔ Your service — what you do
- ✔ Your audience — who you do it for
- ✔ Your best characteristics — what you're known for
- ✔ Your best accomplishments — what your track record proves

Link the pieces together, and you end up with something like this:

> *I'm a computer technology manager and biomedical engineer keeping the water-cleansing machines running smoothly from the desktop to the treatment room. Key trait: super diligence; result: zero costly equipment failures. Not for my health, for yours. — Chris Welch*

As Alison Doyle, Job Search Guide for About.com, explains, "Your professional brand is what matters to a potential employer, networking contact, or anyone who can help you find a job or advance your career."

Where to place your message

You can use professional branding statements in many ways, including in the following dozen documents and verbal presentations:

- ✔ **Bio:** A short, professional biography
- ✔ **Bio flyer:** A high-impact bio that markets you with flair
- ✔ **Online profile:** A document that's usually longer than a bio
- ✔ **Business card:** A contact card that businesspeople use
- ✔ **Elevator speech:** A spoken, succinct message
- ✔ **Cover letter:** A transmittal letter attached to a resume
- ✔ **Networking letter:** A message for personal relationships
- ✔ **Blog:** A website opinion or editorial
- ✔ **Resume:** A branding statement placed immediately below your name, contact data
- ✔ **Statement in job interview:** A response to a request, such as "Tell me about yourself"

✔ **Social media networking:** A statement placed on such sites as Twitter, Facebook, and LinkedIn

✔ **Interview leave-behinds:** Fact sheets that remind interviewers why you're the best candidate for a job; check Chapter 10 for details.

An extra benefit of writing a professional branding statement is that doing it so wonderfully focuses your mind on answering the questions "Who am I?" and "How well am I competing in this workplace?"

For more information on the use of job search branding, visit top authority Dan Schawbel's website, `PersonalBrandingBlog.com`.

What branding statements look like

Now that you have ideas about where to place branding statements, cast your eyes on the face of branding statements. The first 14 samples were created by Judith L. Gillespie of West Melbourne, Fla., a master of cut-to-the-chase branding statements. The samples that follow are the creations of other talented free-agent writers whose names appear beneath each of their works.

Business Manager / Restaurateur

Ethical professional versed in all aspects of developing and sustaining a profitable business and highly functional in stressful venues. A world traveler who has visited the kitchens of the finest restaurants as well as toured wineries in the U.S.A., Europe, Asia, Australia, and Brazil.

Office Administration / Operations Support

A motivated, dedicated recent honors graduate, loyal team player, and decorated military veteran with a solid reputation of providing quality leadership while "always going the extra mile" who is eager to put business, accounting technology, communication, and computer skills to work.

Journalist

Multimedia savvy, deadline-oriented Journalist with great instincts and sound investigative skills. A charismatic wordsmith known for versatility and clear, concise, and compelling prose.

Law Enforcement Specialist

A trustworthy individual with strong communication skills and understanding of human nature who is dedicated to safeguarding lives and property. Praised for always maintaining a high degree of professionalism and remaining clear thinking and decisive in stressful situations. Technically savvy and practiced in civilian and military security, law enforcement and training.

Project Coordinator / Manager

Adept communicator with a passion for conservation, animals, and nature whose versatility and business acumen helps ensure productive, cost-effective, non-profit animal and conservation efforts.

Virtual Marketing Manager

A communication virtuoso and an indefatigable seeker of information with a proven record of success providing the tools all businesses need to thrive in the 21st Century marketplace.

International Commerce Manager

Results-driven expert in trade, customs, export controls, tariff classifications, pricing, and tax compliance who effectively utilizes a first-rate understanding of the world's individual business cultures and monetary systems to appreciably expand client base.

Chef

A dynamic student (GPA 4.0) who presents a uniquely appealing blend of culinary ability and business acumen. Eager and able to contribute to your Team of Connoisseurs. (Note: long-time small business owner / president who changed careers)

Software Engineer / Manager

High-impact, multidimensional manager of People, Process, and Technology with a verifiable record of significant accomplishments leveraging innovation, growth, and profits.

Mechanical Technician / Heavy Equipment Operator

Enthusiastic, detail-oriented professional with an affinity for technology, up-to-date skills, and a comprehensive knowledge of industrial activities on land, air, and sea ranging from Space Shuttle main engine maintenance and boat construction to railroad and ground transportation.

Business Developer / Administrator

An enterprising, congenial professional recognized for financial savvy, integrity, and the ability to meet stringent deadlines in diverse markets and high stress environments.

Optician

A highly-skilled professional whose focus on patients' needs, unerring eye for accuracy, communication and mathematical prowess, and technical aptitude optimizes profitability.

Journeyman Ironworker

Enthusiastic, highly competent individual who knows how to complete projects on time and safely.

Registered Nurse

An accomplished, empathetic Registered Nurse who is emotionally and physically strong, works calmly and decisively in high-stress environments, and is "hooked on surgery."

A special thanks badge to Judith L. Gillespie of West Melbourne, Fla., for creating the 14 preceding fast-moving branding statements you just read. Be inspired!

See more branding statements

Jeff Bezos, the retailing titan who created Amazon.com, offers this one-liner to explain the nature of personal branding:

Your brand is what people say about you when you're not in the room.

How would you explain the nature and value of professional branding? Think about it as you read the following additional branding statements created by a variety of accomplished writers.

Adoption Agent

I view adoption as an opportunity to create a positive, validating, and sense-of-right placement for all parties concerned; namely, the birth parents, adoptive parents, and the child.

For the birth mother, choosing adoption can be a very difficult decision, with the hope that their child feels loved and has a sense of belonging. From the adoptive parents' point of view, while they desire to love that special child and have the child's best interest at the core of all they do, there can be reservations, concerns, fears, and insecurities.

Last but not least, the child may have complex feelings that are tender and raw because they long to feel loved and valued. The goal of the three parties is really one: to know that the child is valued, loved, and feels a sense of belonging.

Dan Dorotik, NCRW — Lubbock, Texas

Accounting Whiz Optimizes Results

My name is Tony Olifir. For 17 years I have owned and managed a business and accounting firm dedicated to helping small businesses within my home state of Kentucky. In addition to my bookkeeping and accounting expertise, I offer organizational and recordkeeping consulting, QuickBooks training and a full range of business start-up services. My hallmark is the personal attention I devote to each business owner. My hands-on approach and knowledge of every facet of each client's business assure optimal results.

Linda Tancs — Hillsborough, N.J.

Chef

I'm an award-winning catering chef with the perfect blend of culinary precision, imagination, and devotion to the art of fine cooking. I'm not looking to be the next star chef. My desire is to make each of my clients feel like a star.

Tamara Dowling, CPRW — Valencia, Calif.

Science Marketing Specialist

Recognized for 20+ years of success in linking science-based achievements with decisive market leadership to build high-performance organizations with significant financial rewards. Led strategic and operational breakthroughs in proactive health informatics and communications technologies, evidence-based prevention and care management products, and cost-effective healthcare delivery systems. A true pioneer in wellness and prevention programs, disease management and population health.

Wendy Enelow, CCM, MRW, JCTC — Coleman Falls, Va.

Massage Therapist (in six words!)

Strong hands, encouraging words, speedy recovery

Tamara Dowling, CPRW — Valencia, Calif.

A popular request in job interviews is to describe who you are in six words. It does not have to be a sentence; it can be phrases or a string of words. The challenge is to make a six-word branding statement memorable and genuine. This example shows the six words chosen by a massage therapist. He uses this as a headline on his resume, as a tagline under his name on his cover letter, and on his business card. Do it well, and the six-word wonder formula will set you apart from the competition.

Senior Accountant

Meticulous Work Ethic • Adaptable across Corporate Environments • Professional & Disciplined Approach

Reputation for precise work coupled with patient, approachable nature and strong problem solving skills. Career reflects a record of successfully handling multiple and shifting priorities with a willingness to get the job done. Known by peers and managers for logical demeanor with proven ability to ask the right questions at the right time.

Laurie Berenson, CPRW, CEIC — Franklin Lakes, N.J.

Phlebotomist

I'm Annie, a cancer warrior / survivor and top-of-the-class phlebotomist. I transform scary unknowns and situations into welcoming visits with family-like support. At St. Luke's Cancer Center, I drove patient survey satisfaction ratings from 11% to 57% my first 5 months on the job. I did this in tiny and visionary ways, from day-to-day personal care to two patient advocacy programs that cost zero dollars to implement and run.

Barb Poole, CCMC, CLTMC, CMRW, PHR, CPRW — Maple Grove, Minn.

Career Coach

I leverage my avid love of learning and mastery of online technology to facilitate career management for trend-setting professionals who strive to be dynamic and high achieving in their business.

Kristen A. Jacoway, CRC, CPRW, CCC, CPBS — Auburn, Ala.

Change Agent

As a catalyst for positive change, I have a history of engaging board and staff members to generate new ideas and increase overall performance. I am adept at establishing policies, procedures, and technologies to enhance efficiency, financial health, and service to organize constituents. I enjoy building and strengthening strategic alliances. My passion is to guide nonprofits, specifically those focused on youth empowerment, to achieve new heights.

Tamara Dowling, CPRW — Valencia, Calif.

Business writer

Corporate Writer
Maggie Clark 509-555-1111

My corporate writing reads like a
stimulating conversation.

Maggie Clark   509-555-1111
My business letters, copywriting,
and webside copy use plain
language, tame unruly grammar,
and encourage conversation. Give
me a call; I'm available.

(Business card front)

(Business card back)

Stephanie Clark, CRS, CIS — Nanaimo, B.C., Canada

Business Event Specialist

I am a self-motivated and highly organized professional with strategic vision and bottom
line orientation to coordinate all phases of projects that include: corporate
meetings/teleconferences, training/leadership programs, new product launches, academic
events and programs, medical education meetings, conventions and trade shows, as well
as outings and informal events.

I have planned and managed events budgeted up to $1 million and attended by up to
4,000.

Among my accomplishments, I have increased exhibitorship and meeting attendance by
20% through effective sales and marketing efforts and strong follow-through. As a result
of maintaining quality throughout events and satisfying client needs, I have been able to
generate substantial repeat and referral business. I offer:

* Venue selection based on site visits and recommendations
* Contract negotiation for meeting centers and services
* Logistics coordination (guest accommodations, speakers' needs, etc.)
* Scheduling and timelines
* Execution of exhibits and sponsorships
* Budget and quality standards development
* Conference material production
* Meeting room set-up/agendas
* Supplier and service staff management
* Pre- and post-meeting expense tracking/variance analysis
* Contingency planning for emergencies

Contact: brendastevens@eventsrus.com
(503) 555-0001 – Portland, Oregon
www.linkedin.com/pub/dir/Brenda/Stevens

Melanie Noonan — Woodland Park, N.J.

Social Worker

ANNE K. FREEMAN, M.S.W.   MULTILINGUAL SOCIAL WORKER

"Specializing in the Development and Delivery of Quality Clinical Programs"
Intuitive and versatile social work professional with 12 years of hands-on experience as a
front-line caseworker working with diverse populations. Employs multiple modalities to build
therapeutic relationships, safe environments, and empowerment in high risk clients. A gifted
facilitator with outstanding counselling abilities utilizing a feminist approach. A team leader
with strong case management skills who is dedicated to improving the well-being of women,
children, and families as an advocate and contributor to community agencies.

Keen interest in women's issues ~ Fluent in English, Spanish, and French

annief@hotmail.com | Ph. 555.555.5555

Tanya Sinclair, CHRP, MCRS — Pickering, Ontario, Canada

Creating a Marvelous Bio

As air sustains life for living creatures, professional bios sustain careers for
responsible jobs. A *bio* — often called an *online bio* — is a brief but focused
account of a person's life. It is reflective of an individual's brand (which I
describe in the proceeding section). Sometimes a branding statement and a
bio are virtually interchangeable.

Generally, most online bios are pint-size accounts, compared to the usually
longer format of online profiles. But not always. Like beauty, whether you're
writing an online bio or an online profile is in the eye of the beholder.

You may be surprised by how useful bios have become. They pop up
everywhere — from social networking sites, blogs, company and personal
websites, and job boards to book covers, association membership pages,
speech introductions, and job interview leave-behind documents.

A bio is sometimes called an *online executive bio*, *online executive summary*,
or *online executive brief*; but by any name, the bios are used to advance
employment or business objectives. Bios often include a link to a full profile
or resume, but they usually omit a photo.

Why don't women brag more?

A recent study describing a Fortune 500 corporation's recruiting practices tried to explain why the company was hiring far more men than women. The upshot is that women were flunking the preliminary phone screening interview and were never interviewed in person. Some women were failing to cite their accomplishments. The omission caused screening interviewers to judge them as "unaccomplished."

Contingency recruiting executive Tim Sackett (www.timsackett.com/blog) has a theory about why some women don't lead with their accomplishments and miss out on good jobs as a result:

"We tend not to want to brag about our accomplishments, but our society has made it more acceptable for men to brag." I agree. Do you?

What can you do when you're filing a resume in a large bureaucratic system and fear it won't be seen by the right decision maker? Federal job expert Kathryn Troutman (www.resume-place.com) encourages her clients to e-mail a short executive bio as an introduction letter to a federal agency hiring manager and to confirm by postscript that a full resume is available in the official federal system.

Four more bio tips

Before you take keyboard in hand and begin pounding out your bio, consider these pointers, which, when followed, set you up to be perceived as outstanding:

- ✔ Read scads of bios — start in this chapter and scout for more examples online. Do this research before you write your own bio. New ideas pop up every 15 minutes, or so it seems.

- ✔ Mention your accomplishments. Repeat: Mention your accomplishments. For example, include your experience in solving specific problems, or how you made or saved money for a previous employer.

- ✔ Spell the words in your bio kurrectly. Beyond familiar warnings that sloppy is as sloppy spells, today's nearly universal use of keywords in computerized recruiting systems has upped the ante. Incorrectly spelled keywords may not turn up in a system that uses older software. By any measure, "A misspell don't sell."

- ✔ Keep track of all the online places where you have posted your bio. You'll probably want to update it from time to time. And if one day the urge to dramatically shift career gears hits you (for instance, to change your occupation from nursing assistant to truck driver), you'll want to replace your yesteryear bio with a whole new bio.

What bios look like

Bios can be created in a no-frills editorial style, as the first six samples illustrate, or dressed up with graphic design, as displayed in the last three samples. After viewing these nine samples, stick around for a preview of a spectacular new kind of document that Don Burns and I call the *bio flyer*.

LEGAL SECRETARY / PARALEGAL – 5 years of experience

- AS, Paralegal Studies – Sullivan College, Lexington, KY
- Highly proficient in word processing, data entry, and Dictaphone transcription using Microsoft application software; noticed for maintaining consistently superior levels of accuracy
- Organized, efficient, and thorough; maintains flexibility in changing work assignments
- Perform well under stress, taking pressure off superiors and peers
- Proficient in the planning and execution of multi-faceted projects in time-critical environments
- Dependable and successful problem resolution and time-management solutions
- Outstanding record of performance, reliability, confidentiality and ethical business standards
- Computer skills include Microsoft Word 97, 2003, 2007 Windows XP, Word Perfect; familiarity with Excel, PowerPoint, and Access. Typing rate 90 WPM
- Complete resume and superior references available

Criminal / Civil Law, Powers of Attorney, Complaints, Domestic Relations, Divorce, Exhibits / Witness Lists, Affidavits, Adoption, QDRO, Subpoenas. Probate, Personal Injury, Motions, Wills, Client Interviewing, Orders, Estates, Real Estate, Research, Worker's Compensation, Mortgages / Deeds, Title Search.

Contact: sallysmith@yahoo.com; Louisville, KY - 555-555-0111

Debbie Ellis, MRW, Phoenix Career Group — Houston, Texas

Watch what you say

Never in history has so much information been available about so many people. And the information is for all eyes on publicly accessible websites. Corporations use profile information to specifically market products to you. Identity thieves use profile information to rob you. Think before posting.

Scientist / General Engineer / Mechanical Engineer / Project Manager / Program Manager / Naval Architect – BIOTECHNOLOGY

17 yrs in Navy R&D on naval, aerospace and sensor platforms
7 yrs in private sector R&D on Biosensor platforms
Master's in Mechanical Engineering, University of California Los Angeles, 1995
Master's in Engineering Management (EMGT), George Washington University, 1991
Bachelor's in mechanical Engineering, 1985, Virginia Tech, Blacksburg, 1985
NAVSEA Certified Submarine Hydrodynamics Trials Director, 1991
Granted Confidential and Top Secret Clearances

Expertise:
- Biosensor R&D
- Sensor networks and sensor concepts
- Hydrodynamics
- DOD and US Federal Government Contractor
- Small Business Innovative Research (SBIR)
- Program Manager, Program Developer
- Project Manager, R&D, Testing, Evaluation, Intellectual Property Licensing
- Concept demonstration team lead for engineers, researchers
- Innovative Methods Designer

Kathryn Troutman — Catonsville, Md.

Disaster Preparedness Expert

Justin Buber, President of Be Prepared, is the go-to expert on disaster preparedness and business continuity, as readers of his popular blog, Bepreparedforanythingblog.com, attest. Justin's brand of risk management services offers complete and holistic plans designed not only to address disaster recovery theoretically but also to actively assist clients during an event.

Through his disaster management experience and IT background in data recovery and backup, Justin offers unparalleled personalized services that are quickly shaping the standards and best practices of business continuity professionals across the country.

Large and medium-sized businesses benefit from his business continuity planning, disaster recovery planning and off-site secure data backups. For small businesses, Justin offers both free and low-cost planning options to assist with continuity planning.

Linda Tancs — Hillsborough, N.J.

Financial Management Analyst / Budget Analyst / Resource Manager

5+ Years, Bank of America Corporation
5+ Years, Financial Management Services
BS, Financial Services

Areas of Expertise:

- Consolidated operating budget management
- Performance and accountability reports
- Improve internal controls
- Research and analyze budget shortfalls
- Budget forecasting
- Activity-based costing
- Resource management
- Planning and defining objectives
- Monitoring and analyzing trends
- Spreadsheet and report designs
- Narrative writing, briefings and presentations
- Efficiency processes
- Problem-solving, solutions and recommendations for managers
- Customer Service, research and follow-up

Kathryn Troutman — Catonsville, Md.

Tenured Educator: Special Education and Community Outreach

BA - Elementary Education, MA – Administration of Special Education. A dedicated and caring educator with advanced degree and 12 years of classroom experience. Committed to helping all children become successful learners. Recognized for consistently creating and maintaining classroom atmospheres that are stimulating, encouraging, safe, and adaptive to the varied needs of students.

Exceptional interpersonal skills; able to establish and maintain cooperative, professional relationships with students, parents, colleagues, administrators, and community. Rewarded for the ability to incorporate hands-on materials. Provide individualized instruction, cooperative learning techniques, and technology. School Board member and administrator.

Areas of specialty: state and federal law and regulations, individual education plans, problems of low- and high- disability students, mainstreaming, special education curricula, staff management, parent education, communications and community relations, budgeting, professional standards and ethics, Head Start, Title 1, ESS, grant writing. Mentor, tri-athlete, licensed private pilot.

Contact: janedoe@gmail.com for resume and references

Debbie Ellis, MRW, Phoenix Career Group — Houston, Texas

(Blog Bio) Dentist

Hi, I'm Dr. Peter Lin, a West LA children's dentist with a DDS from UCLA. As a father of three, I understand kids! I know their needs - a video screen and headphone on every dental chair. Best "No Cavity Club" in LA, as voted by LA Family Life magazine! When I am not fighting cavities, I coach my kids' Little League teams and play tennis with my wife, Sara. Want to learn more about dental health? Read on. Write me a question. I will answer you.

Tamara Dowling, CPRW — Valencia, Calif.

BRUCE HALDEN

7652 Red Fox Lane
Seattle, WA 98102

brucehalden@email.email
www.linkedin.com/in/brucehaldenlogistics

H: (206) 555-0000
C: (206) 555-1234

LOGISTICS OPERATIONS EXECUTIVE – VICE PRESIDENT
WAREHOUSING OPERATIONS | TRANSPORTATION OPERATIONS | LOGISTICS PROJECT MANAGEMENT

Aligning business visions with today's operational realties
Career legacy of rescuing troubled situations … defining process improvements, fixing the issues… challenge after challenge.

20+-year logistics career highlighted by delivering solutions that consistently work. Expert in steering futuristic ideas across disperse locations. Leadership style underpins full participation in business operations – from assessing risk, driving change, monitoring budgets and coordinating team logistics, through policy development, due diligence and cost controls. Empower national teams (10,000 people) to find solutions behind the scenes and on the front lines. Always influence understanding—never "just do it my way".

Barb Poole, CCMC, CLTMC, CMRW, CPRW, PHR — Maple Grove, Minn.

The B words: Boasting versus branding

To claim that you are the best player in women's singles tennis is bragging. But to back such a claim by being ranked the world's No.1 six times by the Women's Tennis Association and winning over $40 million in prize money as has Serena Williams is branding.

Bragging is boasting, often in an obvious or arrogant manner to make oneself seem more important. Branding, on the other hand, is based on more than empty rhetoric any copywriter can dream up. Believable accomplishment-supported branding must stand up to inspection in the glare of bright light: Do you walk the walk when you talk the talk?

Meet The Big Three Guy: Software, Projects, Solutions

Stan Wilson   Software Engineer

→111 Greenland Crescent → Toronto ON → M3H 3P3 →
→H. (555) 555-0111 → C. (555) 555-0112 → softwareguy@hotmail.com →

Software Development   **Project Management**   **Client Solutions**

Highly motivated software developer with strong programming skills and a talent for identifying and implementing innovative technology solutions that align with client objectives and corporate goals. Outstanding leadership, problem-solving, and analytical skills using cutting-edge development tools and industry knowledge. Diligent project execution with precision and patience.

Tanya Sinclair, CHRP, MCRS — Pickering, Ontario, Canada

An Entrepreneurial Technologist Who Gets Results

I possess keen instincts and intelligence, am results driven, and have an aptitude for solving business technology problems. Years in the trenches have fine tuned my background as a trainer, leader and supervisor. Weighing the combination of these factors, I am certain I can be an impact contributor at the outset.

The following contrasts a "before and after" picture depicting how my background enabled a profit center to grow…and what I can do for you as well:

Before	*After*
2 Video Systems and no integrated AV program or systems, with staff of one (me)	20 Video Systems and 4 integrated AV seminar rooms across 8 buildings, within 2 years and a doubling of connectivity inside of one year. Support team of 4.
Minimal training and support	Established a full training and support program designed from scratch including all user guides and training materials.
A lack of awareness among executives of the technology's usefulness in terms of marketing product	Enlightened executive staff to the point where we now support 200 videoconferences per month and a daily logjam of back-to-back VC meetings every day.
Video success approximating 40%	A consistent 96% resulting in quicker or more imminent market entry per product culminating in millions of dollars of added revenues.

Art Frank — Flat Rock, N.C.

Aiming High with a Bio Flyer

If I asked whether you've ever heard of a *bio flyer,* your response is likely to be crickets.

See, I made up the handle. Not by choice, but because Donald Burns, the inventor of this new job search document, and I are unable to find a commonly understood term to describe it, and we think *bio flyer* works. And since Burns and I hold both of the votes at this point in history, *bio flyer* it is!

Bio flyers trace their marketing ancestry to the product flyers seen everywhere from knockers on your front door, to booths at auto shows, to demos at big-box stores. The notable difference: In a bio flyer, *you* are the product.

The number one reason to consider putting together your bio flyer is that it's a sales champ.

The number two reason is that the bio flyer is a multipurpose document. You can make it work for you in numerous settings:

- ✔ In social media, you can use your bio flyer as a replacement for your bio or profile.
- ✔ In job interviews, you can leave behind your bio flyer to remind the interviewer how perfect you are for the job.
- ✔ In networking and prospecting searches, you can circulate your bio flyer as a full-throated introduction to your talents.

What bio flyers look like

The following two bio flyers are the innovative creations of Donald Burns, an award-winning writer and executive coach in New York, N.Y. Burns also likes the bio flyer for somebody with a highly marketable skill who is always on the market for a consulting gig.

Richard C. Whitman

Motivational Speaker • Management Consultant • Financial Columnist

Available for Hands-on Leadership Coaching for Fortune 100 Executive Teams

During my 20 years as a Navy fighter pilot, I enjoyed nothing more than pushing that throttle forward, spooling up the engines of my F14D–Tomcat, and blasting off the deck of an aircraft carrier (0 to 200 mph in 1.5 seconds).

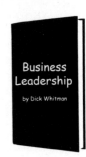

These days – as a Management Consultant and Leadership Coach – I'm no longer driving my F14D. But I get that same feeling of power and exhilaration whenever I start the engines of an under-performing company, rev up the employees and executive team, and watch them blow away the competition.

People often ask me, "How did you catapult from the cockpit of a Tomcat to the corner office of an $8 million management-consulting firm?"

Basically I've applied everything I learned in Naval Aviation – at supersonic speeds – and adapted my Top Gun training and experiences to the challenge of turning around a failing or stagnating business.

Here's Where the Book Comes In

I am passionately interested in the art and science of executive leadership, strategic planning and – most important – flawless execution. After I transitioned from the Navy to management consulting – and, later, running a business – I was shocked to see that so many good companies were wasting time and losing opportunities because of simple mistakes and omissions that resulted in weak execution.

So I started analyzing the differences between Navy pilots and business executives during the planning and execution of critical missions, and eventually published a book about it. I'm forever grateful to my business and leadership mentors and I'd like to convey what I've learned from them, for example:

- **Execution:** How "S-P-A-C-E" consistently improved execution for over 20 Fortune 500 firms.
- **Decision Making:** On the morning of 9-11-01, I was flying an F-14D and dreaded getting an order to shoot down a civilian airliner. Could you shoot down a hijacked plane full of innocent passengers to avoid an even worse catastrophe on the ground?
- **Leadership:** I've had the great fortune to meet – and be led – by some exceptionally good leaders in business and the military. What single quality makes each of them such a great leader?

Career Highlights

- **Startups:** Created three successful businesses, starting from scratch: Sales News Network (SNN.com); Leadership Consulting Division for AB&J; and the Options Trading Channel.
- **Turnarounds:** Overhauled underperforming operations for numerous Fortune 100 clients: Quickly pinpointed problems, streamlined operations, and improved P&L.
- **Transformations:** Shifted the business culture of Martell Investments – from day-to-day trading to long-term strategic planning – which became a key driver in Martell's explosive growth from $150M to $2.5B during 2006–2009.

Boston, MA • E-Mail: dwhitman@DWManagement.com • Cell: 617.743.9020

Donald Burns — New York, N.Y.

Harold S. Otten

Chief Executive Officer • COO • Interim CEO for Private Equity Firms

Board Observer • Turnaround Specialist • Business Builder • M&A Integration Expert

"Good intentions are not enough It's results that count, and I manage by the numbers," says Harold Otten, an Interim CEO and Turnaround Expert.

Shortly after graduating from MIT with a dual B.S. in computer science and business management, Otten joined General Electric (GE). He started as a financial analyst and was quickly promoted through GE's finance and operational ranks.

Halfway through his 20-year career at GE, Otten was handpicked by senior executives for participation in a two-year Corporate Restructuring Project that launched him into general management and, eventually, senior leadership roles.

"I was given an opportunity to learn firsthand from the business world's leading operational and financial minds," he said. His experience at GE provided the foundation for all his leadership, operational, and financial skills.

Although he's earned a reputation for turning around troubled companies, Otten says his greatest sense of satisfaction comes from building businesses. "I love seeing the results of a successful turnaround. Increasing sales, profits, and cash; creating new jobs; and delivering exceptionally great products that serve grateful customers."

Career Highlights

Rosch Corporation	2005–2010	Interim CEO	Three BU Turnarounds
Penn Technologies	2003–2004	VP Operations	Company Turnaround
USST Corporation	1999–2002	General Manager	Increased Sales and Profitability
GE/Aviation Service	1981–1999	General Manager	Increased Sales and Profitability

Top Management Strengths

- **Corporate Turnarounds (Rosch)**: Took charge of 3 troubled business units and reversed a downward spiral for each. Jump-started cash flow and stabilized company within 8 months.
- **People Skills (Penn Technologies)**: Within 1 month, persuaded a hostile union that working cooperatively would benefit all stakeholders. Within a year, the union was touting Penn as a success story at their annual meeting.
- **Dual expertise, Finance and Operations**: Launched three joint ventures, and led 6 major M&A transactions. Led over 250 quality improvement initiatives.

Education

B.S., Computer Science (Minor: Business Management), MIT, Cambridge, MA, 1980

50 Cay Drive • Boca Raton, FL 21077 • Cell: +1 (813) 533-0534 • Email: haroldotten@gmail.com

Donald Burns — New York, N.Y.

Perfecting an Online Profile

Profiles are creatures of many hues. They range from fairly short, keyword-driven text messages to elaborate documents aglow with pictures, eye-catching graphics, video, and embedded links.

Most people — across every age generation — now spend almost all their job search time online instead of offline, according to a random survey of more than 5,200 job seekers conducted recently by Millennial Branding and Beyond.com.

The digital dash in job search is a key factor that explains why attention to online profiles has mushroomed in recent years. If you're in the job market now or expect to be soon, the time's here to get your profile online. As About.com job search guide Alison Doyle says, "If you don't have a professional online profile yet, the best place to start is LinkedIn (www.linkedin.com). Your profile will give you a professional online presence."

Online profiles vs. resumes

Is the resume going to die of old age and be replaced by the online profile? My crystal ball is in the shop, but I don't think so. The two documents serve very different purposes.

The best resume is customized to be company specific. The next-best resume is targeted to be occupational or industry specific. Your customized resume directly informs a relatively small number of hiring authorities that you're the champ to bring on board for a specific job.

Is your profile open for business?

Pay close attention to your social media settings to understand precisely how they affect your visibility to employers.

Those words are good advice from Dean R. DeLisle (www.forwardprogress.net), a well-known business consultant who presents free webinars focused on building the ultimate online profile.

On the LinkedIn website, for example, DeLisle says that two settings are critical when you want to be found:

✔ One is listed under "Email Preferences." Select the sort of messages you're willing to receive. Here's where you specify the types of contacts you welcome, as well as give automatic advice to potential contacts about the times you may be available and the types of positions you're targeting.

✔ The other is listed under "Account Settings." Activate your Public Profile setting and check all the boxes.

Keeping your job search confidential

Are you job hunting on the sly? When you fear firing by your employer if your under-the-radar search goes public, pay heed to the following wise advice from executive talent super agent Debra Feldman (www.jobwhiz.com).

"Make sure that your LinkedIn account is protected. Do not display new connections, and keep your profile updated continuously, not just when you are in job searching mode. Join online communities where your expertise will be visible to those likely to appreciate your contributions and where you can establish new contacts and develop more relationships."

When your credentials are continuously accessible, an employer will not have a specific reason to suspect that you are looking for a new opportunity, Feldman says.

The online profile is not a customized document, but is more like a one-size-fits-all pitch posted on a digital billboard that's located on a busy information superhighway and seen, hopefully, by hordes of unknown viewers.

Unlike the customized resume, the online profile doesn't say, "Dear Hiring Authority, I'm the one to choose and here's why," but "Hey, you, look me over and let me know if you see anything you like."

Both documents have value for job seekers. And both have blowback potential when used in a confidential job search, as well as identity security risk.

 Message consistency matters. Although the two types of documents have different audiences, they should describe the same person. A recruiter's perception of deception is a kiss-off. As Minneapolis executive recruiter Harry Urschel (www.thewisejobsearch.com) explains:

"If your online profile reports your role as an office manager of a small business, and your responsibilities included accounting, your (customized) resume should never make it appear as if your entire role was as an accountant."

Ten tips to improve your profile

Employers can grab a panoramic view of the type of employee you would likely be, based on your experiences, skills, accumulated knowledge, and results portrayed in your online profile. If the person you project shows enough potential to land on a recruiter's A-list, you'll be contacted. Here are ten tips to step up your profile game.

Show your strengths

Focus the content on your professional expertise, benefits, and accomplishments. Itemize your current and past employment, education, industry, and know-how. Don't forget current professional memberships, awards, honors, and certifications. Contact info, including your phone number, is a must. Skip personal information, such as marital status.

Count on keywords

Be generous with relevant keywords throughout your profile so search engines come looking for you. Be sure to explain your job titles so search engines can do their job; merely listing yourself as a "consultant" without adding the keywords that identify the field (such as "consultant medial research") leaves you out in the cold.

Write conversationally

Employers don't hire profiles; they hire real people. Use short paragraphs and bullets. Lead off your profile with your impressive professional ammo. Write a sizzling opening summary loaded with requirements that job ads report to be important to employers in your sights, and then speak of your matching qualifications.

Sizzle with headline power

Pull in readers with energetic headlines, such as these examples:

Experienced software engineer brings green energy to market

Office bookkeeper with 100% accuracy record

Social media manager expert in Twitter, Facebook

Avoid stretching your versatility

Some people throw all their qualifications not on the wall to see what sticks, but into their profile to see what connects. They look like jacks-of-all-trades, but masters of none. Employers usually look for specialists, not generalists. (An exception is a mini-business where each member of the workforce must wear more than one hat.)

Include solid recommendations

Rather than dose your profile with empty self-praise, encourage others to laud your skills and qualities. You're more likely to impress when others comment on your work, such as bosses, coworkers, and customers. Factually explain how you made or saved money for the company. Tell how you delivered on a goal and how you earned top performance reviews. Emphasize provable accomplishments. (Count the number of times I mention accomplishments in this chapter, and you know I'm not kidding about the magic of accomplishments.)

Maintain a complete, updated profile

A half-finished profile is unprofessional and unimpressive. Keep yours fresh and relevant. Most experts advise you to include an attractive and professional photo. But a photo can backfire if it makes you look FOU (fat, old, and ugly).

Omit personal data

Skip status updates that employers can live without knowing. Avoid joining groups or making connections that aren't relevant to your field. Don't put your home address, social security number, driver's or professional license numbers, or family information in your profile. Restrict contact information to your phone number and e-mail and, if you have one, to a postal mail box address. Generally, treat personal identity information like a classified document to keep identity thieves away.

Find rewarding gardens of opportunity

Where should you plant your professional profile? The likely locations of most value are digital networks where you can make connections with people who share your interests in specific professional areas of expertise, such as information technology or journalism, retailing or insurance, medicine or marketing. For job seekers, the social networks at the head of the parade continue to be LinkedIn and Google Plus. Additionally, if you have your own website or blog, post your profile there.

Facebook and Twitter are potential professional hosting perches. But a growing number of doubters aren't enthusiastic about using friendship and dating sites to park professional profiles.

A number of other free websites are available for professional profiles. Many are designed for entrepreneurs who market business products. Some are job-bidding sites. Others specialize in part-time work. Search the Internet to locate "free sites for your professional online profile."

Meet prize-winning profiles

Because some of the best online profiles are spread over many pages (far too many for reproduction in this guide), Career Directors International, the professional writers' association, has posted the winning entries of the six top profile winners of the organization's LinkedIn competition. View CDI'S blue-ribbon profiles at `www.careerdirectors.com/toriLI.htm`.

What professional profiles look like

Check out the two sample one-page profiles that follow. The first sample is a text-only presentation that works well on any platform. The second condenses a longer profile of About.com Job Search Guide Alison Doyle that appears on LinkedIn.

Summary

GLEN FORBES, BSc, PT
CLINICAL LEADER & PHYSIOTHERAPIST

=========================
Maximizing Efficiencies * Developing Leaders * Rejuvenating Healthcare
=========================

* Inspiring, informative, and compassionate clinical leader and skilled physiotherapist
* 20 years of experience in both the public and private sectors
* Skilled at leading a multi-disciplinary team in advancing organizational goals and initiatives
* An articulate and inclusive leader with strong teambuilding and facilitation skills
* Strong business acumen and capacity to generate revenue and identify cost savings
* In-depth understanding of present and future patient and community needs

=========================
PROVIDING QUALITY HEALTHCARE LEADERSHIP
=========================

Noteworthy Recent Accomplishments:

* Established the Physio Centre of Excellence in Ohio centralizing 10 community based programs.
* Championed an award-winning stroke research study.
* Facilitated 50+ education sessions in six months.

=========================

Areas of Medical Expertise:

* Physiotherapy, Acute Medicine
* Private Practice, Sports Medecine
* Paediatrics, Oncology
* Inpatient & Outpatient Neurology
* Cardiac & Stroke Rehabilitation
* Orthopaedics, ICU

=========================

GLEN FORBES, BSc, PT
CLINICAL LEADER & PHYSIOTHERAPIST
glenf@hotmail.com
555.555.5555

=========================
LinkedIn Specialties:
* Physiotherapy Practice Leadership
* Project Leadership & Program Evaluation
* Staff Training & Team Development
* Interdisciplinary Team Collaboration
* Budget Management

Tanya Sinclair, CHRP, MCRS — Pickering, Ontario, Canada

Alison Doyle
About.com Job Search and Employment Expert:
jobsearch.about.com

Summary

I am a job search and employment expert with many years of experience in human resources, career development and job hunting with a focus on job searching, employment issues, and career options, as well as employment trends and technologies for job seekers and employers alike.

I've been the Job Search Guide for About.com since 1998, and have been quoted extensively in major online and print publications.

In addition, I'm the author of Alison Doyle's Job Search Guidebook, Internet Your Way to a New Job: How to Really Find a Job Online and the About.com Guide to Job Searching.

Experience

Job Search Expert at About.com
June 1998 - Present
Alison writes about job searching and careers for About.com. You'll find tips for locating job listings, finding employers, networking and other ways to find the right job. Alison covers job search technology, online job searching, writing resumes and cover letters, references, unemployment, and interviewing skills.
14 recommendations available upon request

Associate Director, Career Services at Skidmore College
September 1991 - December 2010
Develop information technology resources to assist students and alumni with their search for a job or internship.
1 recommendation available upon request

Executive Administrative Manager at Tri-State Retail Systems
1984 - 1991

Skills & Expertise
- **Social Media**
- **Job Search**
- **Career Management**
- **Career Services**
- **Career Advancement**
- **Job Search Strategies**
- **Employment**

Alison Doyle — Albany, N.Y.

Going Up in an Elevator Speech

Simply put, an elevator speech (or elevator pitch) for job search purposes is a brief oral overview of who you are, what you do, and how you can help a hiring authority. It's another branch of the branding concept echoed throughout this chapter.

Elevator speeches are no place to get lost in details. Most often they run 20, 30, or 60 seconds. Highly successful elevator speeches increase the listeners' desire to meet again for a longer exploration of what you, the job-seeking speaker, can do for them.

In case you're wondering how on earth a quick, succinct summation of what you offer ever became known as an elevator speech, here's a clue: Supposedly, the colorful term came about because an introduction speech should last no longer than the average elevator ride. In fact, the precise origin of the elevator speech term is — pun alert — left up in the air.

Eight tips to enjoy the ride

You may not actually be explaining your life's experience and job ambitions in an elevator. But even when your meeting venue is a planned, formal dinner, or a job interviewing office, or a career fair, you want to be primed to capture your listeners' attention. Here are eight tips to be sure you're heard loud and clear.

Create a basic format

Begin writing your elevator pitch by answering the following essential questions:

— Who am I (student, athlete, veteran, rookie, seasoned worker)?

— What do I do, or want to do (to help people who hire me)?

— What is my most important credential (education, award, publication)?

— Why am I qualified (skills, experience)?

— What value do I provide (make money or save money for employer)?

— What stands out about me (dedication to meeting challenges)?

— What type of employer is most likely to see my value (industry or career field)?

Cut to size

When your cup runs over with good things to say about yourself, write it all down. Then keep cutting and editing until you identify three talking points that give a snapshot of your career. Here's an example:

(1) *I spent 22 years as a successful recruiter and HR manager.* (2) *I know how to find and retain top talent.* (3) *Now I'm ready to head up executive talent management in a forward-looking company.*

Hang a hook

Try to include a hard-to-resist hook — a statement or question using words that glue ears to your speech. Use compelling words like the following:

Now I take those financial insider secrets and teach people how to . . ..

Another project I led installed a call center that aided people displaced by the Deepwater Horizon oil spill.

After I recovered missing evidence in a publicized law case, we won, and amazing things happened after that.

Prepare targeted speeches

Although you need a solid elevator speech ready for any occasion, make it listener benefit–oriented by customizing it. The customizing strategy works because human ears perk up when hearing "what's in it for me."

Soak up material

Practice your speech enough to express key points without sounding as though you're reading from a teleprompter.

Go with change

Every career grows and morphs, and your elevator speech needs to grow and morph with it. Updating becomes ever more urgent as the years pile up.

End with an action request

Don't get so caught up in enthusiasm for your speech that you forget to mention what you need. When you're speaking to a hiring authority outside of office hours, the action you want is to set up a job interview. Here are two approaches:

Based on this brief introduction, do you think a future meeting has potential for both of us?

I hope we can speak further about your company's current or potential need for people with my abilities. Can I get on your calendar in the next week or so?

When you're delivering your elevator speech in an interview (answering the "Tell me about yourself" probe), you want clarification of the next step in the hiring decision. Or you want to know whether the interviewer sees any reason why you're not well qualified for the open position, to address any negative issues and perhaps overcome the objection.

Sometimes your action request is for an introduction to an individual who can hire you or open doors for you.

Express appreciation

Frame a gracious exit with your final words:

Thank you for sharing your time with me today.

What elevator speeches look like

The following four 30-second elevator speeches were created by Laura DeCarlo of Melbourne, Fla. DeCarlo is president of Career Directors International, a leading professional writers' association.

Human Resources Generalist

I am an experienced human resources generalist with PHR credentialing from the Society for Human Resource Management. I have full knowledge of employment policies and guidelines which includes eight years of expertise in interviewing, recruiting and counseling. I have been recognized by my prior employers for my ability to partner with them to produce bottom-line savings through staff retention, development, and selection.

Internet Marketing Specialist

"I am Shirley Browne, an Internet marketing specialist. I excel at helping small businesses to quickly remove the roadblocks keeping them from making their websites and Internet presence profitable. With my customized approaches using social media and the marketing of products and services online, my clients typically see at least a 30% increase in revenue within three months."

Marketing Researcher

"Hello, my name is Elaine Slater. I am an experienced marketingresearcher with deep expertise in advertising and product tracking studies. This includes questionnaire design, data analysis and report writing. My major presentations to company executives have repeatedly led to their buy-in on critical studies. When can I set up a personal interview to tell you more about my qualifications?"

Entry Marketing Position

I have worked in the retail industry for the last three years. I am now enrolled in the Marketing program at Thurbridge University. My previous employers have always commented on my strong people skills. Last year I boosted sales by 33% by focusing on providing strategic account management and ensuring proactive service. In addition, I have developed a significant level of knowledge from my marketing courses in product packaging, demographic research, and consumer awareness. I am seeking an entry-level position in marketing using my marketing knowledge, communications, organizational, and selling skills.

Common Threads for Your Search

In today's era of galloping social literacy, the branding linkage between increasing numbers of job search letters is hard to miss. Message consistency becomes not only vital to your image, but necessary to avoid your being discarded as a deceptive job hunter.

Your branding statement should communicate to your bio, to your bio flyer, to your online profile, to your elevator speech, and to your business card, "We're all in this search together."

How to succeed online with really trying

Control of the online candidate image that employers increasingly use to judge you as a person as well as evaluate the talent you bring to the table is largely — but not entirely — your call.

Yes, you, the job seeker, are the chief decision maker who rules what goes in and what stays out of an online presence that hangs a halo over your head. But other people, some of them flat-out strangers, also contribute to your image, sometimes disastrously.

Like it or not, others mention you and tag your photos on Facebook. They upload YouTube videos in which you appear. They spill the beans about you on local websites. They tattle on you in their blogs. In multiple ways there's no escaping the fact that other people impact your online image.

(continued)

(continued)

In a salute to changing times, recent studies reveal that employers now regularly check search engine results to decide whether you're included or booted out as someone they'd like to meet and hire.

That fact is why I include this trio of tips that won't cost you a dime to put a shine on your halo:

- **Reputation protection.** *BrandYourself* (www.brandyourself.com), unlike earlier reputation management services that charged customers thousands of dollars, is free for basic services, which CEO Patrick Ambron explains is just right for the vast majority of BrandYourself users.

  This simple, do-it-yourself service is the only product concentrated solely on helping people control the search results for their name.

- **Expert answers.** *Quora* (www.quora.com) is a free site that allows you to ask and answer questions about any topic, says Chris Forman, CEO of the online job-search organizer StartWire. You can build admirable professional status by answering questions that relate to your professional background. Grab the keyboard!

- **Name of your game.** When you have a common name, such as Joyce Kennedy, you don't want to be mistaken for someone else online. You can avoid much of the potential confusion by adding a middle initial or name to your online name, such as Joyce L. Kennedy or Joyce Lain Kennedy.

"Another strategy is to make sure it's really your information and not someone else's that an employer is judging you on. Try to keep your profile names consistent across all the social networks you're on," advises Dan Schawbel, Managing Partner of Millennial Branding, and author of *Promote Yourself: The New Rules for Career Success* (St. Martin's Press).

Because there are so many names churning about online, there's a good chance that the name you want may not be available on all platforms (websites).

"You may want to use *KnowEm* (www.KnowEm.com), a free site which matches your name against hundreds of social networks so you can see where it's available," Schawbel adds

Chapter 10

Interview Leave-Behind Docs

· ·

In This Chapter

▶ Leaving something powerful to remember you by

▶ Directing hiring attention to your most marketable self

▶ Sampling focused messages that make you special

· ·

Try to seal the deal at the end of a *job selection interview* by proffering a new kind of self-marketing document that your competition may not even know exists: the *interview leave-behind*.

The leave-behind (LB) doc is a new kind of power tool that's muscular enough to win the job in a competitive hiring situation. Why? Unlike your resume, which can be cluttered with all kinds of information, the LB zooms in on specific reasons why, after a job selection interview, you should be hired for the open job.

Typically a single page or two pages filled with data about a topic highly relevant to the specific job for which you are interviewing, the LB describes more details of your accomplishments, skills, or other hiring attractions than does your resume.

Leave-behinds are presented in hard copies at the selection interview.

A Leave-Behind Brings You to Mind

Imagine yourself included in a group of six people on a "short list" for the same job. Now imagine a stretched-thin hiring manager who interviews all of you the same day. All contenders are dressed much the same. All have similar work histories. All seem to ask identical questions. All give cloned replies to questions. All seem to be adequately qualified.

Now put yourself in the frazzled manager's shoes. It's not always easy for the manager to remember one vanilla applicant from another.

Using a leave-behind as a tool to trigger recognition of who you are and what you can do for an employer is a super idea that's rapidly gaining momentum among savvy job seekers. You are no longer lost in the crowd.

Here are three more good reasons to prepare effective leave-behinds.

Reinforce your strengths

Even a knock-out customized resume lacks the space to delve into details that could make the final-cut difference between who's hired and who isn't.

A single-focus LB can step into the void and vividly communicate a key value, such as a likeable personality, an ability to learn new things quickly, or another aspect of your candidacy that a hiring employer appreciates. The leave-behind document is an ideal tool for this purpose.

Distinguish yourself from the competition

A well-crafted LB demonstrates that you're charged up and ready to go all out to achieve your goal. You want this job! You're willing to do extra work to nail it. By example, you demonstrate that you take creative and fresh steps to succeed in your career.

Jumpstart your follow-up

Chapter 7 describes the after-interview self-marketing letters you must write quickly to button up each job-search effort. But sooner is better: The hiring authority will have a visible reminder of you and your value before you're out the door.

15 Leave-Behind Topics to Remember

When you decide to use the power of leave-behinds, your first decision is the choice of topic for the best ROT (return on time). *Hint:* Through research, discover what an employer really values and share what you've done in that area. The following topics are a place to start:

- ✔ **Accomplishment statement.** A listing of your top accomplishments and how they benefited your employers. The CAR (challenge, action, result) true story, set off by bullets, is a favorite format for LBs.

- ✔ **Industry experience close-up.** A summary of your experience in a specific industry. Employers prefer to hire people who have a track record in their industry, presuming that they know how things work there and won't make newbie mistakes.

- ✔ **Occupation highlights.** A brief compilation of high spots in your work history. This approach is the way to go when you're changing industries and your occupation (such as accounting, sales, or teaching) can be applied to many types of workplaces.

- ✔ **Skills summary.** A compilation of skills that are useful in the position you seek, including basic skills, thinking skills, people skills, and personal qualities, such as responsibility, self-esteem, and sociability. (See Chapter 17 for more about skills.)

- ✔ **Targeted profile.** A presentation of who you are and what you've accomplished that will help you reach a specific target. This narrative summary markets your key qualifications and career achievements. (See Chapter 9 for more about profiles.)

- ✔ **Leadership initiatives summary.** A compendium expanding an executive or managerial resume that describes how you excel at being a person others will follow. The summary gives chapter and verse to the favorable results of your leadership.

- ✔ **Cultural fit statement.** A subjective look at how well you're likely to blend in with the home team. It may include clues to your personality, attitude, work habits, mannerisms, dress code references, values, and goals.

✔ **Salary history.** A sheet itemizing your compensation record by job title, employer, dates, and annual pay. (*Tip:* Don't volunteer this doc. And first read salary negotiation guides to protect your best interests, to avoid "giving away the store.")

✔ **Education achievements.** Start with a record of the physical educational institutions you've attended and what you've learned. Typically, this sheet includes brick-and-mortar colleges, universities, and vocational/technical schools.

Additionally, include distance education coursework and degrees, whether free or paid, credit or noncredit, as well as substantial educational lectures.

Do not include fake education degrees from a diploma mill, typically an Internet scam offering worthless credentials for a price. Employers are wise to this fraud.

✔ **Training snapshot.** A document that itemizes job-specific training. Typical sources include on-the-job training, apprenticeship, internship, vocational/technical school, military training and distance study, including online work-related courses.

✔ **Project plan.** A document showing how you planned, executed, and brought to fruition any substantial project, from construction and architecture to software development and company histories. You demonstrate ability, follow-through, and responsibility.

✔ **Mini portfolio.** A multipage showcase of your best work, particularly for creative professionals in marketing, media, advertising, and design. Architects and artists use mini portfolios as LBs, as do interns and new graduates.

✔ **Certification achievements.** A roster of career-boosting certifications that you've earned. Certs are available in most career fields, from technology and health care to financial management and human resources. Certs suggest you're a pro.

✔ **Performance snapshot.** Extracts from performance evaluations, praise from customers and managers, and any other factor showing you're a top performer for the kind of job you want. See Chapter 12 for additional performance-rating sources.

✔ **Strengths summary.** A list of proven workplace abilities, such as good management skills, dedication to meeting deadlines, quick learning ability, skill in solving problems, willingness to do extra, and proficiency in building teams. Include only strengths related to the position you want.

Writing Effective Leave-Behinds

Which topic do you choose for your LB? How much detail do you include? The choice is your call. You're getting in on the ground floor of using leave-behinds to lasso a job, so few guidelines apply yet.

But consider these four common-sense keys to writing successful "self-marketing copy" in job search letters:

- ✔ Select content from the viewpoint of how an employer benefits by hiring you.
- ✔ Write as if you're speaking to one person, and spell the words correctly.
- ✔ Ask a friend with good business judgment to review your copy.
- ✔ Customize your leave-behind for each employer.

Nothing about the topic, writing, or presentation of leave-behinds is chiseled in stone. Some leave-behinds can be conceptualized from other chapters in this book. Some you will discover in other places. Some you will invent based on your own strategic goals.

Many leave-behinds are straightforward and presented in an uncluttered design; others are sophisticated and incorporate graphs, charts, maps, statistical summaries, news clippings, and info graphics.

Review Samples of Leave-Behinds

The six leave-behind samples that follow illustrate a variety of presentations and formats. All but one are single-page presentations; the other is a two-page format.

Make contact management a snap

Use your smartphone to take a picture of new business cards you receive. Smartphones can pull the cards' information into their contact base with such programs as Business Card Reader (businesscardreader.com) and CardMunch (cardmunch.com).

PAULA CLARK

111-555-1111 · paulaclark@newleaf.com · www.paulaclark.com

Career focus: ## COMMANDER/INVESTIGATIONS

Over 23 years of service in a municipal police force with a multi-cultural population of 400K+. Experience distinguished with **international contracts and invitations to act as observer, interviewer, and investigator of serious international crimes.**

Skilled leader, interviewer and investigator, employ respectful and strong negotiating skills. Analytical and decisive problem solver; independent thinker who reliably displays sound judgment and high integrity; and energetic networker who establishes relationships, and seeks input and collaboration.

Facilitate conflict resolutions. Produce well-written and organized security briefs, reports, and summaries.

"I have the ability to set people at ease, to blend into the background when needed, to read into body language, and notice the details. It is these attributes and skills that have led to work in undercover, and to establishing a reputation as an outstanding investigator." —Paula

SKILLS

· Keen observation skills
· Talent for diffusing tension
· Crisis management
· Leadership & program development
· Knowledge of human behavior
· Networking for information
· Collecting evidence
· Evaluating reliability of information
· Teaching and mentoring
· Monitoring budgets

VALUE OFFERED

· Improved internal and external communications and relationships
· Enhanced training, efficiencies, and information tracking and usability
· Introduced new processes and procedures that significantly improved results

CAREER SNAPSHOT

International Experience

Observer	Centre for Genocide Studies, Rwanda
Investigator	United Nations Commission of Inquiry, Sudan
	Coalition for International Justice, Chad
Scenes of Crime Officer	International Criminal Tribunal, Kosovo

CAREER MILESTONES

· Requested by United Nations to participate in Sudanese investigation

· Member of Criminal Intelligence Service of (City Name). As VIP Security Coordinator, liaised with (Major Agency Names), and United Nations Security

· First female officer in (City Name) Police Service Intelligence and Homicide

· Officer of the Year 2006, International Organization of Women Officers

Stephanie Clark, CRS, CIS — Nanaimo, B.C., Canada

SALES SKILLS INDEX™ REPORT SYNOPSIS

Phillip Burns, 505.555.1212   505 Elm St. Pittsburgh, PA 55555

CATEGORY ANALYSIS / RESULTS
Full report available upon request

PROSPECTING / QUALIFY: The first step of any sales system. It is the phase of the sale where prospects are identified, detailed background information is gathered, the physical activity of traditional prospecting is coordinated and an overall strategy for face-to-face selling is developed.

• 8 out of 9 times Phillip selected the BEST two possible strategies.

FIRST IMPRESSION / GREETING: The first face-to-face interaction between a prospect and the Salesperson is the first step. It is designed to enable the salesperson to display his or her sincere interest in the prospect...to gain positive acceptance and to develop a sense of mutual respect and rapport. It is the first phase of face-to-face trust building and sets the face-to-face selling process in motion.

• 7 out of 8 times Phillip selected the BEST two possible strategies.

QUALIFYING / QUESTIONS: The questioning and detailed needs analysis phase of the face-to-face sale. This step of selling enables the salesperson to discover what the prospect will buy, when they will buy and under what conditions they will buy. It is allowing the prospect to identify and verbalize their level of interest and specific detailed needs in the product or service the salesperson is offering.

• 4 out of 6 times Phillip selected the BEST two possible strategies.

DEMONSTRATION: The ability of the salesperson to present his or her product in such a way that it fulfills the stated or implied needs or intentions of the prospect as identified and verbalized.

• 8 out of 8 times Phillip selected the BEST two possible strategies.

INFLUENCE: What people believe enough, they act upon. This step is designed to enable the salesperson to build value and overcome the tendency that many prospects have to place little belief or trust in what is told to them. It is this phase of the sale that solidifies the prospect's belief in the supplier, product or service and salesperson.

• 6 out of 6 times Phillip selected the BEST two possible strategies.

CLOSE: The final phase of any selling system. This step is asking the prospect to buy, dealing with objections, handling any necessary negotiation and completing the transaction to mutual satisfaction.

• 5 out of 8 times Phillip selected the BEST two possible strategies.

GENERAL: This area represents an overall understanding of the sales process. Knowledge of the process can lead to a positive attitude toward sales and a commitment to the individual sales steps.

• 6 out of 9 times Phillip selected the BEST two possible strategies.

ABILITY TO UNDERSTAND AND APPLY EFFECTIVE SALES STRATEGY

**Phillip's overall rating demonstrates that he naturally exhibits knowledge
as to the best selling techniques more than 85% of the time
and his willingness to learn displays a likelihood of improvement with experience.**

www.resumespotlight.com/philburns

Linked in

Jane Roqueplot, CPBA, CWDP, CECC — West Middlesex, Pa.

COLTON DRAKE

cdrake@newleaf.ca ▪ 555-555-1111

MARKETING EXECUTIVE
"an innovative thinker who challenges the business status quo"

Colton Drake is recognized for insightful marketing and business development, acumen in operations, and a natural affinity for crunching and taming forecasting and budgeting financials. His award-winning, innovative processes and products boost both bottom line and top line growth.

In the position of Online Product Manager with ABC Canada, Colton was challenged to turn around the company's largest but most neglected product area, which unfortunately resided in a flat industry sector.

Result: Within two years, Colton led his team to develop a new product road map, restored client attrition by 60 percent, and identified a new market segment that scored an additional 33 percent in revenue. He negotiated a distribution agreement in an unrealized market segment and, within 18 months, realized $1Million in new revenues. Whether in B2B or B2C, Colton is a creative catalyst for unidentified opportunities.

Leadership: Undeniably competitive (a vestige of his days as a contender for Olympic swimming competition), Colton knows how to inspire his team. He dreams big and thinks long term, and firmly recognizes that tangible milestones will motivate to achieve. "Colton's greatest strength as a leader is his ability to communicate his vision and to explain how that vision fits in to the larger strategy at a high level, and the daily work required at a lower level," is how one peer defined Colton's ability to plan and execute.

Metrics: Colton's vision, innovation, and metrics savvy moved a business model from a variable value to a fixed metric that provided new levers to increase revenue and a new tool to manage direct costs. Skilled at leveraging technology and existing assets to maximize revenue and to cut costs, Colton enjoys sharing his investigative process and invites your questions.

Teamwork: Recognizing the value of creative partnerships, Colton leverages others' talents and knowledge for the greatest corporate good. He has led international as well as local teams. The epitome of a strong leader, one who is supportive, inclusive, and laser-focused on profitability, Colton also acknowledges the value of levity in a hard-working environment, and delights his staff with his playful wit.

> **Colton's talents will best be appreciated by a company that demands continuous improvement, exhorts its staff to nurture ideas, champions true teamwork for higher performance levels, and is ready to "break out" of a traditional mold, embracing technology and innovation to spur business growth.**

Stephanie Clark, CRS, CIS — Nanaimo, B.C., Canada

Robert "Bo" Talbot

EXECUTIVE MANAGER

SUPPLY CHAIN / LOGISTICS

"To leverage global resources and technologies to reorganize, streamline, and strengthen supply chain and logistics operations, while ensuring quality of deliverables and increasing profitability"

Behavioral research suggests that the most effective people are those who understand themselves, so they can develop strategies to meet the demands of their environment.

Based on Bo's responses to a professional assessment, this information has statements to provide his broad understanding of his personal style. These statements identify the basic natural behavior that he brings to the job.

GENERAL CHARACTERISTICS

When Bo sees something that is wrong, he wants to fix it. He is oriented toward achieving clear and practical results. He has high personal standards and strives for improvement in everything he does. Accuracy is important to him and he constantly seeks to avoid errors.

Bo is skilled at observing and collecting data on different subjects. If he has a real passion for a given subject, he will read and listen to all the available information on the subject.

Bo has an acute awareness of social, economic, and political implications of his decisions. He gathers data in order to be certain he is correct in his work, communication, and decision-making.

When confronted with a problem Bo will look for a method, a formula, a procedure, or a system to solve it. Bo places an emphasis on the cognitive process and logic when making decisions. He tends to delay making decisions until he has all the facts. Bo's logical, methodical way of gathering data is demonstrated by his ability to ask the right questions at the right time.

PEOPLE FLEXIBILITY

Since people are different, the needs they have, and that must be met, are also different. The information in this section will display that Bo identifies different types of people and how he provides strategies to meet their needs.

When communicating with a person who has the following characteristics:

> ambitious, forceful, decisive, strong-willed, independent and goal-oriented . . .

Bo's communication techniques:
- ✓ Be clear, specific, brief, to the point.
- ✓ Stick to business.
- ✓ Be prepared with support material in a well-organized "package."

Bo realizes what creates tension and avoids:
- ✓ Talking about things not relevant to the issue.
- ✓ Leaving loopholes or cloudy issues.
- ✓ Appearing disorganized.

- -

When communicating with a person who has the following characteristics:

> magnetic, enthusiastic, friendly and demonstrative. . .

Bo's communication techniques:
- ✓ Provide a warm and friendly environment.
- ✓ Doesn't deal with a lot of detail (write it).
- ✓ Ask "feeling" questions to draw opinions or comments.

Bo realizes what creates tension and avoids:
- ✓ Being curt, cold, or tight-lipped.
- ✓ Controlling the conversation.
- ✓ Driving on facts and figures, alternatives, or abstractions.

PEOPLE FLEXIBILITY (*continued*) - - - - - - - -

When communicating with a person who has the following characteristics:

> patient, predictable, reliable, steady, relaxed and modest . . .

Bo's communication techniques:
- ✓ Begin with a personal comment.
- ✓ Present case softly, and in a non-threatening manner.
- ✓ Ask "how?" questions to draw their opinions.

Bo realizes what creates tension and avoids:
- ✓ Rushing headlong into business.
- ✓ Being domineering or demanding.
- ✓ Forcing others to respond quickly to the objectives.

- -

When communicating with a person who has the following characteristics:

> dependent, neat, conservative, perfectionist, careful and compliant . . .

Bo's communication techniques:
- ✓ Prepare his "case" in advance.
- ✓ Stick to business.
- ✓ Accurate and realistic.

Bo realizes what creates tension and avoids:
- ✓ Being flip, casual, informal, and loud.
- ✓ Pushing too hard or being unrealistic with deadlines.
- ✓ Being disorganized or messy.

VALUE TO THE ORGANIZATION

This section of information identifies specific talents and behavior Bo brings to the job.

- ✓ Conscientious and steady.
- ✓ Always looking for logical solutions.
- ✓ "The anchor of reality."
- ✓ Presents the facts without emotion.
- ✓ Always concerned about quality work.

PREFERRED WORK ENVIRONMENT

This section identifies the ideal work environment based on Bo's basic style. This section will identify specific duties and responsibilities that Bo enjoys.

- ✓ Time to be thorough.
- ✓ A team providing solid, tangible, practical evidence.
- ✓ To be approached in a straightforward, direct way; and to stick to business.
- ✓ Proper buzzwords appropriate to his expertise.
- ✓ Others to do what they say they will.

PERSONAL STRENGTHS

Each person brings his/her own strengths to the job. This section identifies Bo's behavioral strengths.

- ✓ Problem solver
- ✓ Precise
- ✓ Diplomatic
- ✓ Organized
- ✓ Responsible
- ✓ Systematic
- ✓ Tactful

Information based on Professional Behavioral Assessment
VALIDATION STUDY & COMPLETE REPORT AVAILABLE UPON REQUEST

ROBERT TALBOT
5555 Mayfield Drive
Sharpsburg, PA 55055
H: (505) 550-0555   C: (505) 550-5550

www.resumespotlight.com/btalbot
botalbot5505@smail.com

Jane Roqueplot, CPBA, CWDP, CECC — West Middlesex, Pa.

Marion Doolittle
Bend, Ore. Mobile 999-888-7777

Currently a Pharmacy Manager for CBS Pharmacy, I am a Pharm.D (University of Southern California, 2004) and actively dual-licensed in CA as a pharmacist and nutritionist with 7 years of retail management experience. I specialize in compounding and am a wellness proponent, passionate about the efficacy and benefits of natural, botanical and herbal products. I am highly motivated, self-directed and effective working independently or in team or leadership roles. As a Pharmacy Manager, I currently supervise 4 techs (per variable shift) to maintain profitable business operations through the accurate and timely dispensation of prescribed medications. I also consult regularly with customers on OTC product selection, while always making sure to provide exceptional service and support to all customers, health professionals, vendors and staff.

PHARMACY MANAGER

Job Description:
You will play an integral role in creating optimal wellness for our patients. You'll be responsible for the management of labor, sales, margin, inventory and normal day-to-day pharmacy operations. Additional duties include learning aspects of compounding, outreach, drug nutrient depletion, drug-herbs/supplement interaction, information on herbal, nutritional and natural remedy supplementation so that the pharmacy staff can consult with the front store practitioners and provide integrative wellness solutions for our patients.

Our business is based on the values of self accountability, teamwork, community involvement, profitability, superior customer service and environmental support. We look for candidates who can succeed and thrive in our values-based organization.

Requirements:

- Clear, active California pharmacist license
- Passion for providing superior customer service
- Prior retail pharmacy management experience
- Great attention to detail
- General business knowledge, ability to make decisions
- Ability to work alternating weekends and adaptable to change
- Willingness to partner with the retail store manager in making the business truly integrative

Debbie Ellis, MRW, Phoenix Career Group — Houston, Texas

DAPHNE MURPHY

25 Rolling Water Lane ✧ Scarsdale, NY 10583 ✧ (914) 335-8624 ✧ daphnemurphy@gmail.com

With a background working with young adults in academic and counseling settings coupled with experience in corporate managerial roles, my strengths align well with the qualifications outlined for your ideal candidate:

✓ **Strong & Inspiring Leadership Skills:** Managed teams nationwide with Bloomberg Markets to support 2,000+ clients and hired, trained, and mentored #1-ranked 15-person sales team with WPS Media.

✓ **12+ Years of Senior-level Management:** Corporate background includes seven years with Bloomberg Markets as a Vice President and Managing Director and five years with WPS Media as the Los Angeles Bureau Sales Manager with a record of achieving consistent, high-quality results.

✓ **Budget & Revenue Planning Experience:** Well-versed in managing P&L responsibility via senior-level managerial roles in two large corporations and as an entrepreneur establishing and managing the day-to-day strategic, financial, and operational aspects of two niche businesses.

✓ **Experience Developing Senior Leadership:** Identified and cultivated rising leaders among strong performers by mentoring, providing opportunities for growth, and grooming for promotion and increased responsibility.

✓ **Collaborative Work Across Departments:** Well-versed in facilitating progress in both academic and corporate settings, including recent committee roles and success connecting an educational nonprofit with the COO and staff of Baruch College for a future partnership.

✓ **Strong Presentation & Communication Skills:** Currently lecture in classroom setting as an adjunct college professor, mentor and liaise with students one-on-one, and volunteer as grief facilitator for children and their families in addition to accepting speaking engagements and delivering presentations in prior corporate roles.

✓ **Knowledge of Higher Education & Educational Access:** My commitment to educating today's underserved youth is part of a career-long focus on education. Presently teaching at an urban college campus and working to set its long-term growth strategy by serving on the school's Advisory and Retention Committee.

As there is nothing more vital than empowering today's diverse young adults to further their education, I fully support the values and mission of The Scholars Foundation and welcome the opportunity to join your management team.

✧ ✧ ✧

Laurie Berenson, CPRW, CEIC — Franklin Lakes, N.J.

Chapter 11

References and Recommendations

. . . .

In This Chapter

▶ Realizing that reputation is everything

▶ Mastering the art of gathering praise

▶ Writing job refs vs. personal refs

▶ Surviving loss caused by lousy refs

. . . .

*I*f you done it, it ain't bragging.

This insightful judgment comes from one of America's most celebrated literary figures, the 19th-century poet, essayist, and journalist Walt Whitman. In a society where modest self-appraisal has been the norm, Whitman's view is materializing often these days in the intensely competitive 21st-century job market where you score only when you can differentiate yourself.

Yet merely bragging about how great you are isn't the same as being able to prove it. If you rely only on your word without presenting tangible evidence to support your self-praise, other people may not believe you or take you seriously when you speak of a past workplace deed — even if you've done it. References and recommendations go a long way toward proving your claims.

Validating claims is why the management of job references has emerged as a hot strategy to promote promising career development. This chapter explains how to maximize the power of your references and recommendations.

Reference ABCs You Don't Want to Miss

When it's no secret that you're going to leave your current job, ask your company's human resources specialist to explain the company's policy for providing references. Here's why you want to know:

✔ Although a former employer legally can say anything about your work performance that's factual and true, legal advice to ward off defamation lawsuits causes many employers to limit reference information to dates of employment, position, and compensation. If you're an ace, that puts you on notice to cultivate recommendations from many sources.

✔ You may find out that your company is outsourcing reference data to private companies that charge a fee to prospective employers for your reference information. For more information about this practice, search for "outsourcing reference checks" on the web.

✔ You may discover that your employer uses software to numerically measure your value, using such companies as SuccessFactors, Halogen Software, and Oracle.

A numerical presentation creates a ranking value. For example, if the ranking scale is 1 to 10 and your performance is ranked at 9.5, you're a star; if you're ranked at 2.5, you're in trouble. A numerical ranking is intended to be highly confidential company information that's used for merit increases and bonus money, for example — *not* as the basis for an employee reference. Confirm that if a numerical rank is in your files, it won't be used in your employee reference.

While you're checking out details on what to expect on the reference front from your current employer, also obtain a written copy on letterhead of your work history before you leave your job. You never know when the work history document will come in handy to save a prospective employer time, money, and frustration.

With the Right References, You Rock!

Without question, little today does more to put a high shine on your hiring halo than strong positive statements others have expressed about your abilities and work value. The following strategies, tactics, and document samples can make that happy glow happen for you:

✔ Reference lists

✔ Reference commentaries

✔ Job search letter quotes

✔ Letters of recommendation

✔ Personal character references

✔ Social media references

Reference lists

Reference lists are "people" lists provided when an employer wants to "check references." Usually a one-page document (sometimes two pages), a reference list is delivered at an employer's request. At a minimum, a reference list provides names with contact information for each person on it.

An ideal reference list adds perspective by summarizing the basis of your relationship with each reference and includes the qualifications you possess that the individual reference can address.

Your reference list can include more than your immediate supervisor, department manager, and HR contacts. Think about obtaining references from second-level management people who direct a division or a unit of a department.

You want to create a reference list separate from your resume to avoid the risk of *reference fatigue.* You don't want to burn out your references by giving too many casual callers access to their names and contact information. Employers typically don't spend the time and money to check references until after you're interviewed and are on the short list of potential hires.

Sending reference lists or recommendation letters with your resume to recruiters isn't a cool idea, counsels Jim Lemke, this book's technical adviser. Recruiters may assume that the documents either are bogus or were written by close friends, to make you come across as a desperate and weak candidate.

Three savvy reference list samples (TEAGUE, JAMES, MORENO) follow in this chapter.

Helping others help you

An efficient way to compile short reference documents and blurbs is to write them yourself and offer a selection of your compositions to the people who want to support you and your career.

If you know the potential recommenders well, you can simply ask if you can save them time by drafting a statement for them, subject to their editing. Busy people often are happy to toot your horn but appreciate your doing the writing for them.

When you don't know the reference giver all that well, tactfully ask if you can suggest a focus (which you choose among a variety of different selling points about you) and provide examples of the short blurbs others have written.

At the very least, enclose a suggestion sheet of points you hope to have each recommender make — and, of course, include your resume.

Reference commentaries

A reference commentary (also called a recommendation report) is a modern format that often appears as a one- to two-page document of short testimonial quotes. Each quote is expressed in a few sentences — and sometimes in a single sentence. The quotes are similar in style to the laudatory blurbs about a book or an author that appear on book jackets.

A reference commentary is useful in multiple phases of your job search, from initial contact through the interview stage. For example, you can present a reference commentary early in an interview, using it as an ice-breaker to kick off conversation and set up a favorable impression during the interview. Say something like this:

> *I'm assuming that at some point you may want to check my references. In the meantime, this commentary reflects a quick glance at the endorsements of people who know my work as it relates to this position.*

Typically, a commentary features a half-dozen or so blurbs — each one focuses on a different selling point about you. Blurbs appear on pages that maximize white space, for speed reading. Some reference commentaries are pitched in straightforward, linear designs. Others are eye-catching, with creative, abstract touches.

The reference commentary is a first-impression marketing tool; it supplements but does not replace full letters of reference from former employers and associates that you may need when hiring is imminent.

This chapter includes two samples of reference commentaries (KENNEDY, MUNROE).

Job search letter quotes

In addition to creating a reference commentary, you can add luster to virtually any of your job search letters with blurbs that zero in on your potential contribution to the type of job you seek. Consider a couple blurb examples:

> *Arthur is the go-to leader in his mastery of state agency financing policy.*

> *Her helpfulness and sunny disposition make Nadine my number one choice when I choose a check-out register at my supermarket.*

Look for samples of blurb-enriched letters throughout this book.

Letters of recommendation

A letter of recommendation isn't wildly effective, but it's better than nothing in cases when a company disappears, your boss dies, or a reference is difficult to contact. Begin now to round up praise in a reference folder, also called a reference dossier. Routinely collect a letter of recommendation whenever you, a supervisor, or a coworker says goodbye.

A recommendation letter affirms your experience and competence, and adds credibility. An excellent letter provides some combination of the following:

✔ Introduces the recommender, explaining the recommender's basis of knowledge for your reference

✔ Confirms dates and job title(s)

✔ Identifies skills, competencies, and other qualifications that make you an ideal candidate for a potential employer

✔ Describes your performance and attitude

✔ Highlights several of your exceptional qualities, using examples

Consider this excerpt of an effective employment recommendation letter:

> *Jane was able to develop her assertiveness skills under my supervision. When she first came into the department as a payroll clerk, she was not as assertive as was necessary in dealing with the other departments.*
>
> *After taking an assertiveness course and developing great self-confidence, Jane was able to develop her conflict-resolution skills, and she was promoted twice in the accounting department before leaving the company to take a manager's position elsewhere.*
>
> *I highly recommend Jane for her willingness to work on areas in which she needed improvement.*

This example — straightforward and sincere — praises a quality of interest to all employers: Willing worker accepts criticism and takes steps to improve job performance.

Interns get specific

For interns, a letter of recommendation is a written statement supporting an application for a specific internship program or fellowship.

You can store reference materials and letters of recommendation online at a for-fee service, Interfolio.com.

This chapter includes two sample recommendation letters (DEVRIES, SMITH).

Personal character references

Employment references come from people who are directly familiar with your work. By contrast, personal references discuss your positive personal attributes. They're written by people who typically are familiar with your behavior outside the workplace.

Although employment references are the heavy hitters in the hiring game, personal references have their uses, as About.com job searching guide Alison Doyle explains:

> If your work record isn't perfect, you can bolster your candidacy with a good character reference. If you are looking for your first job, you can use personal references instead of employment references.

Sources of personal references

Who do you ask to write a personal reference for you? You have many prospects, including the following categories of people who know the real you:

- Relatives and friends
- Neighbors and acquaintances
- Coworkers and trade association acquaintances
- Businesspeople and professionals
- Fellow religious worshipers
- Fellow volunteers at nonprofits
- Professors, teachers, and sports coaches and teammates

Content of personal references

What should a personal reference say? When commenting on general qualities, give an example. One page of several paragraphs is usually adequate. Among the personal attributes your recommender can comment on are the following:

Capable	Helpful	Persistent
Charming	Intelligent	Punctual
Confident	Motivated	Reliable
Conscientious	Observant	Stylish
Creative	Optimistic	Trustworthy

Social media references

You can find all the types of references and recommendations described in this chapter on the social media channels of information distribution.

Customized references are well worth the effort

You probably know that customized resumes aimed at a specific position or career field are leagues more effective than generic resumes. The same principle applies to references and recommendations. The cream of the crop are tailored to fit a specific opportunity.

But reference givers aren't on your payroll. You can't ask them to spend their free time customizing praise for you by rewriting it again and again. So what's the answer? Build a large roster of potential recommenders, and try not to ask too much too often.

Here's what legendary executive job search guru John Lucht (RiteSite.com) recommends:

"No matter who you are, always keep a secret list — with current contact information — of everyone who's a logical reference on every job you've ever held. Your main focus is on the past five to ten years, of course. Except for jobs requiring a security clearance, normally, no one snoops back 15 or 20 years." Lucht illustrates who should be on a manager's list:

- Each of your superiors in each job.

- Some enthusiastic subordinates from each job.

- Prominent coworkers. Perhaps peers. The vice president of finance or the controller, if you're in marketing or manufacturing (or vice versa).

- Third parties, such as customers, suppliers, and even competitors you know from industry committees.

Whether you ask for personal or employment recommendations on social media, be selective by tapping well-regarded recommenders whom you know well — or who at least know the quality of your work.

How valuable are the seemingly endless verbal hugs plastered all over LinkedIn and other social media websites? Aren't they regarded as a dime a dozen? Well, no.

Recommendations found on social media are like money in the bank because people risk their own good names by choosing to go public to recommend you. These people have worked with you, supervised you, done business with you, or have some reason to know how special you are and can verify that you are who you say you are.

Handle Reference Problems Skillfully

References are deal breakers if something goes wrong and you fail to respond to bad news with effective repair moves. References can also hang you out to dry when you're making a secret search and are exposed by the gathering of recommendations. Here's what to do when you get bad news.

Fighting back in reference trouble spots

When you're walloped with an unacceptable reference that seems sure to sink your search, never roll over and play dead. Get up off the mat and start punching, whether the reference-based turndown isn't your fault or whether you deserve the trashing.

Strategy when you're blameless

If you're ever victimized by untrue words that threaten your employment future, fight back with the following script suggested by author and media celebrity Tony Beshara, a top-flight placement and recruiting professional in Dallas (tonybeshara.com).

In Beshara's scenario, personable office clerk Katie and jealous office supervisor Jenny have a toxic workplace history because Jenny thinks the company's owner shows favoritism toward Katie. Jenny fires Katie and lies to prospective employers in reference checks, telling them that Katie didn't do her job and wasn't a good employee. Katie fails to make a new work connection but eventually discovers that Jenny is the villain.

Here's how Beshara suggests that Katie solve her problem:

> *Speaking in a calm, nonthreatening tone, Katie should call Jenny and say nicely but firmly that the negative reference is closing employment doors and must stop.*
>
> *If Jenny is unresponsive, won't come to the phone, or won't return a voice-mail — which is very likely — Katie should write a letter to Jenny with the same message and send a copy to the owner of the company. Katie need not threaten defamation litigation in her letter because the owner, using common sense, will figure out the company's potential risk.*
>
> *Additionally, Katie should call the owner, review the situation, and say that although she doesn't want to cause problems, she does want to be able to go to work and support herself. Katie then can ask the owner to be the one to provide future references for her, since he has firsthand knowledge of her work and she's only asking that he tell the truth.*

Strategy when you're at fault

If you were invited to depart for cause, move immediately to your best damage-control mode. Even if you snagged a basic reference letter on your way out the door, try to arrange a meeting with your previous manager to neutralize your relationship and improve the reference you'll likely receive when potential employers begin inquiring about you.

Because of the uptick in wrongful termination lawsuits, most employers are willing to discuss giving a more positive reference if the booted employee agrees not to pursue litigation.

Ask your old boss if you can meet to reach an agreement on how the company will respond to future reference requests. Detail the great lessons that you've learned from your termination, and thank your ex-boss for helping you to see the light.

Then say, "I'm worried about getting work in the future. Can we come up with something so that this learning experience doesn't stand in my way?" If you get a cold shoulder, be gracious, smile, and thank your ex-boss for considering your request. This sincere effort on your part may prove to be surprisingly helpful on the reference front.

Can't you just forget to mention your former direct boss, who may well blow the whistle on you? No. That omission is a red flag for employers, signaling that something's off base with your performance.

A classic tactic for this dilemma is to crowd out a bad reference with multiple good references. Another tactic: Concentrate your job search on small firms that may not check references or that may be more inclined to take a chance on someone.

Tiptoeing under the radar screen

A stealth job search has always been tricky to pull off without risk. If you give your boss as a reference at your current company, your secrecy jig's up and you may find that pink is the color of your next pay envelope.

Worse, in this age of digital danger, that risk has shot up to red alert.

For example, do you sync your personal and work mail accounts on your smartphone? Are the messages archived? Are sent messages accessible? How far back do they go? Do you have apps installed that provide direct access to your social networking accounts, including Facebook, Twitter, and LinkedIn?

Browse for Google's privacy policy and understand what user data may be spread from one Google product to another, including Gmail. Similarly, revisit privacy policies for social media you use.

Consider four suggestions to rack up references while keeping your job search under wraps:

- ✔ Use the names of former supervisors at other companies, preferably individuals you've kept in touch with and tipped off in advance that you're on the move.

- ✔ Call on reliable contacts you've made at professional organizations.

- ✔ Never ask for praise from coworkers or current vendors. They may innocently let it slip to your supervisor that you've already mentally left your job, or even purposely curry favor with your current management by whispering in the boss's ear.

- ✔ Emphasize to prospective employers that your job search is confidential. When an offer is near, say that, upon receiving a signed offer letter, you'll be pleased to have the prospective employer check with your current management and that, if you don't stack up as advertised, you understand that the job offer is null and void.

Anticipate who you'll need as references, and clue them in on your undercover search as your faith in their discretion allows.

Put Time on Your Side

Three out of five employers (62 percent) report that when they contacted a reference listed on an application, the reference didn't have good things to say about the candidate. Such is the word in a 2012 survey by CareerBuilder (careerbuilder.com), a leading global company in the human capital solutions industry.

Harris Interactive conducted the study among 2,494 hiring managers and human resource professionals, and 3,976 workers across industries and company sizes.

Most employers (80 percent) confirmed that they do contact references when evaluating potential employees. And get this: A majority (69 percent) said speaking with a reference has changed their minds about a candidate.

Now you know why Rosemary Haefner, CareerBuilder's vice president of human resources, urges that it's vital to "Make sure you are including your biggest cheerleaders among your job references."

It's also vital to give yourself as much lead time as possible to drum up reference deliveries from people who admire you and want to cheer you onward and upward. In other words, start now. Your cheerleading team won't respond with the same sense of urgency you feel when you're in full job search mode and need those references yesterday.

Turn the page to begin your review of a tasty collection of reference and recommendation samples.

A surprisingly simple move generates references

When you don't have references from people who work in the company you're leaving, try the "one good word deserves another" approach. After you've made your exit, send your former boss and some coworkers appreciative e-mails. Spell out how much you enjoyed knowing them, how much you learned, how you hope you'll see them in the future, and so on.

By return e-mail, you'll probably receive right-back-at-you good wishes. The e-mail's header will show the author. Print and add each e-mail to your reference folder.

JAMES TEAGUE

5401 68th Street, Lubbock, TX 79424 ◆ 806-783-9900 ◆ jamesteague394@gmail.com

REFERENCES SUMMARY

Reference	Relationship
Stacy Thomas- District Manager, Foods, Inc. 555-485-5096 Stacy4394@gmail.com	Stacy and I worked together to achieve financial, inventory, and customer satisfaction goals. She can verify my ability to deliver results, as well as my determination and commitment to my employer.
John Fench- Store Manager, Wal-Mart, AZ 555-696-4239	I worked to promote John while serving as a Store Manager in Arizona. John can attest to my teaching and mentoring abilities, as well as my in-depth knowledge of operations and merchandising.
Gary Cerrant- Co-Manager, 2006-2010 806-993-3757	Gary was my Co-Manager for 4 years, and I worked closely with him to achieve the results at the Amarillo, TX store. Gary knows me very well and can speak to my ability to foster teamwork and my knowledge of all facets of store operations.
Mary Gonzales- Assistant Manager, 2006-2010 555-678-9495	I have worked with Mary in various capacities over the past 11 years. She can acknowledge my concern and insistence on fairness towards all employees, as well as my ability to lead.
Jerry Hairston- Co-Worker, 1995-Present 806-783-9900 Jerry45@earthlink.net	Jerry would provide information about my numerous management skill areas. He knows my professional abilities as well as being a trusted, caring individual that I have maintained a friendship with for over 16 years.

Dan Dorotik, NCRW — Lubbock, Texas

DAVID D. JAMES, DC, CPC, CCPC, CPMA

555.505.5050 ♦ ddjames@neo.rr.net ♦ 55 Chestnut Drive ♦ Hermitage, PA 55555

REFERENCES ♦ ENDORSEMENTS

Joseph Sudar, J.D., CPC, CASCC, CUC, CHCC, *Owner*   555.555.5555
SUDAR & SUDAR, INC.   josephjd@sudarsudar.com
5555 Island Avenue
Monroeville, PA 55555

Joseph can attest to my knowledge of coding, compliance and documentation...
especially as it relates to the chiropractic field.

Dr. Roger Drew, *Chiropractor/Owner*   555.555.5555
DREW CHIROPRACTIC   rdrew@live.net
5555 Arden Way Blvd.
Meadville, NC 55555

Dr. Drew is qualified to speak to my proficiency in and passion for coding, compliance and
documentation in the chiropractic field and other professional qualifications of interest.

Dr. Kenneth Burger, *Chiropractor/Owner*   555.555.5555
BURGER CHIROPRACTIC   kburgerdr@burger.com
555 River Drive, Suite 5
Butler, PA 55555

Dr. Burger will discuss his knowledge regarding my work ethic and all aspects of my ability
to perform the duties of my position as an employee, plus my knowledge base.

PERSONAL HIGHLIGHTS

Professional Communication and Behavioral Profile identifies specific talents David brings to the job.

". . . anchor of reality" in a "sea of confusion."

David can be extremely tenacious and will stay with his commitments ... He tends to be incisive and
analytical. David can follow through with seemingly unending patience.

Good listener ♦ Persistently seeks logical solutions ♦ Concerned about quality work ♦ Maintains standards
Conscientious and steady ♦ Consistent ♦ Good at reconciling factions—is calming and adds stability

www.linkedin.com/daviddjamesdc

Jane Roqueplot, CPBA, CWDP, CECC — West Middlesex, Pa.

JEREMY MORENO

12309 Brookline Court ♦ New Barrington, NY 10556 ♦ (555) 555-4538 ♦ jeremymoreno@mail.com
jeremymoreno.com ♦ @jremymoreno ♦ linkedin.com/in/jeremymoreno

References

"Jeremy brings enthusiasm, precision, and style to the work he does. He was always looking for ways to improve both effectiveness and efficiency. He started a client training program that reduced service requests by 23%. He is our go-to person for special projects."
Marybeth Claremont
Director of Interactive Services
Manhattan Investments
mclaremont@manhattaninvests.com

"Jeremy is an excellent writer who is constantly coming up with new ideas. He's driven and motivated."
Blair Greenberg
Senior Managing Editor
The Diplomat Monthly
blair.greenbery@thediplomat.com

"Jeremy is a creative, intuitive thinker. Because he is self-motivated and trustworthy, I can rely on him to complete a project on-time and on-target, every time."
Michael Delaney
Managing Editor
Southwest Daily Press
michael.delaney@swdp.com

"Jeremy is a hard-working partner, always focused on the tasks at hand. When he completed his work, he pitched in to help the rest of the team."
Margaret Navarro
Program Director, Campus Activities Team
University of Texas
m-navarro@gmail.com

Tamara Dowling, CPRW — Valencia, Calif.

"An outstanding community leader, Rose was born knowing how to get different groups of people to put aside their differences and work together for the good of all."
Jim Page Rogers
Austin City Council

"Rose is a rising star!" **Jose Alvarez, CEO, Pactory Presh Inc.**

"A first-rate executive, Rose Kennedy never lets projects slide. She understands every part of the word 'deadline'. People like working for her because she's fair."
Velia Acevedo
Administrative Assistant to
City Manager
Crystal Valley, Texas

21 Austin Leaders have their own reasons to applaud Rose Kennedy

"Rose Kennedy is a natural leader who keeps chasing her mission until she brings home the prize."
Betty Jean Morris, Membership Chair
Crystal Valley Chamber of Commerce

"She's personable and you can't help but admire Rose's ability to get things done on time and done right."
Tim Barcelona
Little League Coach
Broward County, Texas

"I've known Rose Kennedy for 20 years and her ethics are the highest. I've never seen her do anything questionable. Her word is her bond. Sign me up as a supporter."
Calle Coho, HR Specialist
Louisiana Corp.

"Rose is a very competent individual who continues to do a bang up job on every task she takes on."
The Rev. Morton Jay
Austin, Texas

JAMES MUNROE

445 Main Street
Suffield, MA 99999

(555) 555-5555
james-munroe@cox.net

PROFESSIONAL REFERENCES

Martha Sutter
Regional Operations Manager
Comcourse
2222 Taylor Road
Westfield, MA 01085
Tel: (555) 555-5555
Relationship: Present Supervisor

*"I have known Jim for over 15 years and have worked closely with him for many of them.
I truly admire his work ethic and attention to detail. He has had major accomplishments
turning around areas with poor productivity, customer satisfaction and sale metrics.
He was always up to the task when given underperforming areas or departments."*

Ronald Lane
Regional Compliance Manager
Comcourse
2222 Taylor Road
Westfield, MA 01085
Tel: (555) 555-5555
Relationship: Former Manager

*"I have known Jim for over 10 years and worked directly with him for 5 years.
He was always someone you can count on, the consummate team player, always had positive
input and feedback. I really enjoyed working with him. He has the ability to communicate
with every level of the organization and portrays himself in a professional manner at all times."*

Forest Miller
Business Specialist
Elmira Electronics
3334 Sullivan Avenue
Worcester, MA 99999
Tel: (555) 555-5555
Relationship: Former Colleague

*"Working with Jim over the past 10 years, both as a direct report to him and eventually a coworker,
he was extremely influential with his teambuilding and employee development skills.
This is just one reason for his continued success as a leader."*

Louise Garver, CPBS, JCTC, CMP, CPRW, CEIP — Broad Brook, Conn.

Janet DeVries
Sales Professional
OuttaTech Products, Inc.

As a Professional Behavioral Analyst who specializes in the career industry, I became acquainted with Janet through her participation in a professional development and career advancement process.

Based on the results of her Personal Behavioral and Communication Styles assessment, I can confidently describe Janet as enthusiastic, outgoing, and articulate. If given the choice, as a professional sales person, Janet would prefer to sell a new account instead of servicing an old account. She can be described as a good closer.

In addition to Janet's behavioral preferences, she also completed a Sales Knowledge and Competency test to determine how well she understands and performs in the sales process. Her results clearly identify her as being an expert in her field of sales. Her scores surpassed those of other top performing sales professionals in the following critical stages of selling: Prospecting, First impressions, Qualification of the decision-maker, Demonstrating and Influencing.

Some may perceive Janet as a natural born salesperson, but beyond her sales skills, what they really see is her natural ability to talk smoothly and readily on most subjects. [Date]

Jane Roqueplot, CPBA, CWDP, CECC — West Middlesex, Pa.

Bob Smith
Regional Sales Manager

I worked with Bob Smith for 3 years at HC Computers, where he was the Regional Director of Sales. He was the best sales person I knew.

He closed more business **(or … he always met his quota … or … he broke into new accounts … or his margins always beat the goals … or … his reports were always on time … you get the picture)** than anyone on the team, and the customers loved him.

He has active industry contacts in CA, AZ and TX, so I believe he would be a perfect solution to reversing our decline in anchor market category sales there. He's willing to travel. He's a superstar.

If you think he might be a fit for our western region sales manager opening and would like to get in touch with him directly, you can reach him on his cell: 123-123-1234. If I can facilitate a connection I'm happy to do it, just let me know.

Thanks,
Luba Taylor

Debbie Ellis, MRW, Phoenix Career Group — Houston, Texas

15 job references you never want

You don't know when you're going to need a reference from the company where you work. Because of legal risk, it's become a widespread policy for large employers to limit their reference comments to a confirmation of employment, time of service, and position. But small firms may not be HR savvy enough to stick to the game plan of name, rank, and serial number. And you never know when a brutally honest blast will pop out of a manager's mouth when asked about a former employee.

Your goal, of course, is for references to salute your talent and character, not the other way around, as these totally made-up one-liners suggest:

Let this not be said about you

✔ "You must be kidding me. He didn't actually give my name as a reference!"

✔ "There's nothing wrong with him that a miracle couldn't cure."

✔ "She insisted on playing loud music throughout work hours."

✔ "He was very insistent on making his own schedule and rules."

✔ "She said she'd worked for a specific agency, and we found out that she didn't."

✔ "She always gave 100 percent at work: 10 percent Monday, 23 percentTuesday, 40 percent Wednesday, 22 percent Thursday, and 5 percent Friday."

✔ "This employee reached rock bottom and started to dig."

✔ "He works well when under constant supervision"

✔ "I've never heard of this person."

✔ "She must have two brains: one is lost; the other is out looking for it."

✔ "He was hyper and off the wall."

✔ "I was told that the candidate didn't do the work she claimed to do during the interview."

✔ "He has the mind of a man who falls for everything and stands for nothing."

✔ "He works eight hours and sleeps eight hours. I fired him because they're the same eight hours."

✔ "She can't be beat. No one is her equal at hitting the nail squarely on the thumb."

Chapter 12

Online Portfolios, Prezis, and Videos

In This Chapter

▶ Marketing yourself online with a work portfolio

▶ Selling your talents in living color with a prezi

▶ Exercising caution with videos in your search

*A*re your space-limited resumes and public profiles robust enough to rake in job interview invitations? If you're not sure recruiters really get you — your super work experience, credentials, accomplishments, skills, competencies, personality essence, and winning track record — think about adding online platform tools. Specifically, consider work portfolios and prezis that include video clips.

If the term "prezi" is a stranger to you, join the crowd. A prezi is constructed with dynamic presentation software that opens a new world between whiteboards and slides. Its zoomable canvas makes it an adventure to explore your marketable qualities. (Check out more prezi details later in this chapter.)

The new types of online platforms this chapter describes don't replace your customized resumes or public profiles, which are — and, for the foreseeable future, are likely to remain — the Western world's dominant job search documents.

Best Prospects for Telling Your Story

Certain occupations benefit from digital getting-to-know-you media far more than others. Although creative professionals steal the show, in random order, here are a few of the many good bets for work portfolios and prezis.

artist, graphic designer, architect, fashion designer, journalist, photographer, actor; manager in advertising, promotions, public relations, marketing, and sales; teacher, chef, baker; real estate professional; fundraising executive; lawyer; business manager; engineer; health care professional, veterinarian; information technology expert; accountant, financial manager; auto body repairer, tree trimmer, gardener, house painter

A common thread for individuals in these types of occupations — whether they work sitting down or standing up — is a requirement to reach goals or solve problems. They devise a plan to do so, carry out their plan, and come up with rewarding results they can show to the world via media and technology. A few specifics illustrate their techniques:

- ✔ Creative workers use all media to show their talent, from broadcast and print, to photos and film, to art and video.
- ✔ Engineers and programmers show results with impressive building projects or new technology developments, perhaps sprinkling in a few audio-recorded references.
- ✔ Accountants and financial managers load up with charts and graphs.
- ✔ Trades workers score with before-and-after photos of their work.

By contrast, even excellent workers who perform repetitive tasks — on a production line, for instance — are challenged to reap a return on investment for their time and expense when creating strong online presentations.

Rewards of Online Presentations

If you think your occupation is a natural for online presentations and decide to try it, four advantages are waiting in the wings for you:

- ✔ **You call the shots.** One of the first moves hiring authorities make after identifying an attractive lead is Googling the person. Displaying your credentials on a work portfolio, a prezi, a video, or even your own website gives you the edge in exerting a degree of control over what they find. Job seekers have a story to tell, and you can best tell it in your own way on your own terms.
- ✔ **You stand out.** Visual examples of your accomplishments, milestones, and completed projects are more believable when seen than merely read. You have visual proof that you can do what you say you can do.
- ✔ **You enlarge the picture.** A resume doesn't have enough space for bullet points, several paragraphs, and a blurb of endorsement to tell your

entire work story. Online presentations have room to show who you are, where you've been to gain your qualifications, and what you can accomplish in the future.

🗸 **You spread the word.** Refer to your online presentation platforms — especially your work portfolio — in all your application materials. Put the word out by using social media; use active links in your social bios to connect potential employers to your presentations. Your chances of inspiring hiring authorities to tap you for interviews expand substantially as you document the talent you deliver.

Researchers say that vision trumps all our other senses and speak of a theory called the picture superiority effect (PSE) to explain how humans absorb information. One PSE report notes that 72 hours after an oral presentation is concluded, only 10 percent of the audience can remember what was said — but when the presentation includes visuals, 65 percent of the audience can recall the information. Visuals apparently not only catch the eye, but also boost the power of memory.

Think about your own information processing: Do you remember more details when a presentation includes images, slides, photos, videos, color, and design?

The next two sections discuss docs that raise your "remember me" score.

Attract Interest with a Work Portfolio

Your goal in presenting an online work portfolio is to make readers feel as if they know you, respect you, and like you. By inviting hiring authorities to view a close-up of your talents and personality, your online presentation opens the door to conversation.

Portfolios can range from something as uncluttered as a long version of your resume, to a website well endowed with materials. Keep your portfolio up-to-date, with no broken images, broken links to other sites, or stale information.

Company business stays company business

Even if you don't work in a highly regulated industry like financial or legal services, beware of posting details of your company-related accomplishments online without express written permission from your employer.

Stashing online portfolios

Pick your best platform to host your online portfolio, advises popular career authority Heather Huhman (heatherhuhman.com).

"Choose a platform from countless hosts for online work portfolios that is specific to you and your goals," Huhman says.

"Google 'free online document storage websites' and 'free online storage apps.' You'll find many offers of free storage. In the Internet space, what's available today may be gone tomorrow, so periodically check back to confirm that the online storage site or app you select is still up and running."

You can also look at fee-based document storage websites, such as InterFolio.com, and easily present your work online to prospective employers and educational institutions.

For additional helpful advice, search for (1) "The Online Portfolio: How It Can Help You Land a Job," by Heather Huhman, and (2) "Preparing Content for a Website Portfolio," by Eric Miller.

Your basic online portfolio includes your *contact information, your resume, your cover letter,* and a customized assortment of other illuminating content, such as the following information, which I identify in random order:

- ✔ **Career summary and goals.** A capsule statement of where you've been, where you hope to go, and what you bring to the table. Get ideas on what to include and how to express yourself in Chapter 9.

- ✔ **Reference blurbs, letters.** Short endorsements and references, especially potent in a video showing the reference giver speaking. For more ideas, review Chapter 11.

- ✔ **Lists of accomplishments.** A consistent record of success stories on how you have benefited or will benefit employers. Accomplishments aren't job duties and responsibilities or personal achievements, such as college graduation. Find a sample accomplishment sheet in Chapter 3.

- ✔ **Degrees, licenses, and certifications.** A listing of details on how you gained qualifications in your career skills: college, vocational/technical school, state testing, or a professional organization, for example.

- ✔ **Samples of your best work.** A collection of samples in any media, such as video, film, reports, papers, brochures, projects, photos, structures, products, art, designs, published books, and more.

- ✔ **Case success studies.** A showcase of problem-solving talent and leadership qualities. The C-A-R method (challenge, action, result) is a popular format; the candidate uses video and displays documentation.

- ✔ **Marketable skills.** A group of skills, competencies, and qualities that employers will pay for. For example: "Demonstrate technical skills, management skills, and communication skills." Read Chapter 17 for suggestions of skills.

✔ **Awards and honors.** An assemblage of any certificates of awards, honors, and industry recognition. Recent college graduates should include evidence of scholarship awards and elected offices.

✔ **Conferences, workshops, and industry expos.** A roundup of professional or industry conferences, seminars, workshops, expos, and conventions that relate deep interest in and connections to career fields or industries.

✔ **Professional development.** A listing of professional association memberships and participation, including committee memberships and chairs, offices held, and reports written.

✔ **Military records.** A listing of military service, military occupational specialties useful for civilian employment, and badges and awards of personal valor or exceptionalism.

✔ **Blogging.** A blog reflects you professionally and personally. You may be blogging about your concern for animals, or maybe you're on the membership committee for the local Toastmaster's Club.

✔ **Volunteering.** A description of volunteer activities as it relates to your career. Community service can be invaluable for new graduates and for re-entry women who return to work after raising children.

Don't overload your portfolio with information that can't support its own weight in marketing you for employment. If you suspect that a recruiter can't grasp your subject in a few minutes, give it a makeover.

Electrify Employers with a Prezi

Confession: I don't know as much as I should about prezis. *Consolation:* Not many people do. This deficit can well work for you because it offers a chance to jump ahead of the pack and stand out from your competition.

Prezi fundamentals

A prezi is relatively new presentation software that explodes with excitement on a computer screen. At a viewer's direction, topics zoom in and out of the spotlight — what tech buffs call "a zooming user interface." No one falls asleep watching a prezi.

The word *prezi* in lowercase letters is a short form of the Hungarian word for "presentation."

The capitalized word *Prezi* refers to the leading commercial company for prezis: Prezi.com. The company's presentation templates are free to job seekers. If you've never seen an example of this high-octane technology and want to jump right in, the Prezi.com website is the place to start.

Prezi job seeker samples

To quickly grasp how a job seeker's prezi impacts viewers, get blown away by viewing the following samples; use the Google URL shortener assigned to each. The links are case-sensitive and will not work if you do not type them exactly in the capital and lowercase letters shown next.

The basic navigation principle for a prezi is "follow the arrows." (If you still can't figure out how to jump from one stunning attraction to another, do as I do — beg a teenager for help.) Check out this trio:

- ✔ Justin Mason, web design/library specialist
  `http://goo.gl/ukiZK`

- ✔ Marie Maurannes, instructional materials designer
  `http://goo.gl/bq12M`

- ✔ Katherine R. Hale, human resources professional
  `http://goo.gl/qlkbG`

Video: Hiring Tool or Turnoff?

Video resumes are risky for job seekers because they invite discrimination. That's the finding of a recent survey, noting that even the best-trained managers have been known to practice subtle discrimination against candidates. They do it on the basis of race, age, gender, looks, and sexual orientation — or as one responder added "old, fat, ugly."

The discrimination finding was reported in the "2012 Global Hiring Trends Survey" of recruiters, human resources professionals, and business owners. It was conducted by Career Directors International, a leading organization of professional resume and career writers.

So, if a first video look at you can kill your job chances, why does a second video look at you make a big difference? After you've been evaluated and added to a short list of potential hires for a job, hiring authorities now want to discover every useful fact about you. A short videoclip then becomes a welcome addition to your online presentation.

Can you really keep a lid on job search?

Even if you aren't looking for a job, should you maintain an online work portfolio because it showcases your accomplishments and industry activities? And should you then worry that doing so will raise the alarm in your boss's mind that you may not be currently satisfied, are wide open to competitive offers, and are no longer trustworthy to share inside company information? Maybe.

Here's what an experienced manager, who wishes to remain anonymous, says about the secrecy issue:

The online world is now an open kimono. When I look at the LinkedIn profile of an employee and see that 'open to jobs' is in the employee's profile, I get nervous. If there were two competing employees for one position and they had similar capabilities, I would promote the one who did not have 'open to jobs.'

Some career advisers emphasize that everyone's going digital today and that you can paper over a loss-of-confidence threat by letting your boss know about your status statements and making clear that they're part of your long-term career goals. Maybe.

Although the jury's still out on the online potential to expose your secret job search, here's how I see the issue:

✔ When the job market is slim-to-none for your type of work, think hard about how your online presence may reflect on your boss's trust of your veracity and the possible consequences.

✔ In an opportunity-rich job market, seeing your online presence may instead cause your boss to more quickly promote you, or to give you a raise because you're too good to lose.

You can personally create a brief and simple but effective video segment, as the following sample illustrates:

Graeme Anthony, British public relations professional
`http://goo.gl/WbBya`

View more samples of basic videos by hopping onto YouTube.com and searching for "job search."

Virtual Job Search is Racing Ahead

New tools and practices, many of which evolved from the explosion in the use of social media, are shaking up the ways jobs and people find each other, as the growth of online presentations illustrates.

Job seekers who don't want to be left behind history's hill will commit themselves to learning more about how technology is changing the job market day by day. Some will self-educate, others will line up tutors, and still others will seek out continuing education courses and workshops.

Sell the steak along with the sizzle

When you're marketing yourself in glamorous and creative new kinds of presentations, don't forget about the fundamentals of selling yourself. And give earlier generations a pat on the back for knowing plenty about selling when telling.

The most famous piece of sales advice ever — "Don't sell the steak, sell the sizzle" — is a maxim popularized by American super sales trainer Elmer Wheeler in the 20th century. It means that, when selling a product or an idea, smart sellers focus the audience's attention on the benefits (the sizzle), not on the features (the steak).

Selling the sizzle for a standby electric generator, for example, may look like this:

Protect your home and family against power outages every day, whether you are home or away.

But after the sizzle's hook has captured the consumer's attention, the question is how the generator can protect home and family. How does the consumer know the claim has a basis in reality?

A good start on answering the how question is to modify the maxim and sell the steak, like this:

Our top-rated standby generator reliably provides whole-house backup power within 10 seconds of a power outage.

When building job-search presentations, the product you're selling is you and your ability to do a superior job. Don't be stingy with the sizzle — but don't overlook the steak. When you claim status as a top candidate for anything, remember to give the reader a basis for believing that you aren't making the stuff up by including facts and numbers.

Online portfolios, prezis, and videos are ideal platforms to sell both your sizzle and your steak.

Chapter 13

Getting Ahead in the Job You Have

· ·

In This Chapter

▶ Creating a range of workplace communications that work like a charm

▶ Skillfully tooting your horn with written words that pull in the cash

▶ Composing documents that make others see you as an up-and-comer

· ·

*N*o matter how much or how little you write on the job, every word you put on screen or paper has the potential to add zing and zip to your career's forward momentum.

Even when you're better at talking than writing, if you don't make good use of written communications, you're leaving opportunity on the table to earn more money, get bumped up to a higher level, and cement good relationships with coworkers and bosses.

This chapter focuses on expanding your use of digital and print letters, memos, notes, reports, and other documents where you now work. The big idea is to impress the higher-ups and give you a future edge if you decide to try moving up a few job titles.

You'll find suggestions ahead that you may not have considered important in bygone days when jobs were falling out of the sky and you could grab them with one hand tied behind your back. Times have changed.

Messages That Grow Your Career

When you've been in the same job for a long time, it's easy to grow stale by drifting into a rut. The rut may be old-shoe comfortable, but do you really want to keep doing the same old, same old in the same old way forever?

Where do you want to go in one to three years? And what if your company lays off gobs of employees, moves to a faraway location, or shuts down entirely —

would you survive? Unlike earlier generations who counted on having a good job for as long as they wanted one, you can't depend on today's employer to keep you onboard until you've finished your working years.

One good answer: Refresh your career development with the types of communications this chapter describes and illustrates.

Asking for a pay raise

As the familiar adage goes, "When they say it's not about the money, it's about the money."

Sometimes the truth is stark. In late 2012, an online Harris Interactive survey for Career Builder sought to pin down which job factors are most important to today's workers.

The survey found that 70 percent of nearly 4,000 full-time workers nationwide said "Show me the money." Employers were sent the message that increasing salaries is rated the best way to keep employees from departing the premises. Other factors count, too, but bumping up paychecks is the name of the game.

So now you know what you need to do if a pay raise doesn't appear automatically as part of a normal performance review cycle: *You raise the issue of your raise.*

Obviously, it's a misstep to burst in on your boss unannounced and exclaim, "Hey, Scrooge, you owe me a pay raise!" You need an appointment to discuss the seriousness of your request. But exactly how to set up that appointment is the great divide where opinion splits. Both sides have merit, depending on differing situations.

Opinion A: Ask to meet, but don't say exactly what about

Face-to-face is always the best way to discuss compensation so that you have the opportunity to develop a two-way dialogue about your hoped-for raise. So when you ask for an appointment, it's a good idea to be a bit vague about your objective.

But won't your manager feel sandbagged if you gloss over the purpose of the appointment only to be put on the spot without advance notice of the topic? It could happen. On the other hand, if you define the topic in advance, it's much too easy for your manager to reply that a raise isn't possible at this time and refuse the meeting. "Don't let *that* happen!" advises Debbie Ellis, MRW, of the Phoenix Career Group in Houston, Texas.

Here's Ellis's sample phrasing for an appointment-seeking e-mail that doesn't shut down your prospects too quickly:

Because being successful in business is a two-way street, I am very interested in talking with you about how I can contribute more to the bottom line of ABC. May we set aside 20 minutes next week to discuss my role and development? I appreciate your advice and am willing to make myself available at a date and time that works for you. With my thanks in advance for your consideration.

Opinion B: Ask to meet, but be direct about the topic

Write the boss an e-mail treating your appointment as a business meeting, which it is:

Working here is my ideal job, and I'm grateful for the opportunity. I would like to meet with you to further discuss the financial value I bring as a player on your team. Please let me know the best time for you.

Alternatively, when you've been tasked with additional duties, try this e-mail approach:

I'm delighted you have chosen me to handle additional responsibilities. I won't let you down. I hope to meet with you as soon as your calendar is open to talk about some details of my new responsibilities and the possibility of a pay increase for accomplishing them to your satisfaction.

Still another approach to set the tone of the raise appointment reflects an employee writing as a mentor for an unpaid intern:

You appointed me to be Karl Witt's mentor during the past five months of his internship. Karl is graduating this year and I'd like to meet with you next week to discuss why I think he should be retained for regular employment at the normal starting rate. When would be the best time for you? My week is jammed Tuesday and Wednesday, but otherwise, I can bend my book to make room for this important conversation.

Regardless of which approach — vague or specific — you choose to book an appointment to discuss your hoped-for raise, begin immediately to compile your persuasive facts.

Right things to say

Keep the following points in mind when preparing your face-to-face statement:

- ✔ You enjoy your job and very much like working here.

- ✔ Your accomplishments matter to the company: Give one or more examples. Especially mention several times when you went beyond your job description to make money or save money for the company.

- ✔ Mention what you've done to overcome your deficits, such as achieving additional education or training, self-study, or practice. Show your commitment. Show that you know how to learn.

REMEMBER

✔ Conduct market research on such free salary websites as salary.com, payscale.com, glassdoor.com, and indeed.com. Knowing current market rates for what you do arms you to speak knowledgably about pay for your job. If you say that you're being paid under market rates, you need authoritative data to back up your claim.

✔ Incorporate such phrases as "I hope you'll consider" and "when the timing is right." You're not demanding; you're negotiating.

Wrong things to say

Never say "Give me my raise or I quit" or "I have another offer. Can you match it?" No one is irreplaceable. When backed against the wall, many managers will simply ask how soon you want to leave. Negotiate on your own merits without a high-drama threat.

Present a request statement at your pay raise meeting

At the beginning of your appointment, hand your manager a short letter that makes your case. Your statement will facilitate the discussion, as well as provide a record of it for final decision makers.

Review two sample raise letters at the end of this chapter (PFAUTCH, CHURINOV).

Requesting a promotion

Did your earlier push for promotion fail? Recover by realistically identifying the reasons your bid went nowhere. Among the possibilities: Were you passed over because of how you're falling short in your current job? Was it because you have certain correctable weaknesses? Was it because you don't project a positive attitude with a smile on your face?

Whatever the cause, you can take three steps to engineer a brighter tomorrow for your career.

First, take an honest inventory of yourself as a candidate for promotion. What can you offer in a higher-level job, such as competencies, skills, judgment, and, most of all, profit-producing behaviors, to put yourself on a fast track with a promotion every couple years?

Second, conceptualize a plan by figuring out how you can magnify your strengths and correct any deficiencies.

Third, work your plan by drafting a statement with your persuasive facts onscreen or on paper.

Right things to say

Keep the following points in mind when preparing your statement:

- ✔ In requesting a promotion, write of your capacity for growth and what you're doing about it, such as taking extension courses, learning through online training, or tapping subject experts in your network. Concentrate on the several most important areas in your work that will allow you to make and be recognized for important contributions.

- ✔ Fine-tune your timing. Commenting that a company expansion is on the horizon, noting that a promising new account has just come in the door, and observing that someone in your logical promotion path is about to leave the company are all examples of opportune times to make your pitch. The right timing isn't when your company has just lost a major account or is surfing bankruptcy.

- ✔ A note of appreciation to an executive for allowing you to attend an industry seminar with your immediate boss is both appreciated and strategic. As career coach and author Donald Asher suggests, "Praise your immediate boss, explaining how much you and your boss learned and accomplished at that Chicago trade show." This great idea is both subtle and effective.

- ✔ When asking for a promotion that would leave your current job vacant, mention that you've trained (or can train) one or more subordinates to seamlessly take over your job when you leave it. The message is clear: The work you accomplish for the company is being left in good hands when you're elevated to the next level.

Wrong thing to say

Never claim that you're indispensable. Your bosses may decide that you're too valuable where you are, that your departure would leave a void, and that you can't be replaced.

Write a formal request for promotion

In this example, the employee seeking promotion doesn't ask for an appointment, but instead hits the issue head-on with a letter to his manager asking for more responsibility and a higher-level position.

Review the sample promotion request letter at the end of this chapter (GORDON).

Applying for an internal job vacancy

When you hope to rise through the ranks to nab a specific internal job, adequate research is a must. Sniff around for information among coworkers in the department housing the vacancy to find out what the job's *really* about and why the previous job holder left. You want to be sure that the job is worth your effort to land and that you will accept it if offered.

The people you're talking to may also be applying for the position and purposely not share the real deal. Discretely try to get the facts before you show your hand.

Stephanie Clarke of New Leaf Resumes in Nanaimo, B.C., Canada, suggests that you seek a meeting and use a short e-mail note to schedule it with the appropriate manager. Here's Clarke's sample phrasing:

*Undeniably keen on continuous improvement, one that includes fostering a lean workforce, I am submitting my application for the position of **Continuous Improvement Coordinator**.*

*My resume and cover letter provide examples of continuous improvements in identifying opportunities, building interdepartmental teams, providing staff training, writing reports, creating presentations — **a full cycle of CI project rollouts**.*

*With results that have, for example, **recaptured $35K in AR write-offs**, **increased assembly by 200%**, and **saved $175K/year in staffing requirements**, I hope you will see the benefit of meeting for further discussion.*

I look forward to hearing from you.

Don't apply for every open position at your company, even if it offers more money, more prestige, and more room to grow. Doing so dims your chances of being taken seriously. Your objective is to show that you're perfect for some jobs and you're cultivating a career path within the company — not merely looking to make more money any way you can.

Right things to say

Keep the following points in mind when preparing your statement:

- Remember to show courtesy, tact, and charm in your writing style.
- Make sure your manager knows that you're pursuing another position within the company. Involve your manager from the beginning, and mention in your statement that you have your manager's support.

> ✔ Highlight your history of positive job performance and your desire to keep expanding your contribution.
>
> ✔ Close the letter with a sentence or two talking about your loyalty to the company and enthusiastic expectation of a continuing relationship.

Wrong thing to say

Never hint that you think the company already has someone lined up for the position. (Even if you're right, they won't appreciate your cynicism.)

Tossing your hat into the ring for an open job where you work and expecting no competition is naive. Instead, take pains to write a first-rate statement of your interest, as the final two sample letters at the end of this chapter demonstrate (MERCADO, PETERS).

Asking for a lateral move

A lateral move is a career positioning tactic. It occurs when an employee changes to an equivalent role in an organization, typically for similar pay and a job title at the same level. It's a sideways move, not a promotion.

Until the last half-dozen years, the good life in the corporate world was achieved with only one direction: up. Ambitious people went "up or out." Now that lateral movement has become a viable career tactic, you can say that "over joins up." The ladder of yesteryear has morphed into a lattice.

The lateral tactic has special advantages for middle managers. A manager who's had cross-training has a leg up on understanding how multiple departments function and interact with each other and is primed for top management.

What's in a lateral move for you? The following quartet of situations unveils some of the most popular reasons:

> ✔ You require additional skills for your target position and need a "feeder" job to beef up your qualifications.
>
> ✔ Your work is being outsourced, but you want to remain in the company.
>
> ✔ You're in school and can't handle the stress of a promotion at this time.
>
> ✔ You're at war with your boss and seek an escape.

Before writing your statement asking for a lateral slot, hop online to read the excellent article "How to Make a Smart Lateral Career Move," by Jena McGregor, Fortune Management.

Right things to say

Keep the following points in mind when preparing your statement:

✔ Show appreciation for what the company has done for you already. Mention specific considerations, kind acts, and your promotions.

✔ Explain why you're applying for a lateral position. Perhaps you're preparing for future career progression and you'll be even more valuable to your company after you hone your talent package in the XYZ function.

✔ Mention your competencies and skills that will be lost to the company if you're forced to work for another company: "My performance reviews have recognized my accomplishments and expertise in [list in bullet form]. I really want to continue my record of job excellence within this company."

✔ If your reason for a lateral move in another locale is actually a personal transfer request (perhaps a member in your family is ill, and the treatment center is in a city where your company also has a facility, or your spouse has been transferred to another locale), say so and offer a written plan for the transition.

Close with a simple assurance that you recognize that the company would be doing you a favor:

You have known me to be conscientious and reliable. I hope we can work together to effect a smooth transition that meets both of our needs. Thank you for your consideration.

Wrong thing to say

In explaining your itch to switch sideways, don't focus on what *you* want — keep the focus on what the company wants.

Cover Your Bases with Workplace Docs

You've just read about the benefits of written requests for raises, promotions, internal jobs, and lateral moves.

But there's much more to using documents to your advantage in a modern workplace. Whether your message is good, not-so-good, or neutral, present it in a positive light. Here are five categories with document examples.

✔ Keeping management current with status reports and time targets. Examples:

- *a project status summary*

- *request for project deadline extension*

✔ Aiding company with risk management issues. Example:

- *request for additional security guards*

✔ Showing you follow company policies and procedures. Examples:

- *request for employer's consent to moonlight*

- *request for clarification of non-compete agreement*

- *request for clarification of company overtime pay rules*

- *rules for use of company credit card*

- *request to see your HR file*

✔ Assuring management you take performance evaluations seriously. Example:

- *concrete plan to improve your performance*

✔ Confirming you're a team builder by introducing top talent. Example:

- *recommendation of candidate to company hiring authority*

What other kinds of helpful written workplace messages did I miss? You can e-mail me at *jlk@sunfeatures.com*.

Smartphone rudeness in the workplace

Want to be popular at work? Show respect for co-workers during talks and walks. No one feels appreciated when forced to compete for attention with your digital device as you text or tweet, or make your digital footprint too loud in the next cubicle. Who will cheer for you when you demonstrate your attitude: "You're not important enough to gain my full attention"?

Paul Pfautch, Customer Service Representative

I have been employed by Fast Electronics since 2007, moving up in responsibility and position three times since my hire. I hope you will agree that I have become an integral member of the Customer Service team and have achieved or exceeded every goal set out for me. For example, I:

- Designed a new call center check list which has resulted in reducing the time to reconcile orders by 28.6%

- Took over responsibility for two laid-off employees during the 2008 – 2010 downturn without loss of data or customer satisfaction

- Consistently met or exceeded processing goals during every quarter in every department

- Won the Fast Electronics Customer Service Achievement Award for outstanding performance in the last two consecutive years

Now that the economy is improving, it is gratifying to see that Fast Electronics can again increase its numbers by hiring new Customer Service Representatives. Doing so can only improve our ability to increase productivity and customer satisfaction.

To stay competitive in our new structure, I have enrolled in the NRF Foundation's National Professional Certification in Customer Service, and will earn my credential at the end of the 40-hour course. I will be the first and only person in my department to hold that certificate.

I am hopeful that my contributions and commitment to training have qualified me for an increase in salary that will be commensurate with the guidelines published this month by the BLS in its Area and Occupation Overview.

Will you support me in my request for a salary increase as it moves through company channels?

Thank you for your consideration, respectfully yours,

Paul Pfautch
Customer Service Department
Fast Electronics

Debbie Ellis, MRW, Phoenix Career Group — Houston, Texas

Lana Churinov, Retirement Benefits Manager

Committed to the continued success of Tomlin Consulting and having very much enjoyed my three years in the Retirement Benefits Department as manager, I am interested in improving my position and compensation moving forward.

To support my proposal, examples of last year's contributions include the following:

- By uncovering serious non-compliance issues in last quarter's leading business acquisition candidate, influenced eleventh-hour price point negotiations to realize a $5 million cost benefit.

- Delivered an 8% increase in employee participation in the company's 401(k) plan — without increasing costs.

- Constructed 300 plans for 180 clients representing 2,500+ employees (union and nonunion workforces) — 20% above goal.

Appreciating the company's policy for annual, Q4 salary reviews, I understand that my request for this consideration may seem to be premature. I suggest, however, that given the company's rapid growth in market share and profitability over the past 24 months; my consistently superior evaluations by both managers and customers; and just-released compensation data for our industry and geography, this may be exactly the right time to address new benchmarks.

Willing to earn an increase and happy to negotiate, I hope you will consider this proposal and contact me with your ideas.

With my thanks, I'm standing by,

Lana Churinov

Debbie Ellis, MRW, Phoenix Career Group — Houston, Texas

JOHN GORDON

405 HOPEWELL AVENUE
FINDLEY, PENNSYLVANIA 16345

(724) 555-0111
FAX: (724) 555-0111

[Date]

Dear Mr. Marsh:

At this time, I would like to take the opportunity to express my goals and aspirations to be considered for a position with more responsibility. I am confident in my ability to perform capably at a higher level. Let me share the reasons why I feel this way.

Five years ago, I came onboard at Health and Medical Care Solutions with a strong work history, a desire to succeed and the confidence that I could make positive contributions to the Health and Medical Care Solutions team. Over the years, I demonstrated dedication to my work and consistently took on additional responsibilities. For example, I took the initiative to acquire my commercial driver's license (CDL), not only for my personal benefit, but also for the success of the company, as I fill in for drivers when needed. Co-workers recognize my skills and aptitude for solution-finding and demonstrate their confidence in my knowledge by coming to me for advice. Three years ago, my dependability, reliability and knowledge were rewarded by advancement from level one pay scale to level two after only two years on the job.

I feel ready for the next step, confident that I can handle more responsibility, and respectfully request a promotion and/or to be considered as a candidate for supervisor should a position become available.

Thank you,

John Gordon

John Gordon
Bio-Technician/CDL Driver

Jane Roqueplot, CPBA, CWDP, CECC — West Middlesex, Pa.

361 19th Street
Flagstaff, AZ 86001
jmercado@email.net

Javier Mercado

Home (602) 555-0111
Work (602) 555-0112
Cell (602) 555-0113

[Date]

Ms. Beverly Higgins, City Administrator
Municipal Building, Suite 204
Flagstaff, AZ 86001

Re: Vacancy Notice 12-084

Dear Ms. Higgins:

I am extremely interested in the position of Police Chief, and hereby present my qualifications in this letter and attached resume.

I have been employed by the Flagstaff Police Department since 1988, progressing to my current position of Detective Captain in 2009. My major skill is in criminal investigations, particularly narcotics and organized crime, where I have achieved my most significant successes. You will note that I played a major role on the investigation team that seized $7.3 million in laundered money destined for drug cartels in South America. Some of these funds were used to purchase new police vehicles instead.

Techniques that have been most effective for me throughout my career include:

- Skill in identifying confidential informants and obtaining evidence for criminal prosecution.
- Constant awareness of surroundings and on the lookout for any disruptive occurrences, helping to thwart illegal activities.
- Adeptness in handling potentially volatile situations using a nonjudgmental approach in dealing with suspects.
- Superior analytical and organization skills to help reconstruct and sequence events.
- Methodical follow-up and proficiency in correlating facts and processing information effectively.
- Sound interview techniques when conducting fact-finding interrogations with suspects and hostile witnesses that lead to admission of criminal activity.
- Empathy and caring attitude toward victims.
- Thoroughness in collection, examination, and preparation of evidence for criminal prosecution.
- Ability to testify in court in an intelligent and reliable manner that is believable by judge and jury.

As head of my unit, I possess an action-driven leadership style that commands presence, yet am approachable and nonthreatening to my detectives. I am recognized by my superiors as a team builder and proactive problem solver, as evidenced by my numerous awards and commendations.

If considered for promotion to Police Chief, I am certain I can fulfill the duties of this position and lead law enforcement efforts that will continue to be a credit to the City of Flagstaff.

Sincerely,

Javier Mercado

Javier Mercado

Enclosure: Resume

Melanie Noonan — Woodland Park, N.J.

WESTON PETERS

51716 Dartmore Drive, Ann Arbor, MI 48103 ▪ 734.229.0060 (cell) ▪ wpeters@aabankgroup.com

[Date]

Ann Arbor Bank Group
Mr. Jason Stockton, Chairman
Board of Directors
110 South Main Street
Ann Arbor, MI 48103

Dear Chairman Stockton and Directors:

Thank you for the opportunity to compete for the position of Chief Executive Officer of Ann Arbor Bank Group.

My enclosed resume outlines an extensive record of diligent performance, and results. Over the last four years, as Senior Vice President of AABG's Investment, Trust, IRA, and Business Services, I committed myself to learning about the other departments of AABG to be ready to step up to this opportunity.

My diverse background in working with a variety of organizations and dealing with a wide spectrum of individuals has given me a wealth of experiences with different business, and community and political leaders. This purposeful cultivation of an outside perspective — while retaining an intimate awareness of what has made AABG great — strengthens my capability to lead this wonderful organization to reach the goals the Board has set.

I offer technical expertise, enthusiasm, and focus, and have always been solutions-oriented, proactive, and eager for new challenges. I have a reputation as a loyal, productive, and disciplined leader, with a magnetic attraction to the best candidates for management teams. I well understand opportunity analysis, capturing market share, and raising the standards of excellence.

My mission as CEO will be to control our expenses, increase our interest income, and expand our delivery system through mergers and acquisition. I welcome an opportunity to discuss these and other complex challenges with the Board. You can be confident that I will provide leadership moving forward, and be a catalyst for AABG's continued growth, increased revenue, and enhanced performance.

I look forward to our conversation.

Best Regards,

Weston Peters

Weston Peters
Enclosures

Vicki Brett-Gach, CPRW — Ann Arbor, Mich.

Part IV
Best Writing Elements

The 5th Wave — By Rich Tennant

"Frankly? I'd stay away from using 'plucky' as a keyword unless you're looking for a job at a chicken processing plant."

In this part . . .

Make your job search letters sing your praises. The chapters in this part guide you toward crafting home run messages. You find suggestions for adding zing to your words, starting your letters with verve, and closing with a line that puts you in command and in demand. You get writing guidelines that make sure your first impression is faultless and great tips for representing your skills at their attention-garnering best.

Chapter 14

Writing Your Way to a Job

In This Chapter

▶ Feeling blocked? Overcoming word jams

▶ Getting a leg up with powerful messages

▶ Knowing what to do in any situation

*W*hen should a resume risk its reputation by going unescorted into the mean streets of the job search without a cover letter? *Almost never.* One exception is when your resume is parked on a job site database where you hope it'll be the reason for a recruiter's *aha* moment.

But when your resume is making the rounds of prospective employers, send along a bodyguard — a cover letter or note. I mean whether you're communicating in response to a job post/ad, or sending an unsolicited prospecting letter, or making a networking effort. Cover letters forever!

Today's cover letter for a resume usually arrives via computer or other digital device, but occasionally it shows up on paper. Whichever medium you use, the important cover letter — as well as its extended family of job search letters — is a vital tool you definitely need to grow your future.

Zooming In on the Basics

"Not so fast!" you say. You can barely write your name, much less a killer job search letter. I'm betting you can do much better than you may think.

If not, consider hiring a professional writer. (See the *Directory of Job Letter Writers* in the Appendix of this book.) Or if you have the strategy but lack language skills, maybe you can find a word-wealthy friend with whom to trade a few home-cooked meals or tickets to a hot event in exchange for well-chosen verbs and nouns.

At the very least, this chapter coaches you to recognize a Stand Out job search communication when you see one.

IF U R interested, plz . . .

Text-speak is a *no* on cover letters. Y? The texting made popular by cellphone-accessorized thumb jockeys is a different language, one not appropriate for business writing. The brevity of language demanded of text messaging doesn't meet writing standards, as in "I'm applying for your GR8 job." Yes, there are still standards, and they are enforced by people who read job search letters. Text-talk, and they won't CU later.

Advantages of Stand Out Letters

When your letter or note attracts interest, employers read your resume to confirm a positive first impression. (Alternatively, other employers turn first to your resume and, when they like what they see, page back to your letter to glean other gems about you.) The trick is to make your letter qualify for the short stack of keepers, not the big pile that gets passed over. So what's the trick?

Five hallmarks define a Stand Out cover letter, separating it from a one- or two-sentence yawner attached merely to restate the obvious — that your resume is attached. These hallmarks are

- ✔ Strong personalization
- ✔ High energy
- ✔ Relevant information
- ✔ Moderately informal
- ✔ Interesting to read

Admittedly, creating these works of job-hunting art takes time. But there are at least ten good reasons why a Stand Out letter is worth every minute you spend working it up:

- ✔ **Making a good first impression:** As your first knock on the door, a Stand Out letter grabs the attention of a hiring professional: "Hey honcho, stop! Look at me! I have the qualifications that you need to make money for you or to save money for you. Here's what I can do for you!"

- ✔ **Putting focus on an employer:** Psychologists are right — we all like to think about ourselves. That goes double for employers. The Stand Out letter focuses on the employer, in contrast to the resume, which focuses on you.

- ✔ **Selling your benefits, not features:** As sales aces know, customers buy benefits, not features. They buy the sizzle, not the steak. Your letter is a great chance to personalize your qualifications in terms of benefits. By correlating an employer's requirements with your top competencies and skills, your knowledge, your work experience, and your achievements, you can believably claim that a specific organization is a perfect place for you to make a valuable contribution.

✔ **Showing savvy without boasting:** A Stand Out letter demonstrates your ability to understand and fulfill a company's specific needs. It shows that you are smart enough — and committed enough — to scout the company's products, services, markets, and employment needs.

✔ **Warming up your audience:** Somewhat like the built-in acceptance that occurs when a studio announcer warms up the audience before a TV star appears, a Stand Out letter presells your attractiveness as a candidate. It predisposes the hiring professional to like you, forming an image of you as qualified, personable, and superior among competitors in a high stack of applications.

✔ **Keeping a measure of control:** A Stand Out letter puts a degree of control in your hands. It sets up a reason for you to contact an employer, if the employer doesn't beat you to it. By promising contact within a given time frame, when you do call, you can truthfully get past a gatekeeper by saying that your call is expected. And when you're blocked by voicemail, a good tactic is to leave another message saying when you will call again. And do it, showing that you are a candidate of your word.

✔ **Indicating that you do good work:** A Stand Out letter is evidence that you're able, knowledgeable, and talented, and that you take pride in your work. By contrast, a poor and boring letter suggests that your work will be poor and boring.

✔ **Confirming critical thinking skills:** A Stand Out letter shows the employer how your mind works — how you formulate ideas and pull them together into a rationale that makes sense. Moreover, your letter proves that you can communicate your thoughts in writing — a useful requirement for sales letters, memos, and reports.

✔ **Taking years off your image:** If you're a job hunter more than 15 years out of school, make a point in your letter of showing that you don't believe the way you worked yesterday is necessarily the best way to work today and tomorrow. Mention major changes that a target industry is undergoing and explain what you've done to keep pace. A letter is an ideal place to convey that you're leaning forward.

✔ **Knocking on new doors:** When your most recent work experience is different from the career field you want to enter, use your letter to accent your skills that best match the new field. Should you mention why you want to switch? Doing so just calls attention to your less-than-perfect match for the job. At times, though, it may be necessary. Suppose that you worked for four companies, each of which was sold. You might conclude your letter by saying something like this:

> *I am well qualified for a small company where wearing many hats is useful. I gained broad experience in different environments during [dates] at four companies: A, B, C, and D. Each company was acquired, resulting in changes of management. Despite departures of key personnel, excellent references about my successful performance at each are available.*

Disadvantages of Stand Out Letters

There aren't any.

Unfreezing Writer's Block

When you find yourself struggling with writing a letter, a very big reason may be that you haven't thought through your career goals. You really can't do your best writing about where you want to go until you know where that place is.

Even when you're certain of your direction, you may be stuck at square one. This phenomenon is called writer's block.

One cure professional writers use to break through writer's block is called freewriting. Writing becomes a problem for some people when they try to start at the beginning. When you freewrite, take about 15 minutes to randomly pound away at your computer keyboard. Do not slow down to organize or edit. After you've keyboarded for the full 15 minutes, read over your work. Highlight ideas, words, and phrases you can use in your letter. You may wish to freewrite several times until your thinking ink warms up.

Another technique to stop staring at a blank screen is to first try to understand the reader's viewpoint. Human images help set up the tone of the letter. Picturing the reader is easy when you know the person, but if your words are addressed to a stranger, take your best guess.

Once you've visualized the reader, kick-start your writing by answering the following questions:

- ✔ Which qualities do you want to emphasize in your letter?
- ✔ Why will your letter be interesting and important to the reader?
- ✔ What benefits do you bring to the reader's company?

✔ What special skills or talents set you apart from the competition?

✔ Why do you think your employability (person-specific) skills will help you fit into a new company?

✔ How are your previous jobs similar to those you now seek? If the jobs are different, what skills are the same and cross over?

✔ What do you like about the company to which you are applying?

Here's a tip for people who speak better than they write. Recruit a friend to engage in a recorded discussion about the target job. Tell the friend why you are a hot prospect to fill it. From that recording may come sound bites that lift your letter out of humdrum oblivion.

As you embark on the process of learning to write Stand Out cover letters, keep in mind that your first draft is probably going to be shredder food for ground squirrels, but your editing and refining can fix *almost* anything.

Ugly Typos, Sloppy Letters, Few Offers

No self-respecting guide to better job letters would dare omit a finger-wagging warning against sloppy word work. So here's a stern but true lecture.

In my contacts over the years with thousands of people who hire people, never have I known even one hiring authority to preach the virtue of goofy grammar, bizarre punctuation, keyboard errors, wayward lowercase, texting abbreviations, or other crimes against accepted business language usage. Everyone who reads jobs letters and resumes for a living is against that sort of thing.

Watch out for these familiar missteps:

✔ **UnAcxeptable spelling.** No large academic studies have confirmed it, but anecdotally, it's no surprise that spelling shockers are responsible for big numbers of rejections for blundering job seekers. My assessment comes from nearly constant reports of such blunders as managers who attempted to describe their previous *rolls* (they meant *roles*) and applicants who could not even spell the word *error* correctly.

If you're writing too fast to be accurate, remember that simple mistakes can put your brand at risk. Fast is good, but accurate sells.

✔ **Grammar gaffes.** Spell checkers can't help letters that say things like "would of known" instead of "would have known." For a crash course in good grammar, see handbooks published for administrative assistants and secretaries; otherwise, retake English 101.

✔ **Poisoned proper nouns.** Addressing a letter to "Mr. Michael R. Forest" (when his name is correctly spelled "Mr. Michael R. Forrest") won't win over an employer; it just convinces him that you have a short attention span. (I actually did exactly that on a book cover.)

The moral to this warning: Proofread until your eyes fall out of your head. Many hiring professionals blow off a qualified candidate if even one typo appears in a letter or resume. Hiring success is in the details.

Overcoming What-If Worries

What-if questions are legitimate puzzlers when writing job search letters. The best answers aren't always obvious. Here are solutions to some of these common concerns:

✔ **What if I'm responding to a recruitment ad? To whom should my cover letter be addressed?**

Send your Stand Out letter with a resume (see my book *Resumes For Dummies*) to the individual named in the ad. Follow instructions.

✔ **What if the ad's instructions say to send the letter and resume to the human resources department?**

Do it. The resume will likely be put into a digital database and stored for a long time; you may be considered for a number of open positions. In addition to following instructions, send a Stand Out letter to the name of the department hiring manager (your prospective boss). Say that your resume is on file with HR. Get the hiring manager's name by anonymously calling, or use the social networking connections I describe in Chapter 2.

✔ **What if I don't know enough about the position to write a Stand Out letter?**

Look up job descriptions for similar positions and read recruitment ads. Try to make online contact with people in the target career field or industry. You can also go after a long shot: Try to get through on the telephone to a person who does similar work for a competitor.

✔ **What if I'm responding to a third-party recruiter? Do I send the same materials?**

Yes, but mention that although you're very interested in this position, you would like to be considered for other jobs if this one doesn't pan out.

✔ **What if I'm initiating a possible opening at a company that hasn't advertised one?**

Research to determine who has the authority to hire you. Send your self-marketing materials to that person. Even more effective is to meet your target at a professional meeting or find a third party whose name you can use as an introduction.

The Anatomy of a Job Search Letter

Every letter contains the same bones beneath its unique skin of qualifications, experience, and focus. The upcoming sections take you from head to toe of a job search letter.

Contact information

Your postal mailing address, mobile and home telephone numbers, e-mail address, Skype number, blog address (if you have a business-related blog, not a party blog), and Twitter address, if you have one, appear first on a job search letter.

When applying for an international position, spell out your state, followed by a comma and USA (as in Mesa, Arizona, USA). A Skype number for video calls on the last line of the contact information encourages response. Also, putting your contact phone number in international format (+1-555-555-5555) shows you are hip to the international scene.

For contact information layout ideas on your letters, look at the sample letters in Part II and Part III.

Date line and inside address

Place the date two lines below your contact information, and place the inside address two lines below the date. Aligned with the left margin of the page, enter the name of the person to whom you're writing.

Traditionally, you include the correct prefix, such as Mr. or Mrs., Dr., or Rev. But this is no longer a cut-and-dried rule — contemporary letters do not always include a prefix, especially when addressed to decision makers in informal workplaces.

If you know the job title of the addressee, include that information on the same line as the addressee's name or on the following line.

The next line contains the organization name and is followed on the next lines by the address.

On the right side of the page, aligned with the inside address information, you can include a subject line labeled *RE:* (which is an abbreviation for *Regarding*) to highlight the reason for correspondence.

Salutation

Your salutation is like the eye contact that establishes a connection and begins the dialogue. Do your best to identify the person who will read your letter and address that person directly. Not only does your reader appreciate being addressed by name, but this personal bit separates your letter from the ones written by people who didn't take the time to do a little research into the company.

If you absolutely can't uncover the name of the hiring manager, write *Dear Employer* or *Good Morning*. It's a cheerful way to begin. Because no one enjoys reading mail addressed to a generic person, never address your letter to *Dear Sir or Madam* or *To Whom It May Concern*.

Try, try, try to discover the name of your reader. It's courteous, it takes initiative, and it indicates genuine interest in the company and, most important, in the job.

Introduction

Your introduction should grab your reader's attention immediately. (See Chapters 16 and 17.) As the kick-off to your letter, it grabs your reader and cements interest to compel a hiring authority to keep reading.

All sorts of rules are given for ways to start your letter. Some say, don't start with *I*. Others advise shock value and creativity, a risky approach unless you're a skilled writer. Still others suggest that you begin with the name of a mutual acquaintance. The most important rule is to compel the reader's interest in sticking with you until you've said what you want to say. (Glance ahead to Chapter 16 and 17 for examples of engaging openings to your letter.)

Body

The body of your letter communicates essential information that the employer should know about you — skills, accomplishments, education, training, and quantified statements. *Remember to focus on the benefits you bring to the employer's table.* Work in a branding statement, if you have one. (See Chapter 9.)

The body of your letter should include a very brief background summary of your relevant experience. This material is information that the reader can get from your resume, so don't spend too much space on it in your letter. But don't be tempted to leave it out. Without this key selling point, your reader may never get to your resume.

Conclusion

The last segment of your letter expresses appreciation for the reader's time and explains what happens next. It says when you will call to set a time for an interview, or it motivates the hiring authority to call you before anyone else does.

Closing, signature, and enclosure line

The closing section is the handshake before parting, sincere and warm. *Sincerely, Sincerely yours,* and *Very truly yours* are the most popular, but other choices include *Best regards* and *All the best* or just *All best.* Don't forget to put a comma after your closing line.

Even if your name appears with your contact information at the top of your letter (highly recommended), type your name below your signature (four lines below the closing) so that there will be no confusion about spelling.

After you've motivated your reader, the enclosure line provides a direction. Indicate the item that you've sent with your cover letter, such as a resume or portfolio. This line directly follows your signature and typed name.

In communicating online, you can sign off with only your typed name, or you can use a cursive typeface. (Search online for "cursive fonts.")

Get Ready to Write

To supercharge your career for takeoff, make your cover letters terrific! Take more risks, offer more surprises, and find fresh ways to sell your benefits and skills. Pledge to never send a run-of-the-mill letter again. From now on, you're in Stand Out mode!

Even great job letter writers can flub

Gonzo journalism is slang for freewheeling, exaggerated, outrageous writing. The term reflects an off-the-wall approach, pushing modernism to an extreme kind of writing. The biggest name in gonzo writing was the late journalist and author Hunter S. Thompson.

In 1958, Thompson applied for a job writing for the revitalized Vancouver Sun newspaper in Canada. He launched his campaign by mailing The Sun's editor a prospecting letter. Here are a few samples from what became a legendary communication.

Giving an frank opinion

Thompson's letter opened with an attention-grabber:

"I got a hell of a kick reading the piece Time magazine did this week on The Sun. In addition to wishing you the best of luck, I'd also like to offer my services," he said. His next paragraph was a doozy:

"Since I haven't seen a copy of the 'new' Sun yet, I'll have to make this a tentative offer. I stepped into a dung-hole the last time I took a job with a paper I didn't know anything about (see enclosed clippings) and I'm not quite ready to go charging up another blind alley. By the time you get this letter, I'll have gotten hold of some of the recent issues of The Sun. Unless it looks totally worthless, I'll let my offer stand."

Pouring salt on wounds

The great gonzo guy continued to say that his arrogance was intentional, that he'd rather offend The Sun's editor now than after he started working for him. Thompson embellished his sentiments, adding complaints about the current state of journalism, which among other choice condemnations, he described as "generally stuck in a bog of stagnant mediocrity." Thompson's description of his current boss — the "lad" he worked for — was even more poisonous.

Thompson's closing paragraphs are memorable:

"Most of my experience has been in sports writing, but I can write everything from warmongering propaganda to learned book reviews. I can work 25 hours a day if necessary, live on any reasonable salary, and don't give a black damn for job security, office politics, or adverse public relations. I would rather be on the dole than work for a paper I was ashamed of."

Is extreme frankness risky?

Did gonzo Thompson land the job at The Sun? No. Although Thompson's letter stood out, he didn't get the job. Why not? A man I'll call Steve, presumably a reader participating in thefuturebuzz.com discussion about the legendary prospecting pitch, said he thought that Thompson's s letter was "funny" and "interesting," and that he might call the writer of such a letter in for an interview just to meet him, but then Steve dropped the bomb:

"I can't see myself hiring someone who so enthusiastically displayed and highlighted their copious baggage."

Chapter 15

Language That Snap-Crackle-Pops

I once asked a friend who writes and publishes career books whether he genuinely likes to write. "Well, no," he responded, "I like *to have* written."

That sentiment sums up everything for many who do almost anything to avoid writing but who know that they can't escape this lifetime without learning to write certain things — self-promotional job letters are some of those things.

Armed with the pointers on language, grammar, and organization included in this chapter, you will be well on your way to writing an awesome job search letter.

Refreshing Your Language

Make the writing task easier for yourself not only by reviewing a few rules of grammar, but also by reminding yourself to answer the big "So why?" and "So what?" questions in every letter.

So why are you writing?

Never assume that the purpose of your letter is obvious to your reader. You are writing a job search letter — or another type of job doc — ultimately aimed at employment or career growth.

Visualize your audience

As you work to get the right razzle dazzle into your cover letter, here's a writing tip from the pros: Visualize your reader and write specifically for that reader. Speaking directly to your reader may seem obvious, but this tenet is said to be one of the most overlooked aspects of effective writing. Writing to a real person makes your letter more personable and interesting to read. It shows that you have considered your reader and want that person to understand what you have to say.

If your blank sheet of paper is beginning to look like the place where you'll spend eternity, rip a page from a magazine featuring a picture of someone who could be reading your letter, tape the picture to your computer, and write to that specific person. Who cares if you select a picture of a conservative middle-aged man with gray hair when, in reality, the reader of your letter is a vivacious young woman with bouncing red curls? No matter. The process — the visualization allowing you to target a particular human being — is what counts.

If you're writing a cover letter, you want to land an interview. Say so. Try to maintain control by saying that you will be in touch at a specified time to see whether an interview is possible. When this approach seems impractical, like when you respond to a blind recruitment ad, close with a benefit you offer — "My former boss describes me as the best multimedia designer in the state. Can we talk?"

If you are writing another type of job letter, tell your reader exactly what you want. Leave no room for guessing.

So what? How does it matter?

For each sentence you write, ask yourself, "So what? What does this information mean to my reader — a benefit gained, a loss avoided, a promise of good things to come — what?" Don't, for instance, merely list a bunch of skills and achievements — what good will those skills do for the person who reads your letter?

Must you always interpret for the reader the benefit of your skills and accomplishments?

✔ Yes, if a ghost of an outside chance exists that the benefits of your skills and achievements will not be evident to the reader.

✔ No, if the listing of your skills and achievements is so strong that an eighth grader will get the message.

For more illustrations of when you must interpret your benefits, look over the sample cover letters in Part II.

Getting into the habit of asking yourself "So why?" and "So what?" boosts the power of your job letters by 100 percent.

Technical versus nontechnical language

Tailor your language to your reader. If you're an engineer writing to another engineer, use technical language. If you're an engineer writing to a director of human resources, your reader may not understand technical engineering language; explain any technical terms in simple, everyday language.

Concise but thorough

Because your reader may be pressed for time, aim to write a concise but thorough letter. In a cover letter, for example, tell your reader as much about yourself as you can, but don't make your reader wade through extra words and unnecessary details. Consider the following example:

> *I am a person who believes that the values of fervent dedication, cooperative teamwork, dynamic leadership, and adaptive creativity really make up the cornerstones and are the crucial components of any totally successful sales venture.*

Revised using concise but thorough language, the same sentence now reads:

> *Dedication, teamwork, leadership, and creativity are essential to successful sales.*

Use short words, sentences, and paragraphs. Avoid cramming too many ideas into each paragraph. Logically break long paragraphs into several short ones.

Write in specific terms; avoid vague descriptions. Use numbers, measures, and facts — detailed information rather than unquantified generalities. Consider the following example:

> *I saved the company a fortune when I instituted a new system for scheduling.*

Now read the same example, revised for specifics:

> *I saved the company more than $1 million in production when I instituted a new system for production scheduling.*

Table 15-1 provides a list of word baggage to avoid and Stand Out words to replace them. Avoid using the words marked with "eliminate."

Table 15-1	Stand Out Replacements
Instead of	*Write*
able	can
about	approximately (be precise)
above	this/that
absolutely	(eliminate)
according to	said
ad	advertisement
advance planning	planning
advise	write/perform
aforementioned	this/that
ahold	reach/get hold of/obtain
along the lines of	like
alot	a lot
a lot of	many/much
alright	all right
arrived at the conclusion	concluded
as per	according to
as to whether	whether
at a later date	later
at the present time	now
at the present writing	now
attached herein	attached/enclosed
attached hereto	attached/enclosed
Bachelor's degree	Bachelor's
bad	poor/inappropriate
beneficial success	success
better than	more than
between each	between every/beside each
between you and I	between you and me
bit	(eliminate)

Instead of	Write
but however	but or however
but that	that
cannot but	(eliminate)
can't hardly	can hardly
city of San Francisco	San Francisco
close proximity	close or proximity
close scrutiny	scrutiny
close to the point of	close to
cohese	cohere
concerning	about
concerning the matter of	concerning/about
continue on	continue
disregardless	regardless
due to the fact that	because
each and every	each or every
end result	result
entirely completed	completed
equally as	as or equally
estimated at about	estimated at
every other	every (second) day
ex-	former
fewer in number	fewer
file away	file
for the purpose of	for
for the reason that	because
for your information	(eliminate)
gather together	gather or together
good success	success
he is a man who . . .	he . . .
he or she	he
idea	belief/theory/plan
i.e./e.g.	that is/for example
if and when	if or when

(continued)

Table 15-1 *(continued)*

Instead of	Write
important essentials	essentials
in accordance with a request	as you requested
inasmuch as	since/because
in connection with	about/concerning
in excess of	over/more than
in order to	to
in respect to the matter of	about/regarding
in spite of	despite
in the amount of	for
in the area of	about
in the field of medicine	in medicine
in this day and age	now/today
irregardless	regardless
join together	join *or* together
keep continuing	continue
kindly	please/very much
kind of	rather/somewhat
know-how	knowledge/understanding
known to be	is/are
large portion/number of	most of/many
last but not least	(eliminate)
like for	like
like to have	(eliminate)
lot/lots	(eliminate)
love	(eliminate)
magnitude	importance/significance
Master's degree	Master's
more essential	essential
more perfect	perfect
more specially	specially
more unique	unique
most carefully	(eliminate)

Instead of	Write
most certainly	(eliminate)
mutual cooperation	cooperation
mutual teamwork	teamwork
near future	soon
needless to say	(eliminate)
new innovation	innovation
new record	record
now pending	pending
of between/of from	of
optimize	increase efficiency
outline in detail	outline or detail
overall	comprehensive/final
per	(eliminate)
per annum	yearly
per diem	daily
period of	for
plan ahead	plan
please be advised	(eliminate)
point in time	now
presently	now/soon
qualified expert	qualified or expert
rather unique	unique
reason is because	because
reason why	because
regarding	about
represent	composed/made up of
respecting	about
revert back	revert
scrutinize closely	scrutinize
seem	(be more specific)
seriously consider	consider
several	many/numerous

(continued)

Table 15-1 (continued)

Instead of	Write
should/would/must of	should/would/must have
spell out in detail	spell out *or* detail
subject	(be more specific)
subject matter	subject
subsequent to	after
sufficient enough	sufficient *or* enough
take for example	for example
take into consideration	consider
target	goal/objective/quota
thank you in advance	(eliminate)
that	(eliminate if possible)
there is/are/was/were	(eliminate)
true facts	facts
try and	try to
unknown	unidentified/undisclosed
unthinkable	unlikely/impossible
very unique	unique
was a former	was/is a former
way in which	way
whatsoever at all	whatsoever
with the exception of	except/except for
yet	(eliminate if possible)
you know	(eliminate)

Active versus passive voice

Passive voice indicates a state of existence with words like *be, is, was, were, are, seem, has,* and *been* — the 90-pound weaklings of verbs.

Instead of mucking up your cover letter with wimpy passive-voice verbs ("Production processes were reformed by my innovation, and $12,000 per month was saved by the company."), choose active-voice verbs to show off your accomplishments: "My innovation reformed production processes and saved the company $15,000 per month."

Active voice does the heavy lifting you need in your letter; it's strong, vibrant, and vigorous — qualities you want to show off to hiring managers yourself.

Past versus present tense

For the most part, use present tense as you're writing. After all, your letter is something you're creating now. When you refer to accomplishments, use past tense.

When your resume says you are currently employed (20XX–Present), remember to use present tense if you refer to your current job in a cover letter. If you slip and use past tense, the reader may assume that you've left the job and are pretending to be currently employed.

Tune Up Grammar and Punctuation

Grammar slips sink jobs. Many employers see language skills as an important aspect of potential job performance, and nothing says language skills like attention to grammar and punctuation. To help you over some areas that many job letter writers find tricky, here's a brief overview of frequently made mistakes and how to correct them.

Sentence fragments

Sentence fragments signal incomplete thoughts. They neglect essential components. For example,

> *Although I work in Detroit, making $200 an hour.*

This fragment is missing the subsequent subject and verb needed to finish the "Although I work . . ." component.

> *Although I work in Detroit, making $200 an hour, I would prefer to work in Atlanta to be near my family.*

To test your sentences, speak each one aloud, out of context. Imagine walking up to someone and saying that sentence. Would the sentence make sense, or is something missing? If so, add the missing information.

Run-on sentences

Run-on sentences are two complete sentences written as one. For example,

I finished writing my cover letter, it's great!

This run-on should read:

I finished writing my cover letter. It's great!

Each sentence contains a complete thought and stands on its own.

Run-on sentences stand out as grammatical errors.

Dangling participles

Dangling participles are words ending in *-ing* that modify the wrong subject. For example,

Running across the water, we saw a huge water beetle.

This sentence literally means that we saw a water beetle while we were running across the water — a *Guinness Book of Records* feat! Try this instead:

We saw a huge water beetle running across the water.

Dangling participles are good for laughs, but they indicate imprecision or lack of care.

Misplaced modifiers

Like dangling participles, misplaced modifiers modify the wrong subject, often resulting in hilarious miscommunications. For example,

Ben taught the dog, an inveterate womanizer, to bark at all blonde women.

The dog is an inveterate womanizer? Probably not. Revised, this sentence makes more sense:

Ben, an inveterate womanizer, taught the dog to bark at all blonde women.

Semicolons

Semicolons can be tricky, so avoid them if you don't feel comfortable using them. In essence, semicolons are weak periods; they indicate a separation between two complete sentences that are so closely related they shouldn't be separated by a period.

As you can see, this definition is not specific. You may simply use periods between every sentence. You won't break any rules, and you'll avoid using semicolons incorrectly.

The only rule for semicolons is as follows: When you introduce a list of complete sentences by using a colon, separate each sentence with a semicolon. For example:

> *I accomplished the following: I networked all the computers, company-wide; I designed a new system for scheduling; and I broke the world record in typing speed.*

Again, you can avoid this use of semicolons in your cover letter by placing each item on a separate line set off by bullets. No punctuation is necessary at the end of each line. For example,

> *I accomplished the following:*
>
> - *I networked all the computers, company-wide*
> - *I designed a new system for scheduling*
> - *I broke the world record in typing speed*

Punctuation in parenthetical expressions

If a parenthetical expression occurs in the middle or at the end of a sentence, place the punctuation outside the parentheses. Some examples include the following:

> *Cover letters are essential (see Chapter 4).*
>
> *Cover letters (and resumes) are essential.*
>
> *Cover letters (and resumes), essential to the job search, are important.*

Question marks and exclamation points, when part of a parenthetical expression occurring in the middle of a sentence, are the exception to this rule. Some examples include the following:

The interview (or was it an inquisition?) was a disaster.

My cover letter (a masterpiece!) took four hours to write.

If a parenthetical expression stands alone as a sentence, place the punctuation inside the parentheses. For example,

(I will discuss these skills in a moment.)

Hyphens

When you use two words together as a description of another word, use a hyphen. Examples include

next-to-last job

long-range plan

To test whether you should use a hyphen, take out one of the descriptive terms and see if the description still makes sense. For example,

next-to-last job

without one descriptive term, becomes

to last job

Doesn't make sense, does it? Because the three words "next to last" cannot be used individually as a description and still make sense, you need hyphens between them.

The same rule applies for two nouns used together to express a single idea. Examples include

light-year

life-cycle

For greatest accuracy, check a dictionary, such as `www.Dictionary.com`.

Abbreviations

Use abbreviations only if you have previously written out what the abbreviation stands for. For example, do not write *UCSD* if you have not previously written *University of California, San Diego (UCSD)*. Never assume that your reader knows or will be able to figure out what an abbreviation stands for.

Exceptions: Abbreviations such as *AIDS* and *DNA* are so well known that they do not have to be defined. Also, some technical jargons commonly use abbreviations. In that case, write to your reader. If your reader will understand the abbreviation, use it.

Numbers

When you use two numbers in a row, avoid confusion by writing out the shorter of the two numbers:

> *six 9-person teams*

Or revise your sentence to separate the numbers:

> *six teams of nine people*

Whenever a sentence begins with a number, write out the number instead of using numerals. Better yet, revise the sentence so that the number does not appear at the beginning.

Commas

In general, use commas anywhere you would pause if you read the sentence aloud. If you're a person who pauses often while speaking, this quick tip probably won't work for you. My advice is to ask several people to read your letter for punctuation and grammar, and follow their suggestions. Or get a good punctuation guide and follow it.

Whenever you have a series of terms separated by commas, use a comma after the next-to-last term for clarity. Some examples include the following:

> *Cover letters, resumes, and interviews make up part of the job search process.*
>
> *Dear Mr. Barnes, Ms. Collins, and Ms. Schultz:*

This technique is called the *serial comma.* Newspapers don't use serial commas because they slow down reading. Be consistent in your use of commas. Don't use a serial comma in one paragraph and no serial comma in another that calls for one.

Capitalization

Any official name of a company, department, agency, division, or organization should be capitalized. Examples include

> *U.S. Department of Labor*
>
> *Department of Safety*

Don't capitalize words such as *department, company,* or *organization* when used as a general word rather than as part of a specific title. For example,

> *I work for a division of Toyota.*

Getting Your Grammar Guide On

Table 15-2 provides a handy chart to guide you through grammatical thickets.

Table 15-2	Stand Out Grammar Guide		
Error Term	*Definition of Term*	*Don't Do This*	*Do This*
Subject–verb disagreement	Subject and verb don't agree, resulting in a grammatically incorrect sentence.	Our team, as well as the company, *value* ambition.	Our team, as well as the company, *values* ambition.
Active voice vs. passive voice	Active voice relates an action (good); passive voice relates a state of existence (bad).	I *was trained* in all aspects of public relations.	U.C.I. *trained* me in all aspects of public relations.
Sentence fragment	Phrase lacks a subject and/or verb, revealing an incomplete thought.	Unlike some applicants.	Unlike some applicants, *I bring* talent and diversity.

Error Term	Definition of Term	Don't Do This	Do This
Run-on sentence	Contains more than one complete thought; may lack punctuation.	Every writer knows how important grammar is, I know that you really value marketing, and sales skills, in your business correspondence.	Every writer knows the importance of grammar. I also understand that you value marketing and sales skills in your business correspondence.
Subject–pronoun disagreement	Pronouns don't agree with subject, resulting in a confusing or easily misunderstood sentence.	When someone reads, they should pay attention to details.	When someone reads, he (or she) should pay attention to details. *Or:* When people read, they should pay attention to details.
Misplaced modifiers	Incorrect placement of a description of one subject in a sentence with two subjects; result is confusion.	Falling more than 500 feet, we watched the daredevil bungee-jump off a cliff.	We watched the daredevil bungee-jump, falling more than 500 feet off a cliff.

Organizing Your Information

Following are several formats to suggest how to organize your letter. You can use any organizational format with any occupation:

- **Problem/solution:** The problem/solution format starts with "Here's the problem" and ends with "Here's how I solved it." Case histories and success stories blossom in this favorite format for job search letters and resumes.

- **Inverted pyramid:** News stories use this format. You start with a lead paragraph summarizing the story, with the following paragraphs presenting facts in order of decreasing importance. In your cover letter, you state a comprehensive goal, career desire, or position at the beginning and then provide specific examples in the following paragraphs to support your aim.

✔ **Deductive order:** Much like the inverted pyramid, the deductive order format starts with a generalization and ends with specific examples supporting the generalization. For example, you can start by making a general statement about a skill and then support that statement with facts.

✔ **Inductive order:** Begin your letter with a story or anecdote, and then lead the reader to the conclusion you want him or her to draw from the story or anecdote. Explain how that story or anecdote supports your ability to succeed at the job you've targeted.

✔ **List:** Separate your letter into distinct points and set off the points with headings, lines, bullets, or numbers. Put the most important point first, as illustrated in the Gerard Kelham letter in Chapter 4. This format is especially effective for enumerating experience and skills.

Alternately, you can combine distinctive point data with the two-column format of the T-letter, as shown in the Lori Armstrong letter, also displayed in Chapter 4.

Reading for Smoothness

When you finish writing your letter, read it over just to check its organization. When you read it, each line should fit into the other. You shouldn't really notice that a new sentence has begun. You should feel prepared to understand everything that you're about to read.

To avoid jarring the reader with an abrupt change of subject, ask yourself, "Why did I place this sentence or paragraph after the one before it?" If the answer isn't obvious in your letter, the flow of your text is probably choppy and unclear to the reader. Analyze what's not working, and rewrite until the letter reads smoothly.

Three simple tips to improve your letters

Highlight short sentences and lists with bullets, asterisks, or em dashes. For example,

. Won Orchid award for building

* Won Orchid award for building

— Won Orchid award for building

✔ Start with a short quote that reflects the employer's policies or values.

✔ Reword portions of the employer's mission statement or other documents, and work these phrases into your letter as you describe your skills, work ethic, and values.

Chapter 16

Great Lines for Success

· ·

· ·

Suppose you open a novel that begins with this sentence:

It was a bright cold day in April, and the clocks were striking twelve.

That line might not entice your reading interest.

But suppose you open a novel that begins like so:

It was a bright cold day in April, and the clocks were striking thirteen.

That line is different. That line is ominous. That line provokes curiosity. That line lassoes your attention and ropes you into reading further to find out what message is being communicated with such an odd statement. That opening message begins George Orwell's classic *1984* and is ranked as one of the 100 all-time best first lines from novels.

I'm not suggesting that you launch job letters with odd-ball quotes or wacky claims.

I'm pointing out that you must work to immediately grab the reader's attention and then hold it tightly throughout the complete text of job search correspondence.

This chapter outlines strategies and words designed to do exactly that. You can use a variety of approaches, ranging from riding on the coattails of a personal connection, to responding to the requirements of a job ad, to creating drama with words that intrigue, words that excite, words that *zing!*

Great Starts for Your Letter

Get your job search letter started with a great opening. You want to grab your reader's attention right away so you don't lose him from the get-go. Check out the following notable letter openers to get you started. (Read "A Sampling of Grand Openers," in this chapter, for specific examples.)

Dropping names

The best information to pop into your opening line is a known name. A personal referral works wonders. In this approach, you begin with the name of a mutual connection — someone whom the letter's recipient likes or respects or, at least, has heard of. Name dropping virtually guarantees that your letter will be read. Additionally, you can score points by identifying yourself as a member of an affinity group, such as the alumni of a college or member of a civic organization. Name is the game!

Defining your wants

In addition to dropping names, here's another high-octane approach: Launch your letter with a clear statement of what you want, quickly followed by the qualifying benefits you offer that directly relate to the requirements the hiring company seeks. Or turn it around — lead with the skills and benefits you offer before saying what you want.

Telling a story

Still another way to energize your opening: Create a narrative hook (. . . *and the clocks were striking thirteen*).

In the broadest sense, a narrative hook is a literary technique in the opening of a communication that "hooks" the reader's attention to keep eyes scooting down the page or screen. It often is a thematic statement of who you are in the world of work: butcher, baker, or candlestick maker.

Here's an example of a successful thematic opening hook for a woman who, after a two-year absence, wanted to return to her original career in the automotive industry:

> *Any claim that the grass is greener outside the auto-industry fence is a myth! At least, it is for me. After 20 years of rock-solid experience in our industry, a series of outside opportunities briefly tempted me to cast eyes elsewhere. But not for long.*

My inner voice keeps shouting loud and clear that the auto side is where I belong, and that's why I'm selectively contacting you. I hope you will see how adding me to your quality operation will be a big win for Stanford Motors.

Sell, don't tell! Job search letters in today's marketplace are really sales letters. Or they should be! Instead of whispering through an old-school letter of transmission — *Please find my resume attached, Your Royal Honor* — open your job search messages with a strategic bang!

A Sampling of Grand Openers

As your mom probably told you, you really don't get a second chance to make a good first impression. Openers count!

So what do contemporary openers look like? Review the following Stand Out opening line examples that are sure to make a job letter jump out of the pack right from the start. Read and grow creative:

- ✔ I recently met with James Smith from your firm, and he strongly recommended that I send you my resume. Knowing the requirements of your open position for a financial analyst, he concludes that I am the ideal candidate. Your opening does seem to be tailor-made for my experience at CityWide Financial Services.

- ✔ During your visit to UCSB last fall, I had the pleasure of hearing you address the issue of FuelCO oil rigs off the coast of Santa Barbara. As a UCSB June graduate, I . . ..

- ✔ My computer skills developed from childhood, plus my well-honed interest in technology advances and my recently completed education in computer science, make me a strong candidate for a position as an entry-level software engineer at your highly regarded company.

- ✔ I recently graduated with a 3.75 GPA from the University of California, where I was a research assistant to Dr. Joe Famous, engineering department chair.

- ✔ Since you will soon be working on photo sessions for the spring catalog, I enclose my portfolio showing how ideal my background in photography and design is for your marketing strategies.

- ✔ Juliette Nagy mentioned that your company has opened a division of sporting goods and suggested that I contact you. As a former high school coach for several sports, I believe I have the mix of skills and knowledge you're looking for.

- ✔ Your speech was inspiring, Ms. Luna-Mendez. Soon I will have completed my Master's degree in physical therapy, just in time for your entry-level openings in the PT ward.

✔ The breakthrough research being conducted at Hughes Medical Labs is too exciting to miss out on! I'm looking forward to following up our phone conversation with a sit-down meeting to explore how I can make a contribution as a member of the early warning symptoms task force. I provide a link to relevant information about exactly what I can add as a biology researcher who has managed several challenging projects.

✔ I enjoyed our meeting at the Rancho Santa Fe Garden Club and, as you suggested, am sending you this additional information to review before we get together.

✔ Chaim Isenberg of the Grenwich and Co. accounting firm suggested I contact you regarding opportunities in your warehouse division in Champagne. My background documents considerable success in the areas of loss prevention and asset recovery, which I understand are high on your list of requirements.

✔ Noting your posting for a civil engineer with environmental experience, here's my question: Will your environmental services department reach its Green Acres corporate goal of providing a "turnkey" approach to environmental investigation and remediation, or will it always struggle with solving complicated projects, from engineering and design issues through remedial construction? You'll never know without the best person for the job to follow through for you. Arguably, that's me and here's why: (bulleted highlights of achievements, experience, education, awards, and quotations from satisfied clients).

✔ I thrive on challenge. When I read your posting for a corporate fitness trainer, I thought lightning had struck and you wrote about that opportunity hoping to find me. I have three years' experience in freelance fitness training following my military service, and, IMHO, an opinion confirmed by clients, I'm fired up and ready to go!

✔ You mention several things in your posting for a reality show screener that make me think you're looking for someone with my proven assets. Let me briefly explain.

✔ Terry Ann Torre, who supervised my work as an intern with your company, recommends that I apply to you for the position of assistant customer service manager. Here are some of the reasons Ms. Torre is recommending me: (bulleted list of reasons).

✔ Serendipity! As a graduating senior, I am delighted to learn that *Wonderful Merchandising Magazine* has just named Better Bargains Inc., a company I've long admired, one of the top ten best places to launch a career!

After developing good skills in fashion merchandising, personnel practices, and salesmanship in my cooperative education program, I have begun to search for a position in retail marketing. I will graduate June 2 and am crossing my fingers that you'll be one of my first interviews.

✔ After working four years on The Hill as a legislative assistant on the House Rules Committee, I understand the inner workings of the political system and could prove to be a valuable asset to a firm such as yours. A few of my areas of expertise: (no more than six bulleted items).

✔ Are you in the market for a sales pro who has set sales records for four different companies and trained dozens of high-performance sales reps?

✔ Congratulations on the opening of your new insurance branch. Watching your progress over several years, I've seen that A-123 Insurance Company has earned "street cred." That leads me to believe that you and I see the insurance business through the same lens: excellent customer service!

✔ I have a successful and reliable work history dealing with the public that would make me an excellent employee for your new store. Interested? My resume would like to meet you, and so would I. Here's why:

✔ Velia Acevedo has suggested I forward my resume to you for consideration for a current administrative assistant opening in the escrow department. Through conversations with Velia at a continuing education class, I learned what it takes to be a successful support professional at your firm. I am confident that I have the head for numbers and word-processing skills to make the grade.

✔ Road-tested but not battle-scarred, I offer the necessary qualifications and experience to deliver real revenue results during my first 30 days as a senior sales representative. Please allow me to document my abilities when we sit down and talk about my becoming part of your team.

✔ Preparing to respond to your ad in today's (name of publication) newspaper, I did some research and discovered that we're both (name of college) grads. Is this serendipity or what? I hope our mutual alma mater is a harbinger of good things to come and that we'll be cheering on the same side in the workplace as well. As this letter very briefly outlines, my qualifications and your requirements for an industrial engineer are joined at the hip.

✔ Chances are excellent that I'm the multitalented graphic designer you seek in your "multitalented graphic designer" post on (name of website). With extensive experience in multimedia, marketing, and print design, I work within budget to deliver world-class catalogs and brochures, logos, website design, Flash, video photomontages, mobile websites, and cover design.

✔ As a new (name of college) graduate, I've been hoping to find the kind of position you're staffing because I have exactly the background you're asking for. Specifically, the following columns match item for item: (List the company's requirements in the left column and, in the right, list your matching qualifications.)

✔ I understand that your firm is in search of individuals with (skills) and (qualifications). I think I've hit the jackpot, and maybe you have as well. Don't you love finding the perfect match?

✔ In reviewing my resume, you will find that I possess all the attributes of a perfect match, from (skills) to (experience or attributes). I am excited to learn of your job opening because I have been searching for a company just like yours to make real use of my experience.

✔ (Mutual contact) thought my resume measures such achievement in the function you supervise that he assured me he would pass it on to you; in the event it hasn't yet reached your desk, here's a copy.

What makes these opening lines work?

✔ Some drop names.

✔ Some connect to a common experience.

✔ Some reveal knowledge of the company involved.

✔ Some use a narrative hook.

✔ Some aim at alumni of a graduate's college.

✔ Some ask a question.

✔ Some refer to the content of an employer's ad.

All show that the person writing the letter is someone who goes the extra mile to do a superior job, a person who has just the kind of motivation that employers hope to hire. But not everyone gets it. Read on.

Leadoff Losers

PRATFALL

This section shows you how *not* to open your letters. These leadoff losers are snatched from real correspondence supplied by recruiters and HR specialists. Comments in italics that follow each line colorfully express the employer's silent point of view. Read and be warned!

✔ I was recently let go due to a reduction in force, which is why I wish to apply for your position in merchandising.

Nothing like starting on an upbeat note.

✔ Having recently completed an assignment in the Commonwealth of Independent States (the former Soviet Union), I am interested in pursuing and advancing my career opportunities into this arena.

Arena? What arena? Here . . . there . . . where?

✔ In most organizations, job performance, whether excellent or inept, doesn't count, as long as you conform and play politics. I believe that performance does count! I have recently been notified by Dunnie Pharmaceuticals that my R&D position will be eliminated in the near future.

Does this translate to, "I wasn't much of a team player?" Is that why the job seeker's position is being eliminated?

✔ I am currently in search of a job; I have no particular preference for any area, for as you can see from my included resume, my experience includes a broad range.

One who will take anything masters nothing. As movie pioneer Sam Goldwyn once said, "Include me out."

✔ I am writing in response to the advertised position for a production coordinator. I am very interested in advancing in my field and making a transition into the aspects of the communications profession described in your ad.

Do you want to advance in your field (which is what?*), or do you want to make a transition, or do you want to do the work I need done?*

✔ If you or someone you know could use a graphic designer, please pass my resume to interested parties, or call me as soon as possible.

If you're asking me to be your agent, remember, agents get 15% off the top.

✔ My partner and I are dissolving our business after 15 years of working together. I am interested in a position at Fred & Associates and have enclosed a resume for your review.

A business divorce is rarely just one person's fault: Are you a pain-in-the-back-country? And what is it you want to do for me?

✔ When a customer calls for a quote, your firm's future is in the hands of the sales staff. I have big hands.

Huh? Close, but no cigar. And keep your hands to yourself.

✔ To maintain solid growth, a company must have marketing and sales professionals who can jump on a market before the competition does. My background proves I can do that.

Tell me something I don't know. I've been in this business for 30 years.

Learn from your false starts. As the Japanese proverb has it, "Fall seven times, stand up eight."

Salutation Snoozers

Although not the dead-letter-walking mistakes of the leadoff losers in the preceding section, these salutation snoozers do have sedating effects:

✔ In response to your recent job posting for a hospital clown, please accept the enclosed copy of my credentials.

Earth to bozo: The sick kids in this hospital need cheering up by an imaginative, funny clown who colors outside the lines. Next!

✔ In a recent edition of Craigslist, your ad for a television producer piqued my interest, and I have therefore enclosed a copy of my resume.

Yawn.

✔ Please accept this letter and resume for the product marketing manager position as referenced on your company's website. I am sure that my work history and educational background will benefit the future endeavors of your company.

Your letter is boring; you're probably boring, too. About 500 people answered our ad, and most are just as mediocre as you seem to be.

✔ I am very interested in opportunities within your company. Enclosed please find my resume for your review.

Sure you are — you and hundreds of other unfocused job hunters who will take whatever jobs they can get.

Letters and resumes begin to blur after skimming a dozen or so of them. Just imagine the glazed-over eyes after a hiring professional reads hundreds of job search letters! Some letters jump out of the stack, enticing the reader to tackle the resume; in other words, they make the cut. Others may as well be stamped with invisible ink: *Ignore me.*

Power Phrases to Use Anywhere

After you've punched out your openers, keep your job search letter mojo going as you flesh out the middle with paragraphs and lines that strongly emphasize your belief in yourself and your strengths.

Don't be shy about listing education and training, skills, competencies, and accomplishments. Use numbers wherever you can.

When you spot a concept you like in the following examples, think of a way to adapt it to your situation. Or mix and match the ideas expressed:

✔ I am particularly well qualified for your (job title) position, as the following highlights illustrate. I would enjoy the opportunity to meet with you to explore how I can contribute to your organization.

✔ For your convenience, I will keep this letter especially brief. The job you're trying to fill (job title) seems to have my name on it, thanks to my qualifications in (skills) and (experience).

✔ Your position for (job title) strongly appeals to me because (tell why).

✔ If our meeting confirms my understanding of your open position for (job title), I am confident that, with my skills in (name skills), I can make an immediate and valuable contribution to (name of employer).

✔ My successful background demonstrates the skills you require in (name of position). Briefly, I offer (bulleted lists of accomplishments and achievements).

✔ As my resume shows, I have substantial and successful experience in (career field/industry/position/skill).

✔ As we discussed earlier, my extensive professional experience can benefit virtually any employer. However, (company name) is of special interest to me because (explain why).

✔ (Name of employer's company) ranks number one in companies I prefer to join.

✔ I look forward to meeting with you to further discuss my background and to show you some of the (skills or competencies) that I have developed.

✔ I'm working to be a part of a company that wants to be recognized as a leader in both ___ and ___. When I have the opportunity to meet with you, I believe you will agree that you want to use my skills and competencies on your watch.

✔ What you're asking for and what I can deliver sound like a match!

✔ As one of six siblings, I was born in a team environment and understand the payoff of pulling together for a successful endeavor.

✔ During my three years in purchasing with Tidewater Productions, I've been credited with yearly savings in the $50,000-to-$75,000 range. This resulted from a combination of skillfully negotiating and replacing underperforming vendors. Wouldn't you like me to save money for your company?

✔ My experience with women's health issues, coupled with demonstrated successful performance in the offices of medical school clinics, suggests that I could make a significant contribution to your practice. Perhaps we could meet to more thoroughly explore this possibility.

✔ Because I haven't yet notified my current employer of my intent to leave, I count on your treating this response to your posting with appropriate sensitivity. *(Note: Employers often prefer to hire employed candidates rather than unemployed candidates.)*

✔ I am happy with my job and am considered to be a high performer by my current employer. Unfortunately, I do not see a path to advancement in the foreseeable future. That is why I am contacting you about future openings in (career field or functional area) at (name of organization).

✔ One of my friends, Salvador Rondavi, works for your company. He recommends that I contact you about a position as a management trainee. He is more than satisfied with his work and, from what he says, I am sure I would like it as well. I will do my utmost to win your professional praise.

✔ Please allow me to highlight some of my accomplishments that are relevant to your requirements.

✔ Staying current with new technologies and products, and applying those that offer improved profit results, is a point of pride for me.

✔ As a versatile IT trainer, I bring significant experience and fast-moving flexibility as new products are introduced to your workforce. Additionally, my B.A. in psychology has given me a useful depth of knowledge in successful motivation practices.

✔ I am long on effort and enthusiasm, although short on experience. Examples of my passion for doing the job well are in references I gained as a student from my employers and customers for the following accomplishments: (list three references and a brief accomplishment statement for each).

✔ I completed a number of successful projects for the physics department in my capacity as student administrative monitor. I believe the knowledge I acquired there would transfer extremely well to your engineering department.

✔ Jason Luo, my former manager, now retired, complimented me for being the hardest-working and most reliable assistant he'd had in his 40 years in the casino business. He was especially impressed with my (name top accomplishment).

✔ As a member of The World Tomorrow Society's Green Futures Committee, I focused on the impact of reusing and recycling waste on various industries, including ours. I'd be delighted to share that data with you when we meet to explore ways I could be useful to Command Construction.

✔ When my last fundraising goal went over the top, I was credited with a big slice of its success because I encouraged everyone's input and buy-in. My talent for inclusiveness brings in record contributions.

✔ I'm proud of a track record that's tops with managers, clients, and coworkers, as this single example from Shelly Kornfield, my former supervisor, illustrates: "Give the assignment to Pam, and you won't have to think about it anymore."

✔ In my last position, managing an assisted-living facility, I saved 8 percent of the annual budget without compromising care; I would welcome sharing the details with you in a meeting to discuss the possibility of my joining your well-respected organization.

✔ After completing two baccalaureate degrees in just four years, I believe that my education, student employment experience, and dedication to hard work and problem solving make me an A-list candidate to join your workforce.

✔ My senior year's academic result: A 3.7 GPA with President's Honors, despite my student job requiring 30 hours a week, illustrates that I know how to dig in and get the job done.

✔ Given my global supply chain experience, I believe that we may have mutual interests.

✔ With my technical skills and understanding of your market, I can step into the position and be immediately productive.

✔ At my previous position on the East Coast, within two years I received praise for playing a key role in raising my branch's basement ranking for customer service (#57 out of 60 stores) to top-ranking customer service (#3 out of 60 stores) in the nationwide organization.

✔ Accustomed to doing more with fewer resources, I can help your firm ride out a financial storm in a tight economy. After meeting with me and assessing my ability to run a tight ship that sails upright, you may decide you can't afford not to hire me.

✔ While I was the fundraising chair for my PTA organization, I planned the campaign, wrote the appeal to potential donors, and organized an e-mail solicitation tree. The result: We raised $27,000, a 130 percent increase over the previous year.

The power phrases in the preceding list are anchored with accomplishments, skills, competencies, the promise of a benefit, or personal characteristics that suggest you will be a likeable model of efficiency, either making money or saving money for your lucky future employer.

An Action Close to Keep Control

After you write a great letter extolling your major match-up for the job you're chasing, maintain momentum with a close that brings you closer to your goal: an interview. You have three basic choices: an action close, an action close plus, and a no-action close.

Action close

Close your letter by telling the reader when you will call for an interview. By setting the agenda, you assure your reader that you will follow up with an action step that brings together a competent candidate with a lucky employer. An action close says that you're on the scene to help and will contact the employer at a specified time:

I'm ready to make money for you and look forward to speaking with you personally. I will call you early next week.

Words that stick when you're stuck

When you're struggling to capture the exact verb that expresses the vigor of your background, glance at this list to jog your wordsmith talents.

Do you need more ways to say what you've done? Try this quick free fix: Type "list action verbs" on Google or another search engine. Stand back for an avalanche of words.

accomplished	achieved	actively participated
administered	codeveloped	dealt effectively
decreased costs	delivered	established
exceeded target	facilitated	formulated
headed up	investigated	led
leveraged	managed	marketed
negotiated	orchestrated	persuaded
planned	played a key role	produced
profitably	project-managed	restructured
scoped out	solved	supervised
took the lead in	turned around	upgraded

Action close plus

Pump up an action close with a suggestion for action sooner rather than later — "I'll call you, but if you're ready to roll, you can call me right away."

An *action close plus* is the best choice for many situations. Your enthusiasm suggests that you're organized and vigorous, but adding a note of urgency by inviting an employer to call you may motivate the employer to prioritize the interview and move up the timetable for a meeting.

Turning an action close into an action close plus is simple, requiring merely one line at the end of the close. The line is, "If you would like to meet with me sooner, you can reach me at (phone number, e-mail, or Twitter)."

I'm eager to sit down with you to discuss the contribution I can make to ABC Organization as it works to create a regional planning group. I'll follow up with a call Wednesday, or you can reach me immediately on my mobile phone, at 888-888-8888. Thank you for your time and consideration.

Let the employer chase you

A-list job seekers with high-demand skills — a rare bunch — can make a case for using a no-action close to avoid looking too eager. The strategic merit of presenting yourself as so attractive a candidate that employers will bust their chops to hire you was straightforwardly expressed by master yogi Baba Hari Dass:

If you chase the world, it runs from you. If you run from the world, it chases you.

Everybody else: Resume cover letters are a form of marketing. Hang on to control of your interviewing process by using an action close.

No-action close

A no-action close hands control of the interviewing process to the employer. It essentially says that you'll sit tight and wait for an employer to call. This is the weakest way to close your cover letter:

> *A copy of my resume is enclosed for your review and consideration. If you have an interest in my background, I would be pleased to hear from you.*

Examples of the Action Closes

You need a competitive edge to get ahead in a competitive market today. You can do that by taking responsibility to follow up. Here are 16 solid closes to help you score that interview:

- ✔ I look forward to our conversation. I'll e-mail you in a few days to coordinate a time that's convenient for you.

- ✔ Because e-mail can't replace face-to-face discussion, I'll call soon to set up an interview.

- ✔ Thank you in advance for reviewing my resume. I enthusiastically anticipate discussing my qualifications in an interview. I'll contact you on Thursday to validate your interest.

- ✔ I look forward to speaking with you personally to discuss your specific needs and my ability to meet them. I'll call your administrative assistant next week to see what time would be most convenient for you.

✔ I welcome a personal interview to discuss how my qualifications can augment your company's excellent reputation for purchasing acumen. I'll e-mail you on Tuesday to see whether we can meet.

✔ I'm excited about employment opportunities within your agency and hope to explore contributions I can make. I'll tweet you within the week to see when your calendar is open.

✔ I hope to play an active role in the future prosperity of your organization. I'll contact you next week to talk about this job or other positions where your needs and my talents meet.

✔ As you requested, here's my resume. I'll check back with you next week to flesh out any blank areas. Thanks for your interest.

✔ My resume follows. I'll telephone you next week to answer any questions you may have and, I hope, set up a time convenient to meet in person.

✔ Recognizing that you may be difficult to reach, I'll check with your office next week to set a convenient time for us to meet. Flexibility is my middle name, and I'll be glad to meet during or outside normal business hours. Thanks, and I look forward to meeting with you personally.

✔ Thank you for calling me back today. I'm sorry I was not in but will telephone you tomorrow to find a convenient time to speak with you on the phone and meet you in person.

✔ I'll contact you within a few days to determine if and when your schedule will allow us to meet. Meeting you will not only be a pleasure, but offers profitable vistas for both of us. My thanks for your time.

✔ As a resume is limited in the information it conveys, why don't we meet in person? If you need additional facts before arranging an interview, call me at 888-888-8888. Otherwise, I'll e-mail you next week to confirm your interest.

✔ My salary needs are in line with the position's description and what I bring in abilities. I'll e-mail you Tuesday to see when we can explore specifics.

✔ Perhaps we can meet and jointly explore the many ways I can save your organization considerable time and money. I'm flexible on timing during business hours or afterward. I'll check your availability next week.

The purpose of a cover letter is to sell an employer on reading your resume and being motivated to take your call for an interview or to contact you for an interview. Without an interview, you're unlikely to be offered employment.

When an ad forbids you to call

How can you use an action close in responding to a job ad that says "No phone calls" or "Don't call us; we'll call you if you match a job opening"? Here are a couple of moves to consider in writing your cover letter:

✔ **Substitute e-mail.** You can still use an action close by changing your promise from "I'll call you" to "I'll e-mail you."

✔ **Play the coincidence card.** Send your cover letter (with an action close) and resume to the company president or hiring manager. Don't mention the ad. The employer's assumption will be that your timing is serendipity — you just happened to apply at the same time the company needs someone with your assets. The company president most likely will forward your material to the hiring manager or HR department with a note calling attention to you. That's a good thing.

P.S. A Final Important Point

Your effort to write a Stand Out letter in your job search is time well invested in your future. And now for one last tip that direct marketing writers have known for light-years — add a P.S. after your signature. And not because you're forgetful.

Adding a P.S. (postscript) to your letter is a spotlighting technique. In this usage, the P.S. doesn't communicate a point that you overlooked; instead, it communicates a point that you want to stand out and be read. What information can you put in your P.S.? You have two basic choices:

✔ Communicate the single most important thing you want an employer to remember about you. Dangle a benefit. Here's an example of dangling a benefit:

> *P.S. I'm eager to tell you how I increased the net profit by 12% for my employer last year. Let's talk soon.*

✔ After your action close *(note, not an action close plus)* and signature, say something to drive the employer to call you first. Here's an example of urging an employer to pick up the phone and check you out:

> *P.S. I would work my heart out to be your best hire of the year. As mentioned, I will call you next week, but if you want to visit sooner, my smartphone is 999-999-9000.*

Letters that give something to get something

The following illustration of a graduating senior's cover letter to the marketing manager of a large private student loan company is a bit of a tease. The letter's promise of a substantial benefit — two unpublished survey data points and the hint of more later — speaks directly to the marketing manager's need to identify criteria that can attract potential customers to his product. All he has to do to gain this benefit is agree to meet with the job seeker.

Dear Mr. Jones:

Students on my campus are scrutinizing private education loans with a new intensity following a batch of high-profile bad press in recent years.

After becoming aware of their increased caution while working as an intern in my college's financial aid office, I followed up with a personal research project surveying 300 students about their criteria for choosing a student loan provider. The project was the basis of a term paper required for my degree in marketing.

Among the marketing conclusions I reached as a result of my research project are these two points:

(Use a paragraph to describe each of the two points).

I hope you will find this information useful, Mr. Jones, and also will consider me for your next marketing associate position. To make that decision, you'll need to know more about my background and abilities; my resume is attached. I'll call you Thursday morning to set up an interview. Many thanks.

Great Lines to Woo Reluctant Readers

If your job search letters fall in a noisy and crowded marketplace and no one is paying attention, will they make a sound? Make your words clear, concise, and interesting to read, and your message will wake up the neighborhood!

Chapter 17

Job Seeker's Skills Finder

Are skills central to driving your workplace wins? Short answer: Don't let your job search letters leave home without them. As you read this chapter, forget about being a grammar snoot; instead, laser your attention on your developed abilities.

No matter which niche you occupy in the workplace — technician or green-collar worker, professional or manager — mastering the discussion of skills you can use and skills that employers are willing to pay you to use translates into a wonderful employment insurance policy, a giant umbrella to keep you from getting soaked when economic thunderstorms rain on your parade.

Learning how to identify your skills and to believably write and talk about them will be transformative to your job hunt. The payoff is moving from the crowd to the choice. This chapter shows you how to do that, beginning with the way skills are classified.

Decoding the Skills Lineup

I'm the first to admit that the classification of skills, like beauty, is in the eye of the beholder. But we have to start somewhere, so based on government and academic classification systems, here's a no-frills framework to guide you through the thicket of workplace skills.

One of the noun terms you often find in a discussion of job requirements is *skill set.* If you've wondered what it means, here's a simple definition: A skill set means the skills needed to accomplish a specified task or perform a given function.

Foundation skills

The foundation skills are appropriate for everyone's skill DNA. They're organized into four groups: basic, people, thinking, and personal qualities.

Basic skills

When you have basic skills, you can read, write, perform arithmetic and mathematical operations, listen, and speak:

- ✔ **Reading:** You can locate, understand, and interpret written information such as manuals, graphs, and schedules.

- ✔ **Writing:** You can communicate thoughts, ideas, information, and messages in writing and create documents such as letters, directions, manuals, reports, graphs, and flow charts.

- ✔ **Arithmetic/mathematics:** You can perform basic computations and approach practical problems by choosing appropriately from a variety of mathematical techniques.

- ✔ **Listening:** You receive, attend to, interpret, and respond to verbal messages and other cues.

- ✔ **Speaking:** You organize ideas and communicate orally.

You have skills because . . .

Here are four springboards for writing and speaking of your skills. You can infer your skills based on history, simply assert your skills, refer to others who identified your skills, or be tested by professional bodies:

- ✔ **Inference:** Your prior education and experience suggest your skills.

  With my degree in civil engineering, I am competent to design bridges.

- ✔ **Assertion:** You claim you have skills.

  I can design and sell a program of services to the Spanish-speaking market.

- ✔ **References:** Others act on your behalf to claim skills.

  My former manager, Carlyle Sangi, says I put together a budget better than anyone she knows.

- ✔ **Certification:** Testing and peer evaluation document your skills.

  As a certified industrial ergonomist, I can evaluate your workplace and make required changes to conform to new OSHA rules.

People skills

These skills allow the "wonder of you" to mesh well with others. They include social, negotiation, leadership, teamwork, and cultural diversity skills:

- ✔ **Social:** You respect the feelings of others, assert yourself when appropriate, and take an interest in what others say and why they think and act as they do.

- ✔ **Negotiation:** You present the facts and arguments of your position, listen to and understand the other party's position, create possible ways to resolve conflict, and make reasonable compromises.

- ✔ **Leadership:** You communicate thoughts and feelings to justify the position you champion, encourage or convince others, and motivate people to believe in and trust you.

- ✔ **Teamwork:** You work cooperatively with others, contribute ideas and effort, and do your share of the work.

- ✔ **Cultural diversity:** You work well with people who have different ethnic, social, or educational backgrounds.

Thinking skills

These skills enable you to think creatively, make decisions, solve problems, visualize, and know how to learn and reason:

- ✔ **Creative thinking:** You generate new ideas.

- ✔ **Decision making:** You have the ability to specify goals and understand reasons not to do something.

- ✔ **Problem solving:** You can recognize a problem and devise a plan of action to deal with it.

- ✔ **Visualizing:** You can picture symbols and organize them in your mind's eye.

- ✔ **Knowing how to learn:** You are able to use efficient learning techniques to acquire and apply new knowledge and skills.

- ✔ **Reasoning:** You concentrate on discovering a rule or principle underlying the relationship between two or more objects and then apply it to solve a problem.

Personal qualities

Classified as skills, these personal qualities include responsibility, self-esteem, sociability, self-management, integrity, and honesty:

- ✔ **Responsibility:** You put forth a high level of effort and persevere toward reaching your goal.

- ✔ **Self-esteem:** You believe in your own self-worth and maintain a positive view of yourself.

- ✔ **Sociability:** You show understanding, friendliness, adaptability, empathy, and politeness in group settings.

- ✔ **Self-management:** You have a realistic view of your knowledge and skills, set realistic personal goals, and monitor progress toward those goals.

Where there's a skill, there's a way

The foundation skills group isn't the end of the story. Other groups of skills are identified by whether they have market value to employers (marketable skills), can be carried around like a mobile phone from one employer to another (crossover skills), or are super-glued to a specific type of work or workplace (job-related skills). Still another term describes skills you're really good at because you love using them (motivated skills):

Understanding competencies versus skills

Competencies, which are also sometimes called *success factors, key characteristics,* or *behaviors,* go deeper than skills, according to one definition. A competency is a relatively enduring characteristic that makes possible superior performance in a particular job or role.

In brief, a competency is the X-factor in why, of two equally skilled employees in the same company, one hits a home run and another hits a double.

Competency recruiting is an evolving human resource management concept. Study corporate websites and determine whether competency recruiting is the policy at your target company. If so, analyze the position you want and develop statements for each competency it requires. If a company is looking for a candidate who has shown "creative leadership," for

example, write examples of when you've demonstrated such behavior. Explain how you did it, distinguishing yourself as a top performer.

As I say in my book *Job Interviews For Dummies,* 4th Edition, in today's world, "The operative words are *skills* (what you can do) and, increasingly a newer and broader employment concept termed *competencies* (how well you do what you do using natural talents). The competencies concept includes skills and such related characteristics and natural abilities as motivation, industriousness, and attitude."

The competency program looks at the whole package as it relates to the job the employer wants done. If a company's website or recruitment materials mention competencies, you mention competencies in your letters. If not, don't refer to competencies, but stick to skills.

- ✔ **Marketable skills:** Simply stated, marketable skills are ones that an employer will pay you to use. They're often identified in job posts and ads. By contrast, unmarketable skills are those that no one is likely to pay you to use — the ability to bounce for a mile on a pogo stick, for example. Also unmarketable or barely marketable: obsolete skills, such as changing the ribbon on a typewriter.

- ✔ **Crossover skills:** You may have heard these skills referred to as *transferrable* skills. To my ear, *crossover* is a more modern term. Crossover skills are portable skills that you can use in a wide variety of jobs.

  For example, employers value communications skills in positions ranging from apple grower to zookeeper. You can transfer these skills from job to job, from industry to industry, or even from one career field to another. I illustrate with a checklist of selected crossover skills in the next section.

- ✔ **Job-related skills:** Job-related skills are also called *technical* or *professional* skills. Because they're suitable for a particular type of job, they assure an employer that you can actually do the job. You can't always move job-related skills from one employer to another, but sometimes you can. (To gauge mobility, ask yourself, "Who would pay me to use this skill?")

  Three examples of job-related skills: the ability to use a certain brand of mold-injection machine, the ability to perform cataract eye surgery, and the ability to spot cheating players in a casino.

- ✔ **Motivated skills:** "Do something you'd do for nothing" is the theme song of motivated skills. These are the developed abilities that you enjoy doing. Describing a motivated skill in a cover letter is a subtle way of saying you'll excel at a specific assignment: *One of my motivated skills is ____.*

Speaking Out about Your Skills

Because spelling out your skills adds substance to your claims of being able to put more money in a company's bank account than it will spend to employ you, I've compiled a couple of checklists to help you claim those you own.

Read through the following checklist of foundation skills and the checklist of crossover skills. Mark the words and terms that truthfully apply to you. Include the terms as part of your skills language to use for job search documents and job interviews.

Speaking of interviews, when you claim ownership of a specific skill, be prepared in interviews to give a brief example of how you used that skill and its benefits. If you're asked and all you can come up with on the spot is babble, the interviewer will think you're an inventor, but not the good kind.

While these checklists aren't exhaustive, they're a good start; you may think of other words and terms to use as well.

Foundation skills checklist

A

- ❏ Ability to learn
- ❏ Accepting criticism
- ❏ Accommodating
- ❏ Affable
- ❏ Ambitious
- ❏ Appealing
- ❏ Aspiring
- ❏ Athletic
- ❏ Autonomy

- ❏ Abstract thinking
- ❏ Accepting freedom
- ❏ Active
- ❏ Agile
- ❏ Amicable
- ❏ Approachable
- ❏ Assertive
- ❏ Attendance
- ❏ Awareness

- ❏ Accepting consequences
- ❏ Accepting supervision
- ❏ Adventurous
- ❏ Alert
- ❏ Animated
- ❏ Artistic abilities
- ❏ Astute
- ❏ Attention to detail

B

- ❏ Benevolent
- ❏ Brave

- ❏ Benign
- ❏ Bright

- ❏ Bold

C

- ❏ Careful
- ❏ Cautious
- ❏ Charming
- ❏ Clever
- ❏ Common sense
- ❏ Composure
- ❏ Conceptualization
- ❏ Congenial
- ❏ Considerate
- ❏ Contemplative
- ❏ Courteous
- ❏ Cunning

- ❏ Caring
- ❏ Charismatic
- ❏ Cheerful
- ❏ Colorful
- ❏ Compassion
- ❏ Comprehension
- ❏ Concern
- ❏ Conscientious
- ❏ Consistent
- ❏ Cordial
- ❏ Creativity
- ❏ Curiosity

- ❏ Casual
- ❏ Charitable
- ❏ Chivalrous
- ❏ Commitment
- ❏ Compliant
- ❏ Concentration
- ❏ Confidence
- ❏ Conservative
- ❏ Constant
- ❏ Courageous
- ❏ Critical thinking

D

❑ Daring ❑ Decisive ❑ Dedicated
❑ Deft ❑ Deliberate ❑ Dependable
❑ Desire ❑ Determined ❑ Devoted
❑ Devout ❑ Dexterity ❑ Dignity
❑ Diligent ❑ Discipline ❑ Dogged
❑ Drive ❑ Dutiful ❑ Dynamic

E

❑ Eager ❑ Earnest ❑ Easy-going
❑ Economical ❑ Efficient ❑ Eloquence
❑ Empathy ❑ Energetic ❑ Engaging
❑ Enjoys challenge ❑ Enterprising ❑ Entertaining
❑ Enthusiasm ❑ Entrepreneurial ❑ Ethical
❑ Exciting ❑ Explorative ❑ Expressive
❑ Extroverted

F

❑ Fair ❑ Faithful ❑ Fast
❑ Firm ❑ Flexibility ❑ Focused
❑ Forceful ❑ Fortitude ❑ Friendly
❑ Funny

G

❑ Generous ❑ Gentle ❑ Genuine
❑ Gifted ❑ Good-natured ❑ Graceful
❑ Gracious

H

❑ Hard-working ❑ Hardy ❑ Honest
❑ Honor ❑ Humble ❑ Humorous
❑ Hustle

I

- ❑ Imagination
- ❑ Improvisation
- ❑ Industrious
- ❑ Initiative
- ❑ Integrity
- ❑ Intuitive

- ❑ Immaculate
- ❑ Incentive
- ❑ Informal
- ❑ Innovative
- ❑ Intelligence
- ❑ Inventing

- ❑ Impetus
- ❑ Independent
- ❑ Ingenious
- ❑ Inquisitive
- ❑ Interest

K

- ❑ Keen

- ❑ Kind

L

- ❑ Likable

- ❑ Lively

- ❑ Loyal

M

- ❑ Maturity
- ❑ Meticulous
- ❑ Motivation

- ❑ Memory
- ❑ Mindful

- ❑ Methodical
- ❑ Modest

N

- ❑ Neat

- ❑ Nimble

O

- ❑ Obliging
- ❑ Optimistic
- ❑ Outgoing

- ❑ Open-minded
- ❑ Orderly

- ❑ Opportunistic
- ❑ Original

P

- ❑ Patience
- ❑ Persistence
- ❑ Pleasant
- ❑ Positive
- ❑ Pragmatic

- ❑ Perfectionist
- ❑ Personable
- ❑ Poised
- ❑ Powerful
- ❑ Presence

- ❑ Persevering
- ❑ Pioneering
- ❑ Polite
- ❑ Practical
- ❑ Pride in work

- ❏ Progressive
- ❏ Prompt
- ❏ Prudent
- ❏ Punctuality

Q

- ❏ Questioning
- ❏ Quick-thinking

R

- ❏ Rational
- ❏ Realistic
- ❏ Reasonable
- ❏ Receptive
- ❏ Reflective
- ❏ Relentless
- ❏ Reliable
- ❏ Reserved
- ❏ Resolute
- ❏ Respectful
- ❏ Responsible
- ❏ Responsiveness
- ❏ Restraint
- ❏ Retention
- ❏ Reverent
- ❏ Risk taking
- ❏ Robust

S

- ❏ Safety
- ❏ Savvy
- ❏ Scrupulous
- ❏ Self-esteem
- ❏ Self-motivating
- ❏ Self-reliant
- ❏ Self-respect
- ❏ Sense of humor
- ❏ Sensible
- ❏ Sharp
- ❏ Showmanship
- ❏ Shrewd
- ❏ Sincere
- ❏ Smart
- ❏ Sociable
- ❏ Spirited
- ❏ Stalwart
- ❏ Stamina
- ❏ Staunch
- ❏ Steadfast
- ❏ Steady
- ❏ Striving
- ❏ Strong
- ❏ Studious
- ❏ Sturdy
- ❏ Style

T

- ❏ Tactful
- ❏ Tasteful
- ❏ Tenacious
- ❏ Thinking
- ❏ Thorough
- ❏ Thoughtfulness
- ❏ Trustworthy

U

- ❏ Unbiased
- ❏ Understanding
- ❏ Unprejudiced
- ❏ Unpretentious
- ❏ Unselfish

V

- ❏ Venturing
- ❏ Versatile
- ❏ Vigilant
- ❏ Vigorous
- ❏ Visualizing
- ❏ Vivacious

W

- ❏ Warm
- ❏ Wary
- ❏ Watchful
- ❏ Willingness to follow rules
- ❏ Wisdom
- ❏ Work ethic
- ❏ Work habits
- ❏ Working alone
- ❏ Working under pressure

Crossover skills checklist

A

- ❏ Accelerating
- ❏ Accomplishing
- ❏ Accounting
- ❏ Accuracy
- ❏ Achieving
- ❏ Activating
- ❏ Active
- ❏ Active learning
- ❏ Active listening
- ❏ Adapting
- ❏ Addressing
- ❏ Adjusting
- ❏ Administering
- ❏ Advertising
- ❏ Advising
- ❏ Aiding
- ❏ Allocating
- ❏ Altering
- ❏ Amending
- ❏ Analyzing behavior
- ❏ Analyzing costs
- ❏ Announcing
- ❏ Anticipating
- ❏ Appearance
- ❏ Application
- ❏ Appointing
- ❏ Appraising
- ❏ Appreciation
- ❏ Arbitrating
- ❏ Argumentation
- ❏ Arranging
- ❏ Articulation
- ❏ Assembling
- ❏ Assessing cost
- ❏ Assessing damage
- ❏ Assigning
- ❏ Assisting
- ❏ Attaining
- ❏ Attending
- ❏ Auditing
- ❏ Augmenting
- ❏ Authoring
- ❏ Automating

B

- ❏ Balancing
- ❏ Bargaining
- ❏ Blending
- ❏ Bookkeeping
- ❏ Boosting
- ❏ Bridging
- ❏ Briefing
- ❏ Budgeting
- ❏ Building

C

- Calculating
- Calibrating
- Cataloging
- Categorizing
- Chairing
- Charting
- Checking
- Clarifying
- Classifying
- Clerical ability
- Coaching
- Coaxing
- Cognizance
- Coherence
- Collaborative
- Combining
- Comforting
- Commanding
- Communicating
- Comparing
- Competence
- Compiling
- Complimenting
- Composing
- Compromising
- Computing
- Condensing
- Conducting
- Confidentiality
- Conflict resolution
- Conforming
- Confronting
- Consolidating
- Constructing
- Consulting
- Contingency planning
- Contracting
- Controlling
- Converting
- Convincing
- Cooperation
- Coordinating
- Copying
- Correcting
- Correlating
- Corresponding
- Counseling
- Counteracting
- Counterbalancing
- Counting
- Creating
- Creative writing
- Crisis management

D

- Data collecting
- Data entry
- Debating
- Decision making
- Deductive reasoning
- Defending
- Defining problems
- Delegating
- Delivering
- Demonstrating
- Depicting
- Describing
- Designating
- Designing
- Detecting
- Developing ideas
- Devising
- Diagnosing
- Diagramming
- Diplomacy
- Directing
- Discretion
- Discussing
- Dispatching
- Dispensing
- Displaying
- Distributing
- Diversifying
- Diverting
- Documenting
- Drafting
- Drawing
- Duplicating

E

❏ Editing

❏ Educating

❏ Effecting change

❏ Elevating

❏ Eliminating

❏ Empowering

❏ Enabling

❏ Enacting

❏ Encouraging

❏ Engineering a plan

❏ Enhancing

❏ Enlarging

❏ Enlisting

❏ Enlivening

❏ Enriching

❏ Envisioning

❏ Equalizing

❏ Escalating

❏ Establishing objectives

❏ Establishing priorities

❏ Estimating

❏ Evaluating

❏ Examining

❏ Exchanging information

❏ Executing a plan

❏ Exhibiting

❏ Expanding

❏ Expediting

❏ Extracting

F

❏ Fabricating

❏ Facilitating

❏ Figuring

❏ Filing

❏ Finding

❏ Finishing

❏ Fixing

❏ Fluency

❏ Following through

❏ Forecasting

❏ Foresight

❏ Forging

❏ Forming

❏ Formulating

❏ Fostering

❏ Founding

❏ Framing

❏ Fulfilling

❏ Fundraising

❏ Furthering

G

❏ Gauging

❏ Generalizing

❏ Generating

❏ Grammar

❏ Graphics

❏ Grouping

❏ Guessing

❏ Guiding

H

❏ Handling complaints

❏ Harmonizing

❏ Heading

❏ Healing

❏ Helpful

❏ Hypothesizing

I

- ❑ Identifying alternatives
- ❑ Identifying causes
- ❑ Identifying downstream consequences
- ❑ Identifying issues
- ❑ Identifying needs
- ❑ Identifying principles
- ❑ Identifying problems
- ❑ Illuminating
- ❑ Illustrating
- ❑ Impartial
- ❑ Implementing
- ❑ Improving
- ❑ Incitement
- ❑ Increasing
- ❑ Indexing
- ❑ Indoctrinating
- ❑ Inductive
- ❑ Inductive reasoning
- ❑ Influencing
- ❑ Information gathering
- ❑ Information management
- ❑ Information organization
- ❑ Information receiving
- ❑ Informing
- ❑ Infusing
- ❑ Insightful
- ❑ Inspecting
- ❑ Inspiring
- ❑ Installation
- ❑ Instilling
- ❑ Instituting
- ❑ Instruction
- ❑ Integration
- ❑ Interaction
- ❑ Interceding
- ❑ Interpersonal skills
- ❑ Interpretation
- ❑ Interrupting
- ❑ Intervening
- ❑ Interviewing
- ❑ Introducing
- ❑ Investigation
- ❑ Isolating
- ❑ Itemizing

J

- ❑ Joining
- ❑ Judgment

K

- ❑ Keeping deadlines
- ❑ Keyboarding
- ❑ Knowledge of subject

L

- ❑ Language
- ❑ Launching
- ❑ Laying
- ❑ Leadership
- ❑ Learning
- ❑ Lecturing
- ❑ Listening for content
- ❑ Listening for context
- ❑ Listening for directions
- ❑ Listening for emotional meaning
- ❑ Listing
- ❑ Locating
- ❑ Logical reasoning
- ❑ Long-term planning

M

- ❏ Maintaining confidentiality
- ❏ Maintenance
- ❏ Managing
- ❏ Maneuvering
- ❏ Manipulation
- ❏ Mapping
- ❏ Marketing
- ❏ Masking
- ❏ Matching
- ❏ Mathematics
- ❏ Measuring
- ❏ Mechanical ability
- ❏ Mediating
- ❏ Meeting
- ❏ Mending
- ❏ Mentoring
- ❏ Merchandising
- ❏ Minding machines
- ❏ Minimizing
- ❏ Modeling
- ❏ Moderating
- ❏ Modifying
- ❏ Modulating
- ❏ Molding
- ❏ Money management
- ❏ Monitoring
- ❏ Motivating

N

- ❏ Negotiating
- ❏ Nonpartisan
- ❏ Number skills
- ❏ Nursing
- ❏ Nurturing

O

- ❏ Objectivity
- ❏ Observing
- ❏ Operating vehicles
- ❏ Operations analysis
- ❏ Oral communication
- ❏ Oral comprehension
- ❏ Orchestrating
- ❏ Organizational
- ❏ Organizing
- ❏ Outfitting
- ❏ Outlining
- ❏ Outreach
- ❏ Overhauling
- ❏ Overseeing

P

- ❏ Pacifying
- ❏ Paraphrasing
- ❏ Participating
- ❏ Patterning
- ❏ Perceiving
- ❏ Perfecting
- ❏ Performing
- ❏ Persuasion
- ❏ Photography
- ❏ Picturing
- ❏ Pinpointing
- ❏ Planning
- ❏ Plotting
- ❏ Policy-making
- ❏ Polishing
- ❏ Politicking
- ❏ Popularizing
- ❏ Portraying
- ❏ Precision
- ❏ Prediction
- ❏ Preparation
- ❏ Presentation
- ❏ Printing
- ❏ Prioritizing
- ❏ Probing
- ❏ Problem solving
- ❏ Processing
- ❏ Producing
- ❏ Professional
- ❏ Prognostication

❏ Program design　　❏ Program developing　　❏ Program implementation

❏ Projection　　❏ Promoting　　❏ Proofreading

❏ Proposing　　❏ Protecting　　❏ Providing

❏ Public speaking　　❏ Publicizing　　❏ Publishing

❏ Purchasing

Q

❏ Quality control

R

❏ Raising　　❏ Ranking　　❏ Readiness

❏ Reading comprehension　　❏ Reasoning　　❏ Reclaiming

❏ Recognition　　❏ Reconciling　　❏ Recording

❏ Recovering　　❏ Recruiting　　❏ Rectifying

❏ Reducing　　❏ Referring　　❏ Reformative

❏ Regulating　　❏ Rehabilitating　　❏ Reinforcing

❏ Relationship building　　❏ Remodeling　　❏ Rendering

❏ Reorganizing　　❏ Repairing　　❏ Repeating

❏ Reporting　　❏ Representing　　❏ Researching

❏ Resolving　　❏ Resource development　　❏ Resource management

❏ Response coordination　　❏ Restoring　　❏ Restructuring

❏ Retrieving　　❏ Reversing　　❏ Reviewing

❏ Revitalizing　　❏ Rhetoric　　❏ Rousing

❏ Running

S

❏ Saving　　❏ Scanning　　❏ Scheduling

❏ Schooling　　❏ Science　　❏ Scientific reasoning

❏ Screening　　❏ Scrutiny　　❏ Searching

❏ Selecting　　❏ Selling　　❏ Sensitivity

❏ Sequencing　　❏ Serving　　❏ Setting up

❏ Settling　　❏ Shaping　　❏ Shielding

- ❏ Situation analysis
- ❏ Solidifying
- ❏ Sorting
- ❏ Specialization
- ❏ Speech
- ❏ Stirring
- ❏ Strengthening
- ❏ Substituting
- ❏ Supplementing
- ❏ Surveying
- ❏ Systematizing
- ❏ Systems perception

- ❏ Sketching
- ❏ Solution appraisal
- ❏ Speaking
- ❏ Specifying
- ❏ Stabilizing
- ❏ Storing information
- ❏ Structuring
- ❏ Summarizing
- ❏ Supporting
- ❏ Sustaining
- ❏ Systems analysis
- ❏ Systems understanding

- ❏ Social networking
- ❏ Social perceptiveness
- ❏ Solving
- ❏ Spearheading
- ❏ Speculating
- ❏ Stimulating
- ❏ Streamlining
- ❏ Styling
- ❏ Supervising
- ❏ Surmising
- ❏ Synthesis
- ❏ Systems management

T

- ❏ Tabulating
- ❏ Teaching
- ❏ Tempering
- ❏ Theorizing
- ❏ Translating
- ❏ Troubleshooting

- ❏ Taking instruction
- ❏ Teamwork
- ❏ Terminology
- ❏ Time management
- ❏ Traveling
- ❏ Tutoring

- ❏ Talking
- ❏ Technical writing
- ❏ Testing
- ❏ Training
- ❏ Treating
- ❏ Typing

U

- ❏ Unifying
- ❏ Using tools

- ❏ Updating

- ❏ Upgrading

V

- ❏ Values clarification

- ❏ Visual communication

W

- ❏ Word processing
- ❏ Working with others

- ❏ Working with earth
- ❏ Written communication

- ❏ Working with nature

No frills, just skills

Define your skills and what you bring to a new job. When prospecting for your skills, review your last job or college post and think about these issues:

✔ What did you do?

✔ What did you direct others to do?

✔ What did you manage, create, approve, or instigate?

✔ What was the outcome of your actions?

✔ More profits? (How much?)

✔ More revenue? (How much?)

✔ More savings (How much can you claim?)

✔ More accounts (How many? What are they worth?)

You can track down more specific skill words in three main ways:

✔ Search job posts and ads. Pay particular attention to each job's requirements.

✔ Search online for "sample job descriptions." You may have to surf a large number of sites because each typically offers only a half-dozen occupations.

✔ Go to a Department of Labor website, O'Net Code Connector, www.onetcodeconnector.org, where you see the skills required for an occupation of interest. The skills are called "Detailed Work Activities."

Showcasing Popular Skills that Employers Want

After pinpointing the skills that sell your value, how do you know which of those skills most help you stand out from the crowd?

A roundup of several surveys suggests skills and qualities that employers often admire. The following list is representative but not comprehensive:

✔ **Effective communication:** Employers seek candidates who can listen to instructions and act on them with minimal guidance. They want employees who speak, write, and listen effectively; organize their thoughts logically; and explain everything clearly.

- ✔ **Computer and technical literacy:** Almost all jobs now require an understanding, ranging from basic to advanced, of computer software, word processing, e-mail, spreadsheets, and Internet navigation.

- ✔ **Problem solving/creativity:** Employers always want people who can get them out of a pickle. Problem-solving ability can aid you in making transactions, processing data, formulating a vision, and reaching a resolution. Employers need the assurance that you can conquer job challenges by thinking critically and creatively.

- ✔ **Interpersonal abilities:** Relationship building and relationship management are high priorities with many employers. These skills confirm that a candidate can relate well to others, both coworkers and customers.

- ✔ **Teamwork skills:** The ability to work well with others while pursuing a common goal is a long-running favorite of employers. But so is the ability to work with minor supervision.

- ✔ **Diversity sensitivity:** In today's world, employers highly value cultural sensitivity and ability to build rapport with others in a multicultural environment.

- ✔ **Planning and organizing:** Workplace life requires prioritizing and organizing information. Employers value people who, metaphorically, dig a well before they're thirsty.

- ✔ **Leadership and management:** Leadership consists of a strong sense of self, confidence, and a comprehensive knowledge of company goals. These qualities motivate and inspire, providing a solid foundation for teamwork.

Year after year, in survey after survey, employers continue to look for assurances that you can in some way either make money for them or save money for them. If the employer is a nonprofit organization, generally you should substitute the skills you can bring to bear on helping the organization fulfill its mission (unless the mission requires selling products to earn money). Skills useful in saving money are universally desired, including by the nonprofits.

Identifying Personal Qualities That Employers Want

In the Great American Skills Sorting, some list makers mix in personal values, personality traits, and personal characteristics with skills — and that's okay with me. But I've made a second list focusing on a few personal qualities that employers rate highly:

- ✔ **Adaptability and flexibility:** Nearly half of employers in a recent survey gave a high rating to "openness to new ideas and concepts." They also like candidates who can work independently or as part of a team, changing gears when required, whether multitasking or adapting working hours and locale.

- ✔ **Professionalism and work ethic:** Employers seek productive workers with positive work ethics who stick with challenges until they meet them.

- ✔ **Positive attitude and energy:** The last to be picked and promoted are candidates who show gloomy outlooks and emotional immaturity. Exhibit a sunny outlook and energetic, organized behavior.

Everyone wants to hire a paragon of virtue, a model of excellence and perfection. Don't overlook adding your personal qualities — and the behaviors they drive — where appropriate when composing your job search correspondence.

Giving Serious Thought to Certifications

A professional certification can be a kind of passport, identifying you as a citizen of a career field with all its rank and privilege. In other words, professional credentialing is one way to document your ownership of the skills you claim.

Not all credentials are worthy. A credential is worth the effort only if it has industry recognition and respect.

Crash course on certification

Differences in certification exist, but for ease of communication, I include other terms of validation, such as *registered, accredited, chartered, qualified,* and *diplomate,* as well as *certified.* Whether the professional designation carries statutory clout or is voluntary, common elements include professional experience, often between two and ten years, sometimes reduced by education. Education standards are included, which may call for minimum levels of both academic and professional education.

Certification examinations are uninviting to many professionals; generally, they require time-consuming study and may include both experience-based knowledge acquired working in the field and curriculum-based knowledge gained by assigned learning texts.

Shopping for skills

Small businesses are creating most of the new jobs. But small companies have fewer resources to use in training new hires. For most jobs, then, you're pretty much on your own to acquire the skills you need.

Although large companies offer fewer jobs in the aggregate, they're still the best places to work to acquire up-to-date skills you can market on future jobs.

What's certification worth?

Is certification worth your effort?

Certification has strong appeal in your early career — say, the first 12 to 15 years — as a technique to control your earnings environment. But in business, certifications lose their luster at the vice president level and above. Why? Certifications zero in on specific skills, while top managers are more concerned with the big picture.

For consulting, medicine, law, and technology careers, professional certifications never lose their punch, especially for people who hope to work internationally. Continuing education may be required to keep them updated and active.

The credential may be a license awarded by a state board, such as the familiar Certified Public Accountant (CPA), or a voluntary program sponsored by a professional organization, such as the Accredited in Public Relations (APR) designation awarded by the Public Relations Society of America.

Good Luck on the Great Skills Search

When you're really stumped on naming specific skills that make you stand out and need more help than this chapter or your informal efforts provide, the Internet beckons: Call forth the genie of Google and type "discover your skills." More than 2.5 million resources are yours to mine.

Part V
The Part of Tens

The 5th Wave   By Rich Tennant

"I think I write great job letters.
I'm good with details..."

In this part . . .

Turn to the pages in the chapters in this part to discover social media etiquette, and gather tips on job hunting via the massive search engine, Google.

Chapter 18

Remember Ten Social Forget-Me-Not Tips

A dictionary definition explains social media as "forms of electronic communication, such as websites for social networking and microblogging, through which users create online communities to share information, ideas, personal messages, videos, and other content." That's a mouthful!

The formal explanation isn't always crystal clear for newcomers to the social concept — which we all were not so long ago. If you're finding the idea a bit murky, back up to Chapter 8 for additional illumination about social media and social networking.

Job hunters who like getting to the point immediately may prefer the following shortcut to decipher the social concept. (This shortcut is available in a number of versions on the Internet, but its origin is unknown.) Presented here in good fun, this rendition pairs each of seven social media websites with the stereotype of the purpose the site supposedly serves. Smile awhile:

- ✔ **Facebook:** I like donuts.
- ✔ **Twitter:** I'm eating a donut.
- ✔ **Foursquare:** This is where I eat donuts.
- ✔ **Google+:** I'm hanging out, eating donuts.
- ✔ **Quora:** How do you eat donuts?
- ✔ **Pinterest:** Here's a donut recipe.
- ✔ **LinkedIn:** My skills include donut eating.

Going Social on the Job Front

Social media is experiencing astonishing, explosive growth. Facebook alone claims 1 billion users worldwide, and Twitter boasts 100 million users across the globe. Social media and social networking can't be ignored in a world that changes communication models seemingly overnight.

The difference between social media and social networking is *observation* and *interaction*. Social media enables social networking. In other words, social media can exist without social networking, but social networking can't exist without social media. Consider an example: When a recruiting professional views an online profile posted on a social media website such as LinkedIn, the recruiter is *observing* — but when the recruiter is motivated to contact a person he's observing, the recruiter is *interacting*.

To gain more know-how for a successful ride aboard the social job search bandwagon without falling off, bear ten tips in mind.

Spread job search news with caution

When you're between jobs, keeping people in your network alerted through social media that you're looking for a particular type of job is a smart move. It's not so smart when you're employed — unless you don't care whether the boss finds out that you're looking to leave and helps you out the door.

The risk that your employer may get wind of your greener-pastures itch isn't your only concern. Identity theft and fraud have entered the mix in recent years. As one privacy consultant has said, "It's hunting season, and you are the game."

The biggest names in social media websites for job hunters are LinkedIn, Facebook, and Twitter. Newer sites include Google+ and Pinterest. Others are already here or on the way. Look critically at each social media site to assess whether you can live with its privacy protections.

Establish yourself as an expert

Use social media to be seen as someone "in the know" about what's happening in your industry or career field. For example, use your status updates on Twitter to tweet about industry topics, new developments, advice, and anything of interest to people in your line of work.

Find role models and mirror them

Use LinkedIn to identify role model networkers who have the kind of job you want. See which groups they belong to, and join those groups. On the other side of the coin, look at who has viewed your profile and, if appropriate, add viewers to your network.

Send thank-you notes to new connections

Form the habit of sending a quick personal note to every person who accepts your invitation to connect on LinkedIn. Online commercial greeting card services save time. Jacquie Lawson e-cards, for example, include a collection of artistic note cards to make saying "glad to know you" easy, gracious, and fast.

Such human touches set the table for the times when you need favors from your connections for introductions, referrals, and news of job opportunities.

Sleuth for useful company research

Many employers, especially large employers, have a presence on Facebook, Twitter, and LinkedIn. Although their Facebook profile probably is on private status, check it out. Cruise additional social sites for other nuggets of information about a company you hope to join.

Regularly check your social sites

When you're connected — following and friending people, and monitoring favorite companies — stay on your toes. Don't let your Twitter feed, LinkedIn updates, and Facebook Wall wither and go stale with inattention. Keep your eyes open for any mention of job openings at companies you like, as well as advice on how to apply for them.

You can send your Facebook contacts direct messages asking about jobs or where they work. Also look on the Glassdoor website (www.glassdoor. com) at its "Inside Connections" tool to uncover who you may know at companies through your Facebook friends list that can promote your resume or even secure an interview.

Tweet for quality, not quantity

Regular tweets about interesting news, articles, personnel changes, and tools for your industry raise the balance in your professional standing bank. But sending out too much too often draws down that balance.

By another measure, the vast majority of what you share on Twitter needs to be helpful, relevant information, either retweeting followers or connecting with others. You then have acceptance to ask for help whenever you need it.

If your knowledge of how to use Twitter is sketchy, you can get up to speed by watching a few of the many free tutorials on the YouTube website (www. youtube.com).

Use common sense to avoid rejection

You've read plenty of warnings about reputation-management issues, such as the bad judgment of posting photos that show you guzzling alcoholic drinks. Belief issues can be just as damaging to your employment prospects.

While having an online presence is important to your job search, do make sure that anything you post on a social networking site isn't going to alienate a potential employer.

What do you think would happen if you were being vetted by a recruiter whose client is a big bank and the recruiter came across a blog you wrote about your strong belief that no bank should be too big to fail? Look left and right before you write.

Match social media to your type of job

Opinions differ about which social media sites pay off best for which type of job hunter. Following are impressions, not scientific studies:

- ✔ LinkedIn has been labeled the "suit-and-tie network" that's useful for finding professional jobs in traditional industries.
- ✔ Facebook is rewarding for jobs in health care, manufacturing and other blue-collar jobs, and seasonal work in delivery services and retailing.
- ✔ Pinterest is a handy hub for spotting jobs in the design and interior decorating fields.
- ✔ Google+ appears to be tilted toward tech jobs.

Never jump from one social networking site to another on a whim. Just as one joke doesn't make a comedian, one interesting job posting doesn't make a favorite social site. Study and reflect on your options before you spread your time too thinly, unless you have 48 hours in your day to devote to social networking.

Don't assume that social is all you need

Alison Doyle, the respected job search guide for About.com (see her profile sample in Chapter 9), advises balance in your search efforts.

"The reason I'm not recommending you count only on online networking [social media] is that many employers still recruit candidates in what is an old-fashioned way. They expect candidates to apply with a resume and a cover letter via the company website, or on a site where they have posted the job opening," Doyle says.

Susan Heathfield, About.com's guide to human resources, agrees with Doyle's advice: "Despite the proliferation of social professional networking, such as that on Twitter and LinkedIn, some traditional components of the application process still work best for the job searcher to find out about a job, or even ask questions. When you apply, employers still expect a resume and cover letter."

As Doyle explains, "to have a well-rounded job search, you still need to search for jobs and to take the time to apply."

What's Next in Social Search

A decade ago, Friendster, the pioneering social media site, was at the top of the social heap. Fast-forward a few years, when Facebook (and, for awhile, MySpace) grabbed the spotlight. As time passes, new social media sites are likely waiting in the wings to emerge, and some current social media sites will probably age, shed users, and fade.

Here's why you care. After you master the do's and don'ts of job hunting in today's social world, you can't forever count on the hunt you know. Dynamics change. Connections change. Enterprises change. (Friendster is now a gaming site based in Kuala Lumpur, Malaysia.)

Before you plunge into a fresh job search a few years down the road, you'd be wise to confirm that the media sites you now count on for employment mobility continue to be the best tools to take you wherever you want to go.

Clap hands for social media's good news!

Are you hanging back from trying to find a job through social networking because you think it's a loser for you? If so, which of the following reasons fuel your rejection — one or all of them?

✔ You're concerned that you'll waste too much of your time on social networking

✔ You could care less that you don't even have a social media account

✔ You shrug off social networking because you're not good with using technology

✔ You're scared silly that your employer will find out you're on the move and dump you

✔ You're not sure you want to expose yourself to the social world because you're an aging job seeker and unfamiliar with this new way of networking

✔ You worry (with reason) about crooks snatching your personal online information

✔ You're simply a private person and need not explain anything to anyone about your online issues

✔ You suspect that recruiters really cruise social media sites to look for reasons not to hire you

OK. To go social or not is your call. But new information expressed by the hiring crowd of why they scout social media may change your mind.

A 2012 study conducted by job board CareerBuilder.com asked 2,300 hiring managers and human resource professionals if, how, and why they use social media in their hiring process.

About 37 percent said that they screen potential job candidates on social networks, checking out their character and personality on social media profiles.

Beyond sizing up your qualifications, recruiters are on the lookout for a good fit with company culture, reasons not to hire you (your suspicion was right), and whatever else they find, such as indications of the following factors:

✔ Good personality

✔ Well-rounded person

✔ Professional image

✔ Great references

✔ Creative talent

✔ Communication skills

Now here's the good news: the Career Builder survey revealed that 29 percent of the surveyed hiring managers found enough positive factors on a profile that caused them to offer the candidate a job.

The upshot: Social networking advocates say that the time has come to consider putting yourself out there when you're looking for employment bliss.

Chapter 19

Top Ten Google Tips for Jackpot Job Search

In This Chapter

▶ Googling surprising ways to find and win prize jobs

▶ Making sure you're a winner when employers Google you

▶ Working with Google to avoid missing out on hidden jobs

*I*n this fast-paced, digital-everything world, job hunting has become a different pursuit than it was a short dozen years ago. No technology better illustrates the dramatic shift than the search engine Google, with all its services that the vast majority of job seekers don't know about. Here's your chance to gain a "secret" advantage to become what you want to be: *employed.*

Welcome to the Wide World of Google

Google is technology with arms that spider into almost every realm of job search, from standard search function and subject alerts, to job finding and reputation monitoring.

The Google wealth of free services to all who are chasing a new job is so extensive that expert Susan P. Joyce has prepared the following primer to show you how to max out opportunities that have eluded you. She's the chief executive officer of NETability, Inc., and of the websites `Job-Hunt.org` and `WorkCoachCafe.com`. Here are her ten high-performance Google tips.

Learn Google ground rules

Google tries to help you find what you're looking for, but sometimes it helps too much by offering too many options.

Help Google out

When you type your search terms (keywords) into the Google search bar, the search engine busts its digital chops to deliver your target data, but you have to help. The following functions illustrate:

✔ **Ignoring your (bad) spelling and capitalization.** Fortunately for many of us, spelling doesn't count much in your search. Google corrects your spelling mistakes and asks you either "Did you mean . . ." or "Showing results for . . .." Capitalization (or lack of it) usually doesn't matter.

✔ **Presuming *and* — not *or*.** When you type two or more words into its search bar, Google assumes that you want to find pages containing all those words, regardless of how connected or separated they are on a page. In essence, Google thinks you intend to use *and* between your search terms. In Google's mind, your instruction looks like this:

accountant (and) bookkeeper.

When you're actually searching for either an accountant or a book-keeper job, inform Google of your intent by connecting the words with the conjunction *or* in capital letters. Your instruction then looks like this:

accountant OR bookkeeper.

Be sure to capitalize the word *OR* in this situation. If you don't, Google sees *or* as one of the keywords you want it to find.

✔ **Ignoring meaningless words.** Google passes over some of the words in your queries that it considers unimportant. Google ignores words like *the, in, of,* and *for.* You need not use such function words and prepositions.

✔ **Trying to read your mind.** Google may be creative in the different versions of the words it finds for you. If you type "administrative assistant jobs," it may return pages containing "admin assistant jobs" as well as "administrative assistant jobs" because it thinks you probably want those pages as well.

Verbatim stops all that help

If you want to turn off all of Google's help (such as correcting spelling and ignoring some words), you can ask it to search exactly on the keywords you've typed into its search bar.

Google calls this feature Verbatim. Find it by clicking the All Results option in the Search Tools menu above the results on your Google search results page.

Search for bingo! answers

Fine-tune your Google searches to find exactly the answers you want by simply adding punctuation and a few more words. Here are seven easy examples:

✔ **Basic search term.** When you want Google to find exact words in a phrase, enclose the words in quotation marks. You then see only pages that contain the words side by side. Write it like this:

"administrative assistant jobs"

✔ **Don't wants.** To avoid administrative assistant jobs that include receptionist duties, tell Google by attaching a minus sign to the front of the word you want excluded. Write it like this:

"administrative assistant jobs" -receptionist

✔ **Do-and-don't wants.** When you want an administrative assistant job without receptionist duties, but you want it to be in Atlanta, add Atlanta to your query. Write it like this:

"administrative assistant job" Atlanta -receptionist

✔ **Want this *or* that.** Perhaps you've had a change of mind and decided that, although you favor Atlanta, you're also fond of Savannah. Write it like this:

"administrative assistant job" -receptionist (Atlanta OR Savannah)

Enclosing in parentheses the either/or part of your search tells Google to treat that part of the query separately from the other parts.

✔ **Fill in the blank.** If you're not sure about the best words for your query, allow Google to come to your rescue by replacing the void with the asterisk character.

To illustrate, maybe you're thinking that the job title "administrative assistant" is too limiting, and you're curious what other assistant jobs are available. Instruct Google to find out with a new query using the asterisk. Write it like this:

* assistant

assistant *

You must leave a space between the search term and the asterisk.

✔ **Expanded help.** When you prefer that Google become more creative with your search, it's easy to make your wishes known. Merely attach the tilde character (~) in front of your basic search term. Google not only delivers hits on the original query, but also brings back additional results in the neighborhood.

Assume that you want Google to find jobs for drivers — truck drivers, taxi drivers, and chauffeurs. Write it like this:

~driver jobs

Or assume that you want to see jobs for a lawyer, sometimes called an attorney. Write it like this:

~lawyer jobs

✔ **Single-site search.** When you want Google to prowl through a specific website, use the action word *site* followed by the website you want it to search. Suppose that a job as an administrative assistant at a large Atlanta employer Bank of America is on your wish list. Write it like this:

job "administrative assistant" -receptionist (atlanta OR savannah) site:bankofamerica.com

Google often pays attention to the order of your search terms, so put the most important word first in long queries — in this case, *job*.

Search many faces of job titles

Choosing the best job title for your search is more complicated than it seems. Multiple titles may apply to the same basic jobs. Some titles are employer specific. Some are industry specific. And some are illogical.

Using the Google fill-in-the-blank (*) feature described in the previous section, I found 20 variations of the administrative assistant job title. I searched with three queries:

*Assistant * jobs*

*administrative * jobs*

*admin * jobs*

Search examples

administrative assistant	admin assistant
administrative asst	administrative support assistant
staff assistant	office assistant
unit admin	receptionist administrative assistant
administrative assistant / receptionist	office administrative assistant
administrative assistant – junior	junior admin assistant
jr admin assistant	junior office assistant
senior administrative assistant	sr administrative assistant
executive administrative assistant	executive assistant
exec assistant	executive admin

See what's going on? Certainly, there's a difference between "junior admin assistant" and "executive assistant," but there's probably very little difference, if any, between "administrative assistant" and "admin assistant."

Evaluate job descriptions

Are you targeting major universities? The administrative assistant position in major universities seems to be called "staff assistant" fairly often. In a hospital, virtually the same job may be called "office admin" or "unit admin." Read the job descriptions for different titles to figure out which ones best fit you.

Research with Google to find the most appropriate job titles that your preferred employers use often. Use those titles in job search letters and documents.

Monitor your good name

An estimated 80 percent or more of employers use Google to form an opinion of job seekers. At least once a week, practice defensive Goggling. Using the versions of your name on your resumes and profiles, run a query and review the first five pages of results. Additionally, set up Google Alerts (discussed later in this chapter) for your name.

Keep an eye out for bad stuff that seems to be about you, as well as bad stuff that's really about someone else who shares your name. If bad stuff is associated with your name, even if it belongs to someone else, your resume is toast.

A 100 percent complete and public LinkedIn profile is a good defense against online mistaken identity.

Find and use a *clean* version of your name — one that you know isn't associated with evildoing — for your job search. Then quickly research and implement additional methods of reputation repair.

You can't address a reputation problem if you don't know about it. You can't know about it if you don't practice defensive Googling.

Uncover hidden jobs

Jobs are posted across the Internet, especially on job boards and company websites, where they attract intense interest and competition. Look for jobs in less obvious places. Here are several examples of where you may find more elbow room in job hunting:

- **Association websites.** Hundreds of thousands of professional and industry associations exist to unite and inform people who work in the same occupation or industry. The associations offer excellent connections for networking. Usually these organizations have websites, and the websites frequently have job postings.

  When you know of a relevant association for your target job or employers, visit it and look for a "career center" or "job board."

  Can't find job postings in an association career center or job board? Before assuming that you've struck out on association sites, try the

Google single-site search. In this search, pretend that the name of the association you're digging into is Example.org. Write it like this:

(~job OR ~career) site:example.org

✔ **Domain name categories of websites.** Internet domain names are always a part of any website address. They have names like Amazon.com, Yahoo.com, Harvard.edu, and Senate.gov.

Domain names are divided into large categories called top-level domains. The names of top-level domains always have a period placed in front of them. Dot-com (.com) is the largest top-level domain category.

Among thousands of top-level domain names (their numbers keep rising), in addition to the most common .com, the three names .edu, .gov, and .org are likely to be used most often.

The following two examples spell out how to do job tracking by domain name categories.

Higher education job: Say that you're scouting for employment as an administrative assistant in a college or university, but you don't have a particular school in mind. Your search includes only college and university websites. Write it like this:

"administrative assistant job"(atlanta OR savannah) site:.edu.

Don't forget the DOT in *.edu.*

Federal government job: Say that you want an administrative assistant's civil service job with the U.S. federal government. (Start at the feds' official website, `www.USAJOBS.gov`, but don't stop there.)

A domain category search may reveal jobs that the official government website may not mention, for some reason. Write it like this:

"administrative assistant job"(atlanta OR savannah) site:.gov.

Don't forget the DOT in *.gov.*

Unless you specify otherwise, Google assumes that you don't need only the newest information available in your search results when older information remains accurate and relevant. When you want to see only jobs posted in the past 24 hours or so, activate the Search Tools feature on the Google search results page and choose the time frame you prefer from the "time" options.

Pinpoint recruiters and hiring managers

Software technology impersonally rejects most job seekers today, creating one of the most frustrating problems job hunters everywhere face: the challenge of uncovering the names of human job deciders to whom they can present their qualifications.

With a job and an employer in mind, calling on Google's long research arms shifts the odds in your favor of finding the names of the relevant recruiting and hiring managers.

Recruiter search

Recruiters may be "internal" employees who work in a company's human resources department or "external" professionals who work in independent third-party firms. To find recruiters no matter where they office, tap into the following search suggestions:

- **LinkedIn single-site search.** Using Google to search LinkedIn (www. linkedin.com) is often useful to identify recruiters for large employers. Suppose you want to spot the recruiter(s) at Amazon. Write it like this:

    recruiter amazon site:linkedin.com

    Look for a search result titled "Amazon Recruiter profiles l LinkedIn" (or something similar).

    The more LinkedIn connections you have, the more details you see about the recruiters Google finds when you click the LinkedIn results page.

- **Company (employer) single-site search.** Hunt for recruiters on the target company's website using the Google single-site search method. In the following search query, *example* is the name of the company you're targeting. Write it like this:

    ~recruiter site:example.com

    "human resources" site:example.com

    "~staff directory" site:example.com

    Be sure there's no space between *site:* and the domain name, which, in this case, is *example.com.*

    Attaching the tilde to the front of the word *recruiter* tells Google to look for all variations of the word, as described in a previous section of this chapter. Be sure to substitute the correct domain name for *example. com*, or use the appropriate domain name category, like *.gov* or *.edu*, for a search across all government agencies, or colleges and universities.

- **General search.** Perform a standard Google search on the employer's name plus the word *recruiter* so that Google will look over every digital hill and dale as it searches the entire Web.

    For example, if you want to spot the recruiter(s) at Amazon, write it like this:

    amazon.com ~recruiter

    "recruiter at amazon.com"

    ~recruiter amazon.com

Double-check the age of the results you find, to be sure you aren't pulling up obsolete data.

Reminder: Attaching the tilde to the front of the word *recruiter* gives Google free rein to find variations on the word *recruiter*, like "head hunter" and "staffing manager."

Hiring manager search

Spot hiring managers based on their job title or department. Start with the information provided on a recent job description for important details, such as the hiring manager's job title ("job reporting to . . .").

For this illustration, assume that the position you seek is in the marketing department. You can employ the following queries:

- ✔ **LinkedIn single-site search.** Because job titles vary (remember administrative assistant earlier in this chapter), using a multipronged search strategy is wise. Consider six examples. Write it like this:

  "(vp OR vice president OR director) marketing" "employer name" site:linkedin.com

  "[probable hiring manager title, like "engineering director" or "customer service manager"]" "employer name" site:linkedin.com

  "marketing manager" "employer name" site:linkedin.com

  *"marketing * manager" "employer name" site:linkedin.com*

  *"marketing *" "employer name" site:linkedin.com*

  manager -project "employer name" site:linkedin.com

- ✔ **Company (employer) single-site search.** Also search the employer website using the Google single-site search option for the same search queries as the LinkedIn searches, plus these six additional queries:

  "[probable hiring manager title]" site:example.com

  "marketing contacts" site:example.com

  ~contacts site:example.com

  ~team site:example.com

  "~directory" site:example.com

  ~organization site:example.com

- ✔ **General Google search.** Set Google loose on the whole Web to find the names you need. You can ask Google to find the answers to these six queries:

  "(vp OR vice president OR director) marketing" "employer name"

  "[probable hiring manager title]" "employer name"

> *"marketing manager" "employer name"*
>
> *"marketing * manager" "employer name"*
>
> *"marketing *" "employer name"*
>
> *"~staff directory" "employer name" marketing*
>
> Check the date on your results to be sure the information isn't several years old. You don't want to be sending a letter to the person who left the job in disgrace five years ago. As a double-check, consider calling the employer's general number and asking, "Is So-and-So still working there as the [whatever job title you have]?"
>
> If the person is still there, you're good to go. If not, ask for the name of the new person in that job. You may or may not get the new name, but it's worth a try.

In the previous examples, replace *marketing* with the department the job description indicates: accounting, administration, purchasing, customer service, engineering, production, and so on.

Think like a detective for interview prep

Employers go for candidates who are really interested in working for them, as opposed to candidates who merely show up for the interview. Many hiring managers view the job interview as a demonstration of the kind of employee you would be.

Get the edge on the competition by spending a couple hours transforming yourself, demonstrating to decision makers that you're Number One on going the second mile.

After you scour the organization's website, call Google in to help by using queries like these:

> *"employer name" "(ceo OR president)"*
>
> *"employer name" officers*
>
> *"employer name" "expanding in *"*
>
> *"employer name" (announced OR introduced)*
>
> *"employer name" "new * announced"*
>
> *"employer name" (growing OR planning)*
>
> *"employer name" (launched OR launching)*
>
> *"employer name" (awarded OR won)*
>
> *"employer name" (chosen OR selected)*

> *"employer name" "opening *"*
>
> *"employer name" "venture funding"*
>
> *"employer name" "quarterly financial results"*
>
> *"employer name" "beginning production"*
>
> *"employer name" "acquiring *"*
>
> *"employer name" ~competitors*

The last query about competitors brings back interview kudos plus. By identifying the target company's competition, you can discuss how much better the target's products and services are than those of their competition.

And if the interview doesn't spark a job offer, you'll have a head start on researching competitors where you might next apply. It's a win–win.

Avoid layoffs and sidestep bad jobs

The last thing you want to do is land a job with a company that needs to lay off staff. You may be conducting a new job search much too soon! So do this research as part of your interview preparation, and then possibly do a double-check before you accept a job offer.

You have no guarantees, of course, but Google may find signs of recent or pending layoffs. Basically, you're looking for bad news.

Do these searches:

> *"employer name" (~layoff OR "laid off")*
>
> *"employer name" layoff **
>
> *"employer name" "~head count reduction"*
>
> *"employer name" "closing *"*
>
> *"employer name" "resigned unexpectedly"*
>
> *"employer name" ~losses*
>
> *"employer name" "ending production"*
>
> *"employer name" restructuring*
>
> *"employer name" "acquired by *"*
>
> *"employer name" "indicted"*

If Google shows you bad news, double-check that the timing of the bad news is new news. This research also enables you to *carefully* ask about what's planned for the company's future.

When you *are* employed, tracking this kind of information can be helpful for your own self-defense so that you aren't the proverbial last person jumping off a sinking ship.

Sometimes job postings aren't genuine. When you find a job posting that looks promising but is listed by an employer you've never heard of, use Google to do your own verification that the job is real before you entrust the company with your resume or fill out an application.

Search for the employer name. If all Google shows you are job postings — no employer website, no employees on LinkedIn, no products or services for sale — neither the employer nor the job are likely real.

Use alerts to stay alert

You can see what employers are finding out about you when they track what's visible for your name. You can also monitor what's happening in your industry or to a competitor. The Google Alert site explains the mechanics, including the following two key options:

- ✔ Do you want Google to search for one or more versions of your name? (*Hint:* Choose all versions of your name.)

- ✔ Do you want Google to send you updates as they happen, once a day, or once a week? (*Hint:* Once a day works well for most job seekers.)

As a job seeker, you can find many uses for Google Alerts, as the following three categories suggest:

- ✔ **Research employers.** When you're interested in employers that are reputed to be good places to work, that pay reasonably well, and that hold good prospects for the future, set up a comprehensive Google Alert for the employer by name, followed by the word *jobs*.

  When you want to shadow more than a single company, you can specify as many as eight companies, as long as you string them together with the word *OR* spelled in capital letters. Write a three-company query like this:

  jobs "Company A" OR "Company B" OR "Company C"

- ✔ **Research new local jobs.** Suppose that you live in Michigan — or want to relocate to Michigan — and want to get a heads-up when a Michigan employer plans to expand and add new jobs. Write it like this:

  "new jobs" OR "expansion" Michigan

  If you're interested in only jobs in Detroit, change *Michigan* to *Detroit*.

- ✔ **Research industries.** When you're interested in a specific industry, set up a Google Alert for that industry (or career field). Google then keeps you in the loop with industry updates, and you'll be the smartest candidate in the interview room.

Explore the Google universe

Most of us don't use 0.01 percent of the endless and expanding cosmos of Google. In addition to Google's default general search, it offers plenty of options to reach out for facts, figures, and futures, as you'll vividly realize by examining the following two websites.

Google Local (local.google.com)

A Google local page features a map you can adjust to highlight your own target work area. Type the city and state or Zip Code you want into the Google search bar.

Use the Google search bar at the top for your query. For example, if you want to work for a hospital, type the word *hospital* into the search bar; the map then lights up with dots indicating the locations of hospitals near you.

On the map, the dots that Google thinks are more relevant to you have little lettered flags that correspond to information in the left column of the page (usually), like the website, contact information, and sometimes reviews. *Result:* Potential target employers' locations and commute.

Google News (news.google.com)

This website is another tip-off to what's going on in a local job market: local employers that are growing bigger companies (or shrinking them), business-people who are becoming increasingly visible, and changing laws that may impact your work life.

More Google Secrets

Latch on to still more job-finding nuggets from search authority Susan P. Joyce. Look online for "Guide to Using Google for Job Search," a free collection of how-to articles on job-hunt.org.

New Game: "Hide and Seek and Find"

Comedian Jimmy Wales comes close to today's digital reality with his statement, "If it isn't on Google, it doesn't exist."

Susan P. Joyce comes closer: "If you can't find it on Google, give up. Wait . . .. No! Keep trying! The job jackpot is there somewhere."

Not only are job search letters tools of our times, but knowing where to send them makes all the difference between a winning move and a writing exercise.

Appendix

Directory of Job Letter Writers

• •

*T*he talented professional letter writers whose work appears in Parts II and III are experts at creating the quality of self-marketing job search documents you need to stand out from your competition.

The writer's name and locale appear at the bottom of each sample. When you want to contact a specific professional, refer to this appendix. It presents each writer's contact information, a glossary of professional certifications, and a directory of professional writing and career-development organizations to which many of the sample writers proudly belong.

About the Sample Writers

The following directory lists each sample writer's name, stated certification designations, location, telephone, and e-mail address. The writer's firm name, fax and toll-free phone numbers, and website are included when available.

Deborah Barnes, CPRW, JCTC
Nahant, Mass.
Phone 781-598-1127
E-mail debnahant@comcast.net

Karen Bartell, CPRW
Best-in-Class Resumes
Massapequa Park, N.Y.
Phone 800-234-3569 or 631-704-3220
Fax 516-799-6300
E-mail kbartell@bestclass
resumes.com
Website www.bestclassresumes.
com

Laurie Berenson, CPRW, CEIC
Sterling Career Concepts, LLC
Franklin Lakes, N.J.
Phone 201-573-8282
Fax 201-255-0137
E-mail laurie@sterlingcareer
concepts.com
Website www.sterlingcareer
concepts.com

Marian Bernard, CPRW, JCTC, CEIP
The Regency Group
Aurora, Ont., Canada
Phone 905-841-7120
Fax 905-841-1391
E-mail marian@neptune.on.ca
Website www.resumeexpert.ca

Sharon M. Bowden, CPRW, CEIP
SMB Solutions
Atlanta, Ga.
Phone 404-264-1855
Fax 404-264-0592
E-mail Sharon@startsavvy.com
Website www.startsavvy.com

Vicki Brett-Gach, CPRW
Best Resume, LLC
Ann Arbor, Mich.
Phone 734-327-0400
Fax 734-913-0633
E-mail bestresume12345@aol.com
Website www.BestResume12345.com

Donald Burns
Career Defense, LLC
New York, N.Y.
Phone 917-519-0487
E-mail dburns1@donaldburns.com
Website www.careerdefense.com

Freddie Cheek, CCM, CPRW, CARW, CWDP
Cheek & Associates, LLC
Amherst, N.Y.
Phone 716-835-6945
Fax 888-227-9957
E-mail fscheek@cheekand associates.com
Website www.CheekandAssociates.com

Stephanie Clark, CRS, CIS
New Leaf Resumes
Nanaimo, B.C., Canada
Phone 855-550-5627
E-mail newleafresumes@gmail.com
Website www.newleafresumes.ca

Laura DeCarlo, CMRW, MCD, CCMC, CP-OJSRM, CEIC, JCTC
Career Directors International
Melbourne, Fla.
Phone 321-752-0442
E-mail laura@careerdirectors.com
Website www.careerdirectors.com

Dan Dorotik, NCRW
100 Percent Resumes
Lubbock, Texas
Phone 806-783-9900
Fax 806-993-3757
E-mail dan@100percentresumes.com
Website www.100percentresumes.com

Tamara Dowling, CPRW
Seeking Success
Valencia, Calif.
Phone 661-263-8709
E-mail td@SeekingSuccess.com
Website www.SeekingSuccess.com

Debbie Ellis, MRW
Phoenix Career Group
Houston, Texas
Phone 281-571-3223
Fax 866-856-1878
E-mail ellis@phoenixcareer group.com
Website www.phoenixcareer group.com

Wendy S. Enelow, CCM, MRW, JCTC
Career Thought Leaders Consortium
Resume Writing Academy
Coleman Falls, Va.
Phone 434-299-5600
E-mail wendy@wendyenelow.com
Website www.wendyenelow.com

MJ Feld, CPRW
Careers by Choice, Inc.
Huntington, N.Y.
Phone 631-673-5432
Fax 631-673-5824
E-mail mj@careersbychoice.com
Website www.careersbychoice.com

John Femia, CPRW
Custom Resume & Writing Service
Schenectady, N.Y.
Phone 518-357-8181
E-mail customresume@nycap.rr.com
Website www.customresume writing.com

Arthur I. Frank
Resumes "R" Us
Flat Rock, N.C.
Phone 866-600-4300 or 828-696-2975
Fax 828-696-2974
E-mail af97710@bellsouth.net
Website www.PowerResumesand
Coaching.com

Louise Garver, CPBS, JCTC, CMP, CPRW, CEIP
Career Directions, LLC
Broad Brook, Conn.
Phone 860-623-9476
Fax 860-623-9473
E-mail LouiseGarver@cox.net
Website www.
CareerDirectionsLLC.com

Judith L. Gillespie, CPCC, CPRW, CEIP
Career Avenues by Judy
West Melbourne, Fla.
Phone 850-524-2917
Fax 321-953-8361
E-mail judy@careeravenuesby
judy.com
Website www.careeravenuesby
judy.com

Susan Guarneri, MRW, CERW, CPRW, CPBS, NCCC, DCC
Guarneri Associates
Three Lakes, Wis.
Phone 715-546-4449
Skype susan.guarneri
E-mail Susan@Resume-Magic.com
Website www.Resume-Magic.com

Divya Gupta, ACPEC, CCC, PCC
Confident Career
Herndon, Va.
Phone 703-953-1154
E-mail divya@confidentcareer.com
Website www.confidentcareer.com

Gay Anne Himebaugh
Seaview Secretarial Solutions
Corona del Mar, Calif.
Phone 949-673-2400
Fax 949-673-2428
E-mail resumes@seaview
secretarial.com

Phyllis G. Houston
The Resume Expert, Mobile Resume
Service Upper Marlboro, Md.
Phone 301-574-3956
Fax 301-574-1191
E-mail phyllis_houston@msn.com

Kristen A. Jacoway, CRC, CPRW, CCC, CPBS
Career Design Coaching
Auburn, Ala.
Phone 334-610-0105
E-mail Kristen@careerdesign
coach.com
Website www.careerdesign
coach.com

David J. Jensen, CEIP
Ascension Writing Services
Salt Lake City, Utah
Phone 801-755-4364
E-mail djensen962@msn.com

Erin Kennedy, MCD, CMRW, CPRW
Professional Resume Services, Inc.
Lapeer, Mich.
Phone 877-970-7767
E-mail erin@exclusive-
executive-resumes.com
Website www.exclusive-
executive-resumes.com

Wendi W. McAfee, CPRW
SMB Solutions
Atlanta, Ga.
Phone 404-351-1360
E-mail wendi@startsavvy.com
Website www.startsavvy.com

Karen Mitchell
Limelight Career Consulting
Lititz, Pa.
Phone 717-468-9601
Fax 717-626-3443
E-mail karen@limelightcareers.com
Website www.limelightcareers.com

Kevin R. Morris
Career Mobile
Naples, Fla.
Phone 239-207-5149
E-mail Kevin@goCareerMobile.com
Website www.goCareerMobile.com

Melanie Noonan
Peripheral Pro, LLC
Woodland Park, N.J.
Phone 973-785-3011
Fax 973-256-6285
E-mail peripro1@aol.com

Don Orlando, CPRW, JCTC, CCM, CCMC, CJSS, MCD
The McLean Group
Montgomery, Ala.
Phone 334-264-2020
E-mail dorlando@yourexecutivecareercoach.com

Barb Poole, CCMC, CLTMC, CMRW, CPRW, PHR
Hire Imaging, LLC
Maple Grove, Minn.
Phone 877-265-2750
E-mail barb@hireimaging.com
Website www.hireimaging.com

Haley Richardson, CPRW, JCTC
Resumes Done Right
Minneapolis, Minn.
E-mail resumesdoneright@rocketmail.com
Website www.resumesdoneright.com

Jane Roqueplot, CPBA, CWDP, CECC
JaneCo's Sensible Solutions
West Middlesex, Pa.
Phone 888-526-3267 or 724-528-1000
E-mail janeir@janecos.com
Website www.janecos.com

Barbara Safani, CERW, NCRW, CPRW, CCM
Career Solvers
New York, N.Y.
Phone 347-480-1827
E-mail info@careersolvers.com
Website www.careersolvers.com

Joellyn Wittenstein Schwerdlin CCMC, JCTC
Career-Success-Coach.com
Worcester, Mass.
Phone 508-459-2854
Fax 508-459-2856
E-mail joellyn@career-success-coach.com
Website www.career-success-coach.com

Tanya Sinclair, CHRP, MCRS
TNT Human Resources Management
Pickering, Ont., Canada
Phone 416-887-5819

Billie R. Sucher, CTMS, CTSB, JCTC, CCM
Billie Sucher Career Services
Urbandale, Iowa
Phone 515-276-0061
E-mail billie@billiesucher.com
Website www.billiesucher.com

Linda Tancs
Get Smart Consulting
Hillsborough, N.J.
Phone 908-428-4475
E-mail info@getsmartconsulting.com
Website www.getsmartconsulting.com

Kathryn Kraemer Troutman
The Resume Place Federal Career
Training Institute
Catonsville, Md.
Phone 888-480-8265
E-mail Kathryn@resume-place.com
Website www.resume-place.com

Edward Turilli, CPRW
AccuWriter Resume Service
North Kingstown, R.I.
Bonita Springs, Fla.
Phone 239-298-9514
E-mail AccuWriter@comcast.net
Website www.resumes4-u.com

**Rosa Elizabeth Vargas, MRW,
CERW, NCRW, ACRW**
Career Steering Executive Resume
Service
Orlando, Fla.
Phone 321-704-7209
Fax 888-448-1675
E-mail writer@careersteering.com
Website www.careersteering.com

A Glossary of Professional Certifications

Ever wonder what the letters behind someone's name mean? Initials behind the sample writers' names designate certifications each has voluntarily earned. A professional organization awards the designations based on a candidate's professional evaluation, usually measured by formal testing, of the candidate's level of expertise in a specific skill area.

The certification examination process generally requires time-consuming study and may include both experience-based knowledge acquired in the field and curriculum-based knowledge gained by study of assigned learning texts.

Certification is an indication that the certified professional is a player in a field's large body of knowledge and that the professional meets documented standards and achievement requirements.

Many — but not all — of the certifications accorded to this book's sample writers were awarded by one of the professional organizations listed in the following section. (Other certifications are awarded by a variety of professional organizations not represented here.)

Certification evaluations are voluntary for professional writers. For their own reasons, not all of the experts whose excellent work appears in these pages have sought credentialing.

ACRW — Academy Certified Resume Writer

CARW — Certified Advanced Resume Writer

CCM — Credentialed Career Manager

CEIC — Certified Employment Interview Consultant

CEIP — Certified Employment Interview Professional

CMRS — Certified Master Resume Specialist

CMRW — Certified Master Resume Writer

CPCC — Certified Professional Career Coach

CP-OJS — Certified Professional in Online Job Search

CPRW — Certified Professional Resume Writer

CRS+X — Certified Resume Specialist

CWPP — Certified Web Portfolio Practitioner

MCD — Master Career Director

MRW — Master Resume Writer

NCRW — Nationally Certified Resume Writer

Professional Organizations

Professional writers of job letters belong to professional organizations to stay current with new ideas, continue professional development, and connect with other serious experts. The professional organizations that follow are responsible for inviting their members to contribute their best work to this book. The certification designations awarded by each organization are noted.

Association of Online Resume and Career Professionals (AORCP)
Certifications awarded:
Certified Master Resume Specialist (CMRS)
Website www.aorcp.com
Contact Karen M. Silins, Karen@aorcp.com

Career Directors International (CDI)
Certifications awarded:
Certified Master Resume Writer (CMRW)
Master Career Director (MCD)
Certified Resume Specialist (CRS+X)
Certified Advanced Resume Writer (CARW)
Certified Employment Interview Consultant (CEIC)
Certified Professional in Online Job Search (CP-OJS)
Certified Web Portfolio Practitioner (CWPP)
Website www.careerdirectors.com
Contact Laura DeCarlo, laura@careerdirectors.com

Career Thought Leaders Consortium (CTL)
Certifications awarded:
Master Resume Writer (MRW)
Credentialed Career Manager (CCM)
Website www.careerthought
leaders.com
Contact Wendy Enelow,
wendy@careerthoughtleaders.com

The National Resume Writers' Association (NRWA)
Certifications awarded:
Nationally Certified Resume Writer (NCRW)
Website www.nrwaweb.com
Contact Marie Zimenoff, President,
president@thenrwa.com;
or Administrative Manager,
adminmanager@thenrwa.com

Professional Association of Resume Writers & Career Coaches (PARW/CC)
Certifications awarded:
Certified Professional Resume Writer (CPRW)
Certified Employment Interview Professional (CEIP)
Certified Professional Career Coach (CPCC)
Website www.parw.com
Contact Frank Fox,
parwhq@aol.com

Resume Writing Academy (RWA)
Certifications awarded:
Academy Certified Resume Writer (ACRW)
Website www.resumewriting
academy.com
Contact Wendy Enelow,
wendy@resumewritingacademy.com

About Hiring a Professional Job Search Letter Writer

Now you know that an effective communications-supported job search counts more than ever in a time when technology seems to change every 15 minutes.

Even so, maybe persuasive writing isn't your talent or keyboard gymnastics your skill. The obvious answer is to get help and move forward with your life.

The 42 contributors of sample letters to this groundbreaking work are at the top of their profession. If you need a hand, you may want to seek the services of the career professional who wrote your favorite sample in this guidebook, or perhaps you'll want to consider several writers before making a choice. Turn the page for suggestions on choosing with confidence.

5 Tips for Choosing Job Search Writers

Selecting a professional writer to move your career forward can be daunting if you've never before called out the heavy artillery. The following tips will help you make a wise choice.

Getting to know you

Many professionals offer a free consultation. To get the most from this opportunity, jot down every question you can think of about job search letters before you meet with any professional. That will insure the time you spend together will be well tailored to your specific needs.

Once hired, a top professional writer spends at least an unhurried hour on the phone with you getting to know your background, what you want in a job, your personality, and other factors that are critical to writing great messages that can change your life.

Getting to your writer

Do check the writers' credentials and references, which services and goods they offer, and how each will benefit your job search. Those who want to write your letters should hold certifications in the field, present workshops to the public and colleagues, write for publication, and be active members of at least one career professional organization.

Ask about a worksheet workload. You may not want to fill out extensive worksheets, effectively writing the basic documents yourself. A writer must spend considerable time with you to capture your word choice and philosophy well enough to reflect the best you.

Industry awareness

Workplace jargon is everywhere. Each industry and career field communicates its own insider language. A strong writer can research and overcome not having a command of the specific lingo, but your messages must sound as though you wear the correct secret decoder ring and know what you're talking about.

Out-the-door price

Follow the taxi principle: Find out what the total ride will cost before you get in. Writers cannot guarantee you'll land a job based on their work because too many other factors — from interviews to background checks — are in play.

Delivery dates

If you must have new employment by a specific date, ask about the writer's delivery schedule. Highly successful writers may have weeks of work lined up that extend beyond your deadline.

Index

• C •

• K •

Kennedy, Erin (job letter writer)
  contact information, 321
  networking letter, 93
  prospecting letter, 111
  reply letter, 72
keywords
  mobile job search message tip, 20
  online profile, 174

• L •

language
  active versus passive voice, 254–255, 260
  concise but thorough, 249
  interpreting your benefits, 248–249
  past versus present tense, 255
  short words, sentences, and paragraphs, 249
  stating exactly what you want, 247–248
  tailoring to reader, 249
  technical versus nontechnical, 249
  vague descriptions, 249
  visualizing the reader, 248
  word replacements, 250–254
laptop, mobile job search, 20
lateral move, 227–228
layoffs, 316–317
leadership addendum, 29, 37–38
leadership initiatives summary, 185
leadership skills, 281, 296
leave-behind doc
  basic description, 183
  branding statement on, 154
  distinguishing yourself from competition, 184
  as jumpstarting the follow-up, 184
  reasons for, 183–184
  reinforcing strengths in, 184
  samples, 188–194
  topics, 185–186
  writing effective, 187

Lemke, Jim (technical reviewer), 12
letter
  body, 244–245
  conclusion, 245
  contact information, 243
  date line and inside address, 243–244
  enclosure line, 245
  getting ahead, 8
  getting hired, 7–8
  getting modern, 8
  introduction, 244
  salutation, 244
  signature, 245
  sloppy, 241–242
  typos, 241–242
letter of recommendation. See recommendations; references
letter writing
  deductive order format, 262
  freewriting, 240–241
  getting ready to write, 245
  grammar importance, 241
  inductive order format, 262
  inverted pyramid format, 261–262
  list format, 262
  picturing the reader, 240
  problem/solution format, 261
  professional, hiring, 238
  proper nouns, 242
  reading for smoothness, 262
  spell checking, 240
  stand out letter advantages, 238–240
  text-speak, 238
  worry, 242–243
  writer's block, 240–241
LinkedIn
  benefiting from, 142–143
  conducting searches, 144–145
  matching to job type, 304
  photo, 144
  Public Profile settings, 172
  single-site search, 313–314
  updates, regularly checking, 303
  useful company research, 303
list format, 262

About the Author

Joyce Lain Kennedy is America's first nationally syndicated careers columnist. Her two-times-weekly column, CAREERS NOW, syndicated by Tribune Media Services, appears in newspapers and on websites across the land. In her four decades of advising readers — newbies, prime-timers, and in-between — she has received millions of letters inquiring about career moves and job search and has answered countless numbers of them in print.

Kennedy is the author of seven career books, including *Joyce Lain Kennedy's Career Book* (McGraw-Hill), and *Electronic Job Search Revolution, Electronic Resume Revolution*, and *Hook Up, Get Hired! The Internet Job Search Revolution* (the last three published by Wiley).

Job Search Letters For Dummies is one of a trio of job market books by Kennedy published under Wiley's *For Dummies* branded imprint. *Job Interviews For Dummies, 4th Edition* won the gold medal, the coveted Benjamin Franklin award for best career book of the year. The other guide in the suite is *Resumes For Dummies, 6th Edition.*

Writing from Carlsbad, California, a San Diego suburb, the country's best known careers columnist is a graduate of Washington University in St. Louis. Contact her at jlk@sunfeatures.com.

About the Technical Editor

James M. Lemke has earned a reputation as a leader in talent strategies and processes. He is Vice President, Human Resources, for Finca International, a global nonprofit financial services organization.

Jim has held executive positions with Opportunity International, Wachovia Bank, TRW, UCLA, Walt Disney Imagineering, and Raytheon. Previously, Jim spent 15 years as a human resources consultant and hiring authority. His client list included: Real Networks, Southern California Metropolitan Water District, Northrop Grumman, Southwest Airlines, Jet Propulsion Laboratory, United Arab Emirates University, and the White House.

Jim resides in Buckeye, Arizona. Contact him at jamesmlemke@gmail.com.

Author's Acknowledgments

Endless thanks to the following superhero-helpful individuals. (Next time, I'm sending each of you a cape along with your copy of this book.)

James M. Lemke, technical advising all-star, human relations vice president of a major international humanitarian organization, and globe-trotting business traveler. Jim vetted the professional practices I describe in this book, and, luckily for thee and me, Jim tracks all the new trends and technology.

Linda Brandon, *For Dummies* editor at the top of her game, shepherded this guide through a myriad of publishing hoops and oops, always making spot-on suggestions and corrections.

Yevgeniy "Yev" Churinov, computer whiz, mobile early adopter, and social networking guru, contributed both technological clarity and practical production assistance.

Lindsay Sandman Lefevere, *For Dummies* executive editor, stands out as this book's wise godmother.

Krista Hansing, five-star copyeditor whose sharp eyes, sound judgment, and editorial skills made this challenging work a far better guide.

Susan P. Joyce delivered invaluable knowledge of contemporary job search in the new digital age; **Kathryn Kraemer Troutman** generously shared her incomparable grasp of the federal job market and its often confusing documents; **Allison Doyle** came through with Doyle alerts to winners and losers in this decade's deluge of new recruiting technology; and **Debbie Ellis** confirmed herself to be a leading career management professional who never met a job search letter she couldn't improve.

Gail Ross, literary agent-attorney and longtime friend, continues to keep me out of trouble in the publishing world.

Special appreciation of the 42 richly talented professional writers who contributed sample letters, notes, emails, and other job search documents to these pages: Deborah Barnes, Karen Bartell, Laurie Berenson, Marian Bernard, Sharon M. Bowden, Vicki Brett-Gach, Donald Burns, Freddie Cheek, Stephanie Clark, Laura DeCarlo, Dan Dorotik, Tamara Dowling, Debbie Ellis, Wendy S. Enelow, MJ Feld, John Femia, Arthur I. Frank, Louise Garver, Judith L. Gillespie, Susan Guarneri, Divya Gupta, Gay Anne Himebaugh, Phyllis G. Houston, Kristen A. Jacoway, David J. Jensen, Erin Kennedy, Wendy W. McAfee, Karen Mitchell, Kevin R. Morris, Melanie Noonan, Don Orlando, Barb Poole, Haley Richardson, Jane Roqueplot, Barbara Safani, Joellyn Wittenstein Schwerdlin, Tanya Sinclair, Billie R. Sucher, Linda Tancs, Kathryn Kraemer Troutman, Ed Turilli, and Rosa Elizabeth Vargas.

Publisher's Acknowledgments

Acquisitions Editor: Lindsay Lefevere
Project Editor: Linda Brandon
Copy Editor: Krista Hansing
Technical Editor: James M. Lemke
Art Coordinator: Alicia B. South

Project Coordinator: Kristie Rees
Cover Photos: © cogal / iStockphoto.com

Apple & Mac

iPad For Dummies,
5th Edition
978-1-118-49823-1

iPhone 5 For Dummies,
6th Edition
978-1-118-35201-4

MacBook For Dummies,
4th Edition
978-1-118-20920-2

OS X Mountain Lion
For Dummies
978-1-118-39418-2

Blogging & Social Media

Facebook For Dummies,
4th Edition
978-1-118-09562-1

Mom Blogging
For Dummies
978-1-118-03843-7

Pinterest For Dummies
978-1-118-32800-2

WordPress For Dummies,
5th Edition
978-1-118-38318-6

Business

Commodities For Dummies,
2nd Edition
978-1-118-01687-9

Investing For Dummies,
6th Edition
978-0-470-90545-6

Personal Finance
For Dummies,
7th Edition
978-1-118-11785-9

QuickBooks 2013
For Dummies
978-1-118-35641-8

Small Business Marketing Kit
For Dummies,
3rd Edition
978-1-118-31183-7

Careers

Job Interviews
For Dummies,
4th Edition
978-1-118-11290-8

Job Searching with
Social Media
For Dummies
978-0-470-93072-4

Personal Branding
For Dummies
978-1-118-11792-7

Resumes For Dummies,
6th Edition
978-0-470-87361-8

Success as a Mediator
For Dummies
978-1-118-07862-4

Diet & Nutrition

Belly Fat Diet For Dummies
978-1-118-34585-6

Eating Clean For Dummies
978-1-118-00013-7

Nutrition For Dummies,
5th Edition
978-0-470-93231-5

Digital Photography

Digital Photography
For Dummies,
7th Edition
978-1-118-09203-3

Digital SLR Cameras &
Photography For Dummies,
4th Edition
978-1-118-14489-3

Photoshop Elements 11
For Dummies
978-1-118-40821-6

Gardening

Herb Gardening
For Dummies,
2nd Edition
978-0-470-61778-6

Vegetable Gardening
For Dummies,
2nd Edition
978-0-470-49870-5

Health

Anti-Inflammation Diet
For Dummies
978-1-118-02381-5

Diabetes For Dummies,
3rd Edition
978-0-470-27086-8

Living Paleo For Dummies
978-1-118-29405-5

Hobbies

Beekeeping
For Dummies
978-0-470-43065-1

eBay For Dummies,
7th Edition
978-1-118-09806-6

Raising Chickens
For Dummies
978-0-470-46544-8

Wine For Dummies,
5th Edition
978-1-118-28872-6

Writing Young Adult Fiction
For Dummies
978-0-470-94954-2

Language &
Foreign Language

500 Spanish Verbs
For Dummies
978-1-118-02382-2

English Grammar
For Dummies,
2nd Edition
978-0-470-54664-2

French All-in One
For Dummies
978-1-118-22815-9

German Essentials
For Dummies
978-1-118-18422-6

Italian For Dummies
2nd Edition
978-1-118-00465-4

Available in print and e-book formats.

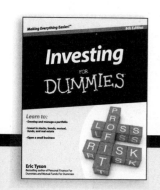

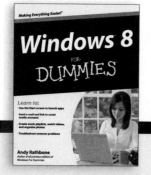

Math & Science

Algebra I For Dummies,
2nd Edition
978-0-470-55964-2

Anatomy and Physiology
For Dummies,
2nd Edition
978-0-470-92326-9

Astronomy For Dummies,
3rd Edition
978-1-118-37697-3

Biology For Dummies,
2nd Edition
978-0-470-59875-7

Chemistry For Dummies,
2nd Edition
978-1-1180-0730-3

Pre-Algebra Essentials
For Dummies
978-0-470-61838-7

Microsoft Office

Excel 2013 For Dummies
978-1-118-51012-4

Office 2013 All-in-One
For Dummies
978-1-118-51636-2

PowerPoint 2013
For Dummies
978-1-118-50253-2

Word 2013 For Dummies
978-1-118-49123-2

Music

Blues Harmonica
For Dummies
978-1-118-25269-7

Guitar For Dummies,
3rd Edition
978-1-118-11554-1

iPod & iTunes
For Dummies,
10th Edition
978-1-118-50864-0

Programming

Android Application
Development For
Dummies, 2nd Edition
978-1-118-38710-8

iOS 6 Application
Development For Dummies
978-1-118-50880-0

Java For Dummies,
5th Edition
978-0-470-37173-2

Religion & Inspiration

The Bible For Dummies
978-0-7645-5296-0

Buddhism For Dummies,
2nd Edition
978-1-118-02379-2

Catholicism For Dummies,
2nd Edition
978-1-118-07778-8

Self-Help & Relationships

Bipolar Disorder
For Dummies,
2nd Edition
978-1-118-33882-7

Meditation For Dummies,
3rd Edition
978-1-118-29144-3

Seniors

Computers For Seniors
For Dummies,
3rd Edition
978-1-118-11553-4

iPad For Seniors
For Dummies,
5th Edition
978-1-118-49708-1

Social Security
For Dummies
978-1-118-20573-0

Smartphones & Tablets

Android Phones
For Dummies
978-1-118-16952-0

Kindle Fire HD
For Dummies
978-1-118-42223-6

NOOK HD For Dummies,
Portable Edition
978-1-118-39498-4

Surface For Dummies
978-1-118-49634-3

Test Prep

ACT For Dummies,
5th Edition
978-1-118-01259-8

ASVAB For Dummies,
3rd Edition
978-0-470-63760-9

GRE For Dummies,
7th Edition
978-0-470-88921-3

Officer Candidate Tests,
For Dummies
978-0-470-59876-4

Physician's Assistant Exam
For Dummies
978-1-118-11556-5

Series 7 Exam
For Dummies
978-0-470-09932-2

Windows 8

Windows 8 For Dummies
978-1-118 13461-0

Windows 8 For Dummies,
Book + DVD Bundle
978-1-118-27167-4

Windows 8 All-in-One
For Dummies
978-1-118-11920-4

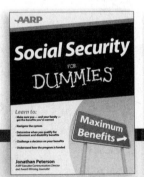

Available in print and e-book formats.

Take Dummies with you everywhere you go!

Whether you're excited about e-books, want more from the web, must have your mobile apps, or swept up in social media, Dummies makes everything easier .

Dummies products make life easier

- DIY
- Consumer Electronics
- Crafts
- Software
- Cookware
- Hobbies
- Videos
- Music
- Games
- and More!

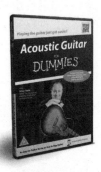

For more information, go to **Dummies.com®** and search the store by category.

FOR
DUMMIE.

A Wiley Bra